Disability/Postmodernity

WITHDRAWN FROM
THE LIBRARY

UNIVERSITY OF
WINCHESTER

D0264037

Disability/Postmodernity

Embodying disability theory

Edited by

Mairian Corker and Tom Shakespeare

continuum
LONDON • NEW YORK

UNIVERSITY OF WINCHESTER
LIBRARY

Continuum
The Tower Building
11 York Road
London SE1 7NX

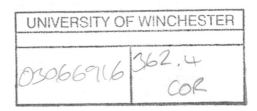
UNIVERSITY OF WINCHESTER

03066916 362.4
COR

First published 2002
Reprinted 2004, 2006

80 Maiden Lane
Suite 704
New York, NY 10038

© Mairian Corker, Tom Shakespeare and the contributors 2002

All rights reserved. No part of this publication may be reproduced or transmitted in any form or by any means, electronic or mechanical, including photocopying, recording or any information storage or retrieval system, without permission in writing from the publishers.

British Library Cataloguing-in-Publication Data
A catalogue record for this book is available from the British Library.

ISBN 0-8264-5056-3 (hardback)
       0-8264-5055-5 (paperback)

Library of Congress Cataloging-in-Publication Data
Disability/postmodernity : embodying disability theory / edited by Mairian Corker and Tom Shakespeare.
       p. cm.
   Includes bibliographical references and index.
   ISBN 0-8264-5056-3 (hbk) — ISBN 0-8264-5055-5 (pbk.)
   1. Sociology of disability.   2. Disability studies.   3. Postmodernism.
   I. Corker, Mairian.   II. Shakespeare, Tom.

   HV1568.2 .D59 2001
   305.9'0816—dc21   2001042270

Typeset by RefineCatch Limited, Bungay, Suffolk
Printed and bound in Great Britain by
MPG Books Ltd, Bodmin, Cornwall

Contents

Contributors

Peter Beresford is a psychiatric system survivor. He works with the Open Services Project and is Professor of Social Policy at Brunel University.

Johnson Cheu is a doctoral candidate in English at the Ohio State University, where he is working on his dissertation, 'Disabling Cure in Twentieth-century America: Disability, Identity, Literature and Culture', on the cultural and rhetorical constructions of cure in twentieth-century American literature and culture. His poetry has appeared in publications such as *Staring Back: The Disability Experience from the Inside Out* and *The Ragged Edge*.

Mairian Corker currently holds Senior Research Fellowships at King's College London, and the University of Central Lancashire. Her work lies at the intersection of deaf studies, disability studies and discourse studies. She is author of many publications, including *Counselling – The Deaf Challenge* (1994), *Deaf Transitions* (1996) (both Jessica Kingsley), *Deaf and Disabled, or Deafness Disabled?* (Open University Press, 1998) and the forthcoming *Disabling Language: Analyzing Disability as Social Practice* (Routledge), and co-editor, with Sally French, of *Disability Discourse* (Open University Press, 1999). She is an executive editor of the journal *Disability and Society*.

John Davis is a Research Fellow in the Research Unit in Health and Behavioural Change, University of Edinburgh. An anthropologist, he has recently engaged in ethnographic fieldwork on two ESRC-funded projects: *The Socio-Economic and Cultural Context of Children's Lifestyles and the Production of Health Variations* and *Lives of Disabled Children*. He is the author of a number of publications on disability and childhood, including journal articles in *Disability and Society*, *Children and Society* and the *International Journal of Children's Rights*.

Anita Ghai teaches in the Department of Psychology, Jesus and Mary College, University of Delhi, India. Disability issues are central to her work as an academic and activist. She is co-author, with Anima Sen, of *The Mentally Handicapped: Prediction of the Work Performance* (Phoenix Publishers, New Delhi, 1996), in addition to several book chapters and articles relating to disability. She is an overseas editor for the journals *Disability and Society* and *Disability, Culture and Education.*

Dan Goodley is a Lecturer in the Centre for Disability Studies at the University of Leeds. His research and teaching focus upon the self-advocacy of people with the label of 'learning difficulties', and their contribution to the politics of disability and the development of a social theory of disability and impairment. Recent publications include *Self-advocacy in the Lives of People with Learning Difficulties: The Politics of Resilience* (Open University Press, 2000) and *Arts against Disablement: The Performing Arts of People with Learning Difficulties* (with Michele Moore, BILD publications, 2001).

Petra Kuppers is Assistant Professor (Humanities) at Bryant College, Rhode Island, USA. She has edited *Performances of Disability* (Harwood Academic Press, 2001), and has published widely on representation, the body and contemporary arts. She is a practising community artist, and teaches cultural theory at the Open University.

Miho Iwakuma is a doctoral candidate at the University of Oklahoma. Originally from Japan, her dissertation is about Japanese people with disabilities. Her research focuses in particular on cross-cultural understandings of disability and communication and she has published a number of articles in both English and Japanese, which include chapters in forthcoming books *Disability and the Life Course* (Cambridge University Press) and *Intercultural Views of People with Disabilities in Africa and Asia* (Lawrence Erlbaum).

Rod Michalko is Associate Professor of Sociology at St Francis Xavier University in Nova Scotia, Canada. He is author of *The Mystery of the Eye and the Shadow of Blindness* (University of Toronto Press, 1998) and *The Two in One: Walking with Smokie, Walking with Blindness* (Temple University Press, 1999). His third book, *Useless Difference: Disability and the Dilemma of Suffering*, will soon be published.

Janet Price is an Honorary Fellow at the Liverpool School of Tropical Medicine. She has written individually, and with Margrit Shildrick, on feminist theory and the body, postmodernism and disability, biomedicine and bioethics, most recently co-editing the collections *Vital Signs* (Edinburgh, 1998) and *Feminist Theory and the Body* (Edinburgh, 1999).

Mark Rapley is a Senior Lecturer in Psychology at Murdoch University in Perth, Western Australia. His research interests are in ethnomethodology, analysis and discursive psychology. Much of his work has focused on the interactions of psychologists and people described as 'intellectually disabled'. His most recent book (with Alec McHoul), *How to Analyse Talk in Institutional Settings: A Casebook of Methods*, will be published by Continuum in 2001, and he is currently working on *The Social Construction of Intellectual Disability* (Cambridge University Press).

Jackie Leach Scully studied biochemistry at Oxford and completed her PhD in molecular biology at Cambridge. After research fellowships in the fields of mammary cancer and later in neurodegeneration, she studied ethics and theology and went on to research public attitudes towards ethical issues in genetic manipulation. She is a Research Associate at the Institute for the History and Ethics of Medicine at Basel University, where her current research interests focus on how socially marginalized groups, such as disabled people, construct ethically contentious issues in the new genetics.

Tom Shakespeare is currently Research Development Officer at the Policy, Ethics and Life Sciences Research Institute, University of Newcastle. An active member of the UK disability movement, he has written and broadcast widely on disability issues. His books include *The Sexual Politics of Disability* (Cassell, 1996), co-authored with Kath Gillespie-Sells and Dominic Davis, and *Help* (Venture Press, 2000), and he edited *The Disability Reader: Social Science Perspectives* (Cassell, 1998).

Margrit Shildrick is SURI Research Fellow at Staffordshire University. She is the author of *Leaky Bodies and Boundaries* (Routledge, 1997) and co-editor with Janet Price of *Vital Signs* (Edinburgh, 1998) and *Feminist Theory and the Body* (Edinburgh, 1999). She works and publishes extensively on the body, including issues of disability, and has just finished a new book called *Vulnerability and Monstrous Embodiment* (Sage, 2001).

Russell P. Shuttleworth has worked as a personal assistant for disabled men since 1984. He is an ardent supporter of the Disability Rights Movement. He holds a BA and MA in anthropology from California State University, Sacramento, an MSW from San Francisco State University and a PhD in medical anthropology from the joint programme at the University of California, San Francisco and Berkeley. His dissertation research dealt with the search for sexual intimacy for men with cerebral palsy.

Anita Silvers is Professor of Philosophy at San Francisco State University. She has published seven books – most recently, *Disability, Difference, Discrimination: Perspectives on Justice in Bioethics and Public Policy* (Rowman & Littlefield, 1998) and *Americans with Disabilities: Exploring Implications of the Law for Individuals and Institutions* (Routledge, 2000) – and more than a hundred book chapters and journal articles on topics in ethics and bioethics, aesthetics, social philosophy, philosophy of law, feminist philosophy, disability studies, education and public policy. In 1978, she was named the California Distinguished Humanist by the California Council for the Humanities, and in 1989 she received the California Faculty Association's Equal Rights Award for her work in increasing opportunities in higher education for people with disabilities.

Carol Thomas is a Senior Lecturer in the Department of Applied Social Science at Lancaster University. Her publications in disability studies include *Female Forms: Experiencing and Understanding Disability* (Open University Press, 1999). She has a particular research interest in the experiences of disabled women, but also researches in the fields of cancer studies and health inequalities.

Tanya Titchkosky is Assistant Professor of Sociology at St Francis Xavier University, Nova Scotia, Canada. She is author of numerous articles, including 'Disability studies: the old and the new' (*Canadian Journal of Sociology*, 25(2): 197–224) and 'Disability – a rose by any other name? People-first language in Canadian society' (*Canadian Review of Sociology and Anthropology*, in press). Tanya is currently revising for publication her manuscript *Disability Stays: An Introduction to the Social Construction of Disability.*

Shelley Tremain received a PhD in Philosophy from York University (Toronto, Canada) and was the 1997–98 Ed Roberts Postdoctoral Fellow at the World Institute on Disability and the University of California at Berkeley. Tremain publishes widely on disability, sexuality, gender, feminism and cultural politics, is the editor of a collection of essays entitled *Foucault and the Government of Disability* (University of Michigan Press, forthcoming) and is writing a book on Foucault, disability, gender and governmentality.

James Valentine is Senior Lecturer in Sociology at the University of Stirling, and has been carrying out research on marginality in Japanese society since 1986. Through the 1990s his research increasingly focused on representations of people conceived as marginal through disability, ethnicity, gender and sexuality.

Nick Watson is a Lecturer in the Department of Nursing Studies at the University of Edinburgh. He has researched and published widely in the health and disability field, and his current research interests include a project on the social history of the wheelchair. A member of the UK disability movement, he was, until recently, Convenor of *Accessibility* Lothian, a leading Scottish organization of disabled people.

Anne Wilson (a pseudonym) is a psychiatric system survivor and college lecturer.

Iris Marion Young is Professor of Political Science at the University of Chicago. She is author of *Inclusion and Democracy, Justice and the Politics of Difference* (Princeton University Press, 1990), *Intersecting Voices: Dilemmas of Gender, Political Philosophy and Policy* and *Throwing Like a Girl and Other Essays in Feminist Philosophy and Social Theory* (Indiana University Press, 1990), and recently co-edited (with Alison Jaggar) *Blackwell's Companion to Feminist Philosophy*.

Foreword

It has taken a long time for the condition of being positioned as 'disabled' to be conceptualized as an oppression, rather than an unproblematic description of the characteristics and functionings of the bodies of some individuals. Even today in the sub-discipline with which I am most familiar, political philosophy, a relatively abstract notion of having a disability still appears in writings concerning justice, desert and responsibility, as the paradigm of the sort of disadvantage people might suffer that is simply a matter of bad luck.

Many philosophers and many actors in politics and social services have argued against a simple-minded notion of justice that would bring everyone under an identical standard of equal treatment, on the grounds that such a 'level playing-field' is patently unfair to many people with disabilities. In the 1980s, feminist critiques of equality as sameness were some of the most elaborated and sustained accounts of how such approaches to law and policy fall short of justice, and some of these readily saw the similarities between the ways the lives of women and the lives of people with disabilities often do not fit the given standards. Martha Minow's (1990) work stands out as defining such 'dilemmas of difference'.

It took some more sustained thinking about such a lack of 'fit' between dominant standards of equality and performance and the lives and functioning of many people with disability before what has come to be called the 'social model' of disability came to challenge a medical model of individualized attributes and functionings. As I understand it, this social model denies that any particular attributes or functionings of individual bodies should be thought to constitute a 'problem' or 'disadvantage' apart from the social environment within which the individuals live. This social environment has both material–physical and symbolic–interactive dimensions. Moving on wheels is a 'disadvantage' only in a world full of stairs. Because many people expect to make 'eye contact' with people they talk to, as a sign of respect and engagement, some of them dislike or even fear persons whom they do not experience as making such contact. The social model of disability notices many such attributes of environments and relations among persons, and the project it has generated would systematically describe the structures and processes of such social environments as they construct some people as 'normal' and others as 'deviant', giving many advantages to the former (Silvers *et al.*, 1998).

The social model of disability has enormous critical power because it shifts attention on issues of justice for people with disabilities from the 'needs' of people with disabilities to others who assume that a certain background of structures and practices is given. Such a shift in perspective has had some practical import in public policy, where a principle that employers and institutions should change their spaces and practices to enable a broader diversity of individuals to participate in this has received a certain measure of legal recognition. Those given responsibilities under such principles, of course, have many ways of denying and avoiding them. After the social model of disability has been articulated, however, it becomes difficult to revert to a world that describes some people as simply and unfortunately having 'special needs'.

These essays collected by Mairian Corker and Tom Shakespeare mark another step in the radicalization of theory and practice regarding persons socially positioned as 'disabled'. While the social model of disability destabilizes the assumption that the 'problem' with some people has to do with attributes of their bodies and functions, it nevertheless continues to presume a certain fixity to these bodies, and thereby understands many of the experiences and self-conceptions of persons positioned as disabled as grounded in such bodily facts. Following some of the moves of recent feminist and queer theories, these essays variously destabilize the image of given bodies inserted in valuable and changeable social contexts implicit in the social model of disability. Experiences of moving, perceiving, interacting with others, manipulating tools, thinking through problems and expressing oneself are all conditioned and constituted by social structures of constraint and enablement, as well as by forms of the representation of persons, as both 'normal' and 'deviant'. The subject of disability herself is constituted as varying and culturally conditioned lived body.

The editors label the tools of analyses they find these essays share 'postmodern'. They recognize, especially at this moment in the history of the academy in North America and Europe, that this label functions more to create antagonists than to situate a set of methods. Some people embrace the label while others are repelled by it and wish to argue against whatever those who embrace it say. While the editors' introduction 'maps the terrain' of what they see to be 'postmodernity', the essays themselves do not draw in a sweeping way from the diversity of contemporary thought in this area. A dominant influence is Foucault, in particular feminist and queer appropriations of his methods. Others apply self-reflective methods of the analysis of everyday discourses, popular culture representation and analysis of microprocesses that have come to be called 'cultural studies'. What they share is a sceptical attitude towards any assumptions about persons positioned as disabled as obvious or given, and a determination to fashion a genealogy of such assumptions that will change the way we all look at the social constraints and particular capacities of many people relatively ignored in theories of subjectivity.

Towards the end of their introduction, Corker and Shakespeare express a worry that academic essays using such cultural studies methods may be perceived as leaving disability activists behind 'as disability is opened up to its own complexity'. Fortunately, the essays themselves are concrete and clear enough that they do not require special schooling in 'postmodern' language to be revealing. It is true, however, that the project of exploring the cultural and discursive constitution of subjectivity goes beyond politics in the sense of groups of persons identifying what they perceive as social wrongs they wish to claim remedy for from others, and proposing policies to enact such remedy. Even though it has significant consequences for the conduct of such politics, reflection on the cultural construction of embodied experience is both prior and posterior to this moment of public claim and policy action. It is prior in the sense that it helps constitute the political subject, and posterior in the sense that it opens reflection onto these many areas of practice life that are not directly involved in proposing and implementing institutional policies – such as love and friendship, play and enjoyment.

Thus I would propose that the assertion of a 'postmodern' approach to disability studies not be concerned as a displacement of the social model of disability, on analogy with the way that social model displaces a model of disability as that of having malformed or unfortunate bodies and function-ings. The social model of disability seems necessary for activists to maintain in their arguments with employers, educators, legislators and judges. Ana-lyses of the subjectivity of those positioned by social structures and practices as having disabilities, such as those this volume offers, are an important complement to and deepening of these political arguments.

Iris Marion Young, Chicago, 28 February 2001

References

Minow, M. (1990) *Making All the Difference*. Ithaca: Cornell University Press.

Silvers, A., Wasserman, D. and Mahowald, M. B. (1998) *Disability, Difference, Dis-crimination: Perspectives on Justice in Bioethics and Public Policy*. Lanham, MD: Rowman & Littlefield.

1

Mapping the Terrain

Mairian Corker and Tom Shakespeare

Introduction

This collection aims to contribute to the development of disability studies by exploring what postmodernist and post-structuralist scholarship can contribute to our understandings of disability and the diverse experience of disabled people. It is our contention that disability studies, particularly in Britain, has suffered from a theoretical deficit, and has been reluctant to take advantage of this scholarship. Our secondary purpose is to offer scholars already familiar with postmodern thought an introduction to the analysis of disability. In this introductory chapter, we seek to do three things. First, we provide what we hope is an accessible route through the terrain of modernism and post-modernism, and we situate the diverse contributions to the collection within this landscape. Second, we give readers some examples of key postmodern texts, which can be used to develop this landscape further. And finally, we reflect on the current state of disability studies, and the benefits that post-modern theoretical insights might bring for the understanding of disability and the empowerment of disabled people.

Modernism and postmodernity

As we enter the twenty-first century, it is argued by many that we are witnessing the emergence of a new age of uncertainty, for which we need new language, new theories and new forms of practice. Globalization, new communication technologies, the collapse of Communism, the techno-industrialization of war, the privatization of public resourses, the advent of universal consumerism: these are only a few of the profound institutional transformations which have taken place at all levels of the economic, social and political system.

Western societies are now, in various ways, said to be 'post-industrial', post-Fordist, 'postmodern', even 'post-historical' and 'post-human'. All these terms identify themselves as something they are not. But to ask exactly how our world may be *postmodern* yields a range of answers. For example, *post-* can indicate a *result* of modernism, or the *aftermath, displacement, devel-opment, denial* or *rejection* of modernism. It is helpful to begin to address this apparent confusion by asking *what*, exactly, has been superseded, displaced, developed, denied or rejected and *why?* In other words, the first questions this book must address are what is modernism, and how is it different from postmodernism?

Modernity describes the social institutions, belief and value systems of capitalist civilization, including the globalization of industrialism, mass sur-veillance and technological warfare, that are entrenched in Western society. *Capitalism*, or the ideological hegemony of market forces and the endless search for profit and capital accumulation, along with its social counterpart *modernization*, runs the risk of a cultural imperialism that submerges trad-itional ways of life. But even in Majority World societies characterized by agrarian economies and traditional moralities, cultures and political struc-tures, pro-modernization elites often look favourably on the centralizing social dynamic and the universalistic moralities and knowledges of the West.

At the heart of modernity is *the culture of the Enlightenment*. This is founded on assumptions about the unity of humanity, the individual as the creative force of society and history, the superiority of the West, the idea of science as Truth and the belief in social progress, and this is what we mean when we refer to *modernism*. These assumptions are said to be *foundationalist* in the sense that they argue for the rational, independent subject as the ground of both *ontology* (being) and *epistemology* (theories of knowledge). *Meta-narratives*, or all-encompassing and totalizing narratives, that are built on *an operational code of binary, 'either/or' thought*, are therefore central to modernism. The *individual and medical models of disability*, which perceive and classify disability in terms of a meta-narrative of deviance, lack and tragedy, and assume it to be logically separate from and inferior to 'nor-malcy', are characteristic of the kinds of epistemologies or knowledge systems generated by modernism.

In spite of the ideology of scientific enlightenment and progress, and the public celebration of a culture of self-redemption and emancipatory hope, large numbers of people remain oppressed within modernism, particularly those who are perceived not to meet the modernist ideal of the rational, independent subject. Modernism is complicit in the creation of social inequalities and systems of privileging and power based on the axes of dis-ability, gender, 'race', class, sexuality and age. Its capitalist underpinnings mean that inequality often manifests itself in terms of a divide between the rich and the poor across all of these axes.

The first challenge to modernism came in the emergence of the modern counter-culture of *socialism*, which in the Communist states of the twentieth century apparently represented another kind of civilization. The counter-culture of socialism is 'modern' in the sense that it retains the binary logic and, in the case of Communism, is based on a Marxist meta-narrative. But in the late twentieth century, Communism no longer offered a viable alternative to capitalism and, in the capitalist states themselves, social democracy has become less socialistic. The *social model of disability*, particularly given its roots in historical materialism, is perhaps an example of the socialist counter-culture. This model makes a conceptual distinction between disability and impairment, similar to the feminist distinction between gender and sex. It sees disability as *socially created*, or constructed on top of impairment, and places the explanation of its changing character in the social and economic structure and culture of the society in which it is found. The body of know-ledge and practice that constitutes the social model is primarily concerned with *the political project of emancipation* and, in some of its interpretations, with the development of an *oppositional politics of identity*.

The second challenge to modernism is targeted not at its underpinnings, but at its heart – the culture of the Enlightenment. This challenge aims to achieve a shift in knowledge and culture – in how we perceive, think and produce – rather than in the material factors of economics and the use of nature. As such, it is concerned more with *how we build inclusive societies* and with *the social role of knowledge* in this process. *Postmodernism*, as this chal-lenge has come to be known, is concerned with the culture of postmodernity. It refers to philosophical ideas, mainly derived from *post-structuralist theory*, and to cultural formations, especially associated with global popular culture. It is not a claim *about* material reality, nor does it always ignore material reality. *Postmodernity*, on the other hand, is an attempt to label contemporary society, and suggests that we are living through the transition from a modern to a postmodern age.

The postmodern terrain is mapped out in detail in the following section, but here it is worth emphasizing the centrality of post-structuralist theories, which call into question the foundationalist assumptions of modern Western thought outlined above. *Post-structuralism* provides a different view of the subject, arguing that subjects are not the autonomous creators of themselves or their social worlds. Rather, subjects are embedded in a complex network of social relations. These relations in turn determine which subjects can appear, where and in what capacity. The subject is not something prior to politics or social structures, but is constituted in and through specific socio-political arrangements. In this sense, in some of its interpretations, the social model can appear to be an example of post-structuralist theory. However, to make sense of the ways in which subjects are at once revealed and concealed, post-structuralism contends that modernism's focus on the individual as an autonomous agent needs to be deconstructed, contested and troubled. This makes for a tension-ridden relationship with versions of the social model that see only 'society', or which stress the agency of disabled people in achieving their own liberation. It is our task in the following section to identify some of the key ideas and approaches of postmodernism, to introduce some of the theorists who have developed them and to suggest why they are important for disability studies.

Mapping the postmodern terrain

Postmodern themes seem especially visible in the realm of knowledge, where there are a number of theoretical approaches, loosely and often incorrectly bundled together, but sharing an implicit sensitivity for the *complexity* of the social world. Instead of taking the modernist approach, which analyses complex phenomena in terms of simple or essential principles, postmodern approaches acknowledge that it is not possible to tell a single and exclusive story about something that is complex. We would broadly characterize the postmodern landscape in terms of the following overlapping themes:

- epistemologies that are based on the troubling of meta-historical narratives and the critique of Enlightenment assumptions, especially those about 'reality' and 'truth';
- an ontological emphasis on uncertainty, instability, hybridity, contingency, embodiment and reflexivity;
- a methodological emphasis on genealogy, deconstruction and situated knowledge;
- the decentring of the subject and the social world, often through an emphasis on language, discourse and culture;
- the incorporation of psychoanalytical ideas into social theory;
- altered relations between knowledge and power;
- de-differentiation and de-territorialization;
- new ideas about cognition, sensation and the body;
- new ideas about ethics and social justice.

That these themes consistently overlap is evidenced in the blurring of disciplinary boundaries, such as those between science, literature and ideology and between philosophy and cultural criticism. It can also be seen in the move of new interdisciplinary, hybrid knowledges such as feminism, queer studies, ethnic studies, urban studies, cultural studies and disability studies to the centre of human studies. Some of the debates about a possible historical transition beyond modernity have concentrated upon institutional dynamics, particularly those that see a shift from industrial production to the production of information as the basis for a new form of political power. In contrast, other debates have concentrated on more cultural and aesthetic issues, especially in the realms of art, architecture and mass culture. But there remains disagreement over whether the postmodern age marks the end of modernity and the dissolution of the Enlightenment culture. It is this disagreement that charts the 'territories' of the postmodern landscape.

Radical postmodernism

As Anita Silvers notes at the start of her chapter, Jean-François Lyotard's *The Postmodern Condition* is a pivotal statement in the debate over knowledge. He identifies a key theme of the postmodern turn: the decline of the legitimating power of 'meta-narratives' as distinctive of postmodern culture. Meta-narratives refer to foundational theories (theories of knowledge, morality or aesthetics) and grand stories of social progress which have been central to the legitimation of modern knowledge, culture and social institutions. In his thesis on the decline of the meta-narrative, Lyotard argues that the meta-narratives such as the philosophical theories of knowledge in the tradition of Locke, Kant, Husserl, or the stories of social progress related by Condorcet, Marx or Parsons, have lost their authority to justify modern social practices. They presuppose an ahistorical standpoint from which to understand the human mind, knowledge, society and history. Postmodernity therefore implies a shift from meta-narratives to local narratives and from general theories to pragmatic strategies. In place of a rational knowing subject and a universal mind, we imagine multiple minds, subjects and knowledges reflecting different social locations and histories. A parallel process of decentring is evident in the social world – both in terms of the self and in terms of politics. In answer to the question 'What form do social knowledges assume in a postmodern culture?', Lyotard proposes two possibilities. First the human sciences may become instruments of bureaucratic social control. In an increasingly risky world, however, it is more likely that the limits, uncertainty and incompleteness of knowledge will be emphasized. In this regard, Lyotard describes the rise of a postmodern science, which favours local, historically contextualized and pragmatic types of social inquiry. The value of postmodern knowledges lies in making us aware of and tolerant toward social differences, ambiguity and conflict.

The *radical postmodernism* of Lyotard is seen by its proponents to create the possibility of escaping from the confines of modernism and of reimagining the world. For some theorists, industrialization is replaced by a simulated world made possible by computer technology. The floating images and narcissistic codes of the mass media come to be seen as that point where technology invades the inner world of the individual subject – the opening of a new post-word era that displaces 'reality' itself. In his critique of modernity, Jean Baudrillard is often brutal and uncompromising in his desire to demonstrate that ontological and epistemological truths are fundamentally flawed. Indeed, Baudrillard's theories of *representation* have been described as 'terrorism' of the real. Baudrillard believes that we have no need of the real in opening up a space for political action and engagement, as Petra Kuppers explores in her analysis of image politics. Baudrillard argues that the cultural transformation brought on by the postmodern age has profoundly affected our sense of self and of place, causing considerable confusion and a loss of meaning. Though he is concerned with issues of power, like Lyotard, he sees postmodernity as a 'post-industrial' society, where the primacy of the mode of production in defining social relations is replaced by the primacy of the mode of information and its transmission through technology. His *ideology of disembodiment* characterizes postmodern society as an implosion of the social into *hyperreality*, or a collapse of the distance between an 'original' object (signifier) and its 'simulacra' (signified). For Baudrillard, social order is code-oriented, and power is conceptualized in terms of cybernetic control. Social experience is only possible as 'spectacle' – it is transitory and rudimentary – and any attempt to theorize it is therefore futile. Baudrillard would view disability, like gender, as a *simulation*, and would therefore refuse the fetishization of people with impairments in the same way that he refuses the fetishization of 'women'. He claims that the more 'difference' circulates in our contemporary hyperreal world as an emancipatory construct, the more we see the inevitability that it will be recaptured by a process of simulation.

The critique of radical modernists

Much of the criticism of 'postmodernism' *per se* has in fact been targeted at the radical postmoderns, in particular at their suggestion that postmodernity marks a 'new age', when capitalism is clearly alive and well. They are also criticized for their 'nihilistic' attitude towards social struggles, and their insistence on *de-differentiation* (the breakdown of boundaries between social and cultural spheres) is seen to exemplify the excesses of *relativism* – a theoretical framework in which anything goes. It is argued that the emancipatory project is compromised through an expansion of the critique of universals to include a critique of *any* identity category. But, as Anita Ghai emphasizes, social movements must be vigilant for cultural imperialism, as they are not exempt from the reproduction of oppressive practices. It is these criticisms that have been central to the concerns of *strategic postmodernists* and *poststructuralists*, who have responded to the radical agenda through critique and modification of the postmodern problematic within a political project of resistance and social change. Instead of making a foundational move in the face of empirical or interpretative conflicts, these theorists consider social, moral and political consequences, the practical purposes of knowledges and their situational impact.

The post-structuralist intervention

Lyotard's theme of the decentred world remains pivotal, though in different ways, to the work of post-structuralists Jacques Derrida and Michel Foucault. Derrida is concerned with ways of thinking about how meanings are established, specifically that meanings are organized through difference in a dynamic play of presence and absence. Meaning includes identity (what it is) and difference (what it isn't) and is therefore continuously being deferred. Derrida invented a word for this process, combining difference and deferral – *différance* (1978). A Derridean perspective on disability would argue that though they are antagonistic, 'normativism' needs 'disability' for its own definition: a person without an impairment can define him/herself as 'normal' only in opposition to that which s/he is not – a person with an impairment. Disability is not excluded from 'normativism'; it is integral to its very assertion. Moreover, when 'normativism' is privileged, 'disability' becomes a derivative, *cultural* arrangement that imposes on the taken-for-granted, *natural* status of the 'normal'. This strategy for revealing the underpinnings of a particular binary opposition is called *deconstruction*. Derrida argues that we are always within a binary logic and, whenever we try to break out of its stranglehold, we reinscribe its very basis. Thus, in addition to making sense of the manner in which 'normativism' is itself a social construct, he might be concerned with the way in which an adoption of (a 'positive', 'proud' and 'visible') 'disabled identity' reinscribes the 'sick role' produced through the normal/impaired binary. This is important because of the large numbers of people with impairments who identify as neither 'normal' nor 'disabled', but nevertheless are individually engaged in resisting the hegemony of normativism in their everyday lives. In other words, Derrida argues for an *ethical response* to difference. This ethical response is central to the chapter by Janet Price and Margrit Shildrick, and is also suggested in the chapter by Jackie Leach Scully, in her examination of the way that medical authority perpetuates itself through the cultural conventions that legitimate its authority.

Michel Foucault did not recognize himself as a 'postmodern' writer. His work is nevertheless significant for its post-structuralist analyses of madness, criminality, sexuality, 'biopolitics' and power, and in his later work, like Derrida, he is increasingly concerned more with ethics. This shift is evident in the three volumes that constitute the *History of Sexuality*, where he moves from an emphasis on sex to what he calls 'techniques of the self'. Foucault argues that the sexual subject is not the natural origin of sexual truths but that discourses on sexuality (for example, sexology and psychiatry) help produce dominant and subjugated sexual subjects. He then explores the new ways of life and the 'techniques', such as reading and writing, through which individuals take care of the self and strive to reconstitute themselves as privileged, suggesting ways in which we might better understand the relationship between private life and broader culture. A Foucauldian perspective on disability might argue, then, that a proliferation of discourses on impairment gave rise to the category 'disability'. Though these discourses were originally scientific and medical classificatory devices, they subsequently gained currency in judicial and psychiatric fields of knowledge. 'Disabled people' did not exist before this classification although impairment and impairment-related practices certainly did. Thus Foucault shows us that social identities are effects of the ways in which knowledge is organized, but his work is also significant for its explication of the links between knowledge and power. In his post-structuralist account of power in modern societies, Foucault uses the term *biopower* to refer to the radically modern form of power, which made knowledge/power an agent of transformation of human life. Modern power is thus not 'sovereign', a result of coercion from outside, but 'disciplinary' because of the ritualized and institutionalized action of the techniques of power and their normalizing effect on modern life. Although Foucault views all forms of power as entailing resistance, biopower lends itself to a bleak version of modern social life as an 'iron cage'. In place of science, he favours *genealogies*, or historical-critical analyses tracing the making of identities, selves, social norms and institutions, which focus on the role of the medical and human sciences in the shaping of a 'disciplinary' society. Foucauldian themes are central to the chapters by Dan Goodley and Mark Rapley, Russell Shuttleworth and Shelley Tremain. They are also present, though less explicitly stated, in James Valentine's chapter, and that by Anne Wilson and Peter Beresford.

The psychoanalytic intervention
Under the broad umbrella of postmodernism, Derrida's attack on *logocentrism*, or what he sees to be the dishonest pursuit of certainty that shapes reason, and Foucault's unveiling of historical exclusion are joined by a third strand of postmodern thought. This emerged out of the union between *structuralist linguistics* of Ferdinand de Saussure, which examines linguistic infrastructure in terms of the *synchronic* (existing now) rather than the *diachronic* (existing and changing over time), and a critique of Freud and psychoanalysis. This strand, which is regrettably not covered in this volume, is particularly visible in the work of Jacques Lacan. Lacan attempted to explain how the mind comes to be structured and inserted in the social order as a departure from the Freudian belief in the materialist biology of the mind. He replaced the Freudian concepts of Id, Ego and Superego with the structures of the Imaginary, the Symbolic and the Real as the stages of human psychic maturation. In this way he saw structure as pre-dating experience, and the individual subject as a product of the discourse of the Other. A Lacanian view on disability might argue that the entire order of disabling culture divides us into two states – impaired and 'normal', in the form of a hierarchy that

privileges the latter. It does so through linguistic structures that are so deep that the 'tyranny of the normal' not only breaks up the impaired/'normal' dyad, but does so to the degree that any possibility of relationship to the normal is repressed in the unconscious as the imaginary. The entire concept of identity takes place through this repression of impairment, in such a way that people with impairments cannot affirmatively identify with others like themselves.

Lacan's idea of the self as fiction or *imaginary* marked the most radical and comprehensive decentring of the human subject through its suggestion that the unconscious, just like language, is an endless process of difference, lack and absence. It runs counter to much received wisdom, specifically in its assumption that experience is unproblematic and meaning transparent. This is central to Lacan's theory that social relations, or what he calls *the Symbolic Order*, depend upon the repression of desire. All self-knowledge is fractured and fragile – put another way, experience lies – as the individual subject is caught between imaginary traps of narcissistic mirroring and symbolic dislocations of language.

Fredric Jameson also draws upon Althusser's Lacanian theory of ideology. He contends that the concept of postmodernity is best grasped as a means of understanding changes to the cultural space of 'late capitalism'. He examines how a flattening of hierarchy, discernment, evaluation and value in postmodern cultural conditions is accompanied by a breakdown in the psychological capacity of human subjects to map and locate themselves in terms of the broader social network. For example, in his work on the built environment and postmodern architecture, he argues that cultural shifts bring about a spatial disorientation by superseding an older, modernist and clearly structured urban space. He argues for an aesthetic of 'cognitive mapping' for constructing a space that allows for systemic connections and structural explanations as the basis for a politics of alliance. Because the notion of cognitive mapping is in part conceptualized in Lacanian terms, the issue is not just one of spatial orientation but also of psychic and social identity. Although she does not specifically mention Jameson, there are elements of his ideas in the chapter by Tanya Titchkosky, which explores spatial orientation and psychic social identity, and also in the chapter by Johnson Cheu.

Voices of difference

The postmodern terrain would not be complete without reference to the very significant contribution that has been made by the often overlapping theories of feminism, queer studies and critical 'race' studies – a contribution that goes considerably beyond rewriting the pre-existing analyses described above, or adding in a sensitivity to difference. Though there is a tense relationship between postmodernism and feminism, many feminist writers take the debates of postmodernity in new and highly original directions. Indeed, as Carol Thomas and Mairian Corker explore through a dialogic interplay between the modern [material] and the post-structural [textual] in contemporary analyses of disability, feminism's position in postmodernity often serves to highlight the artificially constructed nature of the debate between modernism and postmodernism. Feminist writings frequently draw on post-structuralist themes such as the critique of meta-narratives and the challenging of representation, whilst tending to avoid the excesses of radical postmodernism. In its critique of modernism, feminist scholarship is notable for its broadening of the focus of theory and politics on issues of labour, class and political economy to issues related to Foucauldian themes, most notably those related to the body.

For example, Judith Butler's 'queering' of the Foucauldian concept of 'the docile body' has produced the notion of *performativity*, which she develops using the phenomenological theory that social agents constitute 'reality' through social practice. She criticizes the commonly held idea that femininity and masculinity are the cultural expressions of material fact, namely the female or the male body. Instead of the notion of gender as an expressive act, she proposes viewing it as a performative one. Thus, the idea of gender, 'race' and disability as *corporeal styles* makes it possible to examine how individuals live in their bodies and, in this process, constitute gender, 'race' and disability in social relations. She emphasizes that performativity must be understood not as a singular or deliberate act, or performance, but rather as the ritualized practice by which discourse produces the effect it names. In this way, Butler breaks away from the distinction between the 'reality' of sex and the 'appearance' of gender. Butler has been criticized for engaging in purely abstract, apolitical textual analysis. However, she herself notes that language and materiality are fully embedded in each other, and she places considerable emphasis on the *materializing* of corporeal styles. She argues that, when the universal category of the modern body is replaced by the plurality postmodern bodies, none of which is solely determinate, it offers a way of celebrating a politics of creative subversion. But it does so without retreating into identity politics or the tactics of collective rebellion, which belong to body/politics of the 1970s. This is important given that oppression frequently works through closing down difference and choice.

Butler's work is notable for its intersectional analysis of feminism and queer theory. But similar post-structuralist themes have been taken up by post-colonial and critical race theorists, such as Gayatri Chakravorty Spivak and Homi K. Bhabha. Bhabha draws from a diverse range of social theorists, including Derrida, Lacan and Foucault, in his focus on the political effects of various languages of national belonging. His political aim is to disrupt familiar or settled identity myths, primarily by focusing on the multiple forms in which 'nation', 'culture' and 'community' become the subject of discourse, as well as the object of psychic and cultural identifications. For Bhabha, people are caught between subject and object status, and acknowledgement of this opens a potential critical space to undermine and alter communal values of the culturally dominant, and to think through new political possibilities. What follows from this is that ethnic identity, far from being some biological stamp upon an individual, is bound up with dynamic and changing relations of political domination, social exclusion, religious heritages and forms of culture. Thus, for many theorists in this tradition, the question of how to develop anti-racist strategies is an issue that touches on much more than just a mere awareness of possible conflicts in and between dominant and ethnic or subcultural identities. According to Spivak, the production of identity and especially the writing of historical identities – always a process of conflicting and contested narratives – is intrinsically at odds with the received wisdom of hegemony. Conflicts are built into the analysis of minority histories in contemporary historiography; the struggle for inclusion and representation, says Spivak, shields the *cognitive failure* of all claims to knowledge. In her analysis of *the subaltern*, Spivak focuses on the slippages and gaps of some core discursive strategies of the group. By drawing on post-structuralist theories, especially those of Derrida, Spivak seeks to define different configurations of subaltern consciousness; indeed, she points out that the effect of the subject can itself be read as subaltern and thus resistant to historicization. Spivak's ideas are explored in the chapter by Anita Ghai.

Although Butler's analysis, like Foucault's and Derrida's, is inspired by phenomenology, the work of Maurice Merleau-Ponty has been increasingly influential as feminists and others seek to move away from the abstraction of text. Miho Iwakuma's chapter is in this tradition. Merleau-Ponty's phenomenology is one in which the historical opposition between mind and body has no place. However, he seems to privilege a universalized gender-neutral, and thus effectively male, body, which is somehow fixed in time and space and only disrupted by loss of health or impairment. Feminists have critiqued this position by pointing out that the female body is 'naturally' subject to changes in form over the life course, and there is a deep concern in the work of Iris Marion Young with the processes of embodied subjectivity. For example, in her essay *Throwing Like a Girl*, Young explores the phenomenology of feminine body comportment, motility and spatiality. She shows how the constraints of femininity in contemporary Western societies make it impossible for women to use their full bodily capacities in a free and open engagement with the world. In a sense, then, feminine embodiment is dis-abled. Young has attempted to weave insights of post-structuralist feminism with a theory that takes differences between women into account. For Young, the body is central to how dominant cultures designate certain groups as Other.

Subordinate groups are defined by their bodies and according to norms that diminish and degrade them. By imprisoning the Other in a body that is of no account, the privileged are able to take a god's eye view as disembodied subjects who are central to the modernist project. They therefore set the standards. This *aesthetic scaling of bodies*, as Young describes it, is not only central to the construction of difference, but it also underpins the processes of oppression.

Feminists such as Luce Irigaray and Julia Kristeva have attempted to develop theories of female embodiment as a constructive force. In so doing, they have challenged Lacan's more explicitly expressed belief in the inevitability of women's exclusion. Irigaray, in particular, has looked for ways to give expression to women's bodies as the site of pleasure, arousal and sensuality, for example. Her emphasis on touch as the mediating force between embodied selves is an important theme in Janet Price and Margrit Shildrick's chapter. These appeals to differences in women's bodily and sexual experience or to unique modes of feminine desire not only provide insight into the materiality of feminine embodiment, but demonstrate that feminine embodiment is not simply oppressive, but can be heretical and even empowering as well. However, Irigaray has made the female a unitary focus of her work and has therefore laid herself open to criticisms of ahistorical essentialism. Nevertheless, this analysis of the positioning of women outside the process of self-constitution points to an understanding of disabled people's appearance as exterior representations either of something else – monuments of tragedy, deviance or freakery, for example – or as fetishes – the 'marvellous' objects (supercrips) of non-disabled people's desire.

Donna Haraway links these critiques to more general social changes such as the emergence of an information-based economy, the restructuring of work and households and the altered configurations of difference in a globalized world order. But her specific project in relation to the body is queering what counts as nature in a way that speaks to all forms of post-human embodiment. Acknowledging that there have always been bodies that create ontological anxiety in their failure to conform, Haraway also points to technological practices such as xenotransplantation, genetic engineering, transsexual surgery and cloning, and the way in which they blur the boundaries of the fixed human body. To explain this body, she gives us the concept of *the cyborg*, a half-human, half-machine creation that embodies and materializes the breaking of traditional patriarchal distinctions between human and machine, physical and non-physical. The cyborg is simultaneously a living being and a narrative construction. As both a technological object and a discursive formation, it embodies the power of the imagination as well as the materiality of technology. Haraway also critiques the way in which science has projected men as the norm of all humanity, ignoring women's lives and the way in which these lives have historically differed in important ways from those of men. She warns against appeals to traditional doctrines of objectivity for the grounding of feminist knowledge and politics. Modernist doctrines of objective vision, she suggests, have underpinned the deployment of fixed identity categories. Yet there is nothing about being 'female' that binds women together politically and ideologically. Her commitment to 'situated knowledges' and partial truths does not give way to extreme relativism but works towards conceptualizations, mainly of the object of science, that allow for connectivity and interdependence. These ideas are central to Rod Michalko's chapter, but they are also present in John Davis's and Nick Watson's analysis of the situatedness of disabled childhoods.

Embodying disability theory

Whereas theorists of race, gender and sexuality have embraced and explored the contributions of postmodernism, disability theorists have proved reluctant to take on board new perspectives. Disability and impairment have been largely excluded from mainstream postmodern analysis and this analysis has so far failed to impact significantly on how we perceive, think about and produce disability and impairment in the twenty-first century. In British disability studies, 'postmodernism' has become a dumping ground for anything and everything that appears to challenge the orthodoxy of neo-Marxism, historical materialism and the social model. The assumption of this volume is that this failure to engage with post-structuralist and postmodernist thought is to the detriment of disability studies.

Though the social model has changed the way many disabled people and their allies think about disability, even the most ardent social modellists agree that it is not a comprehensive social theory of disability. It is perhaps because of this that its considerable *conceptual* power lacks a strong theoretical base, and this has been an important reason for its exclusion from mainstream social theory. We believe that it is time to attend both to a theoretical deepening and to a local responsiveness of disability studies, and this collection aims to demonstrate some ways forward. The chapters presented in this volume contribute much to this process in their examination of ideas such as embodiment and impairment, culture and discourse, identity and resistance, and in showing how postmodern and post-structuralist theory can benefit this process. They also show how thinking in this way blurs the boundaries between theory, culture and practice – so much so that organizing the book into discrete sections has been an almost impossible task.

This blurring of boundaries is one example that demonstrates the danger of this enterprise. A strength of disability studies has been its close connection between scholarship and activism. Within the disability movement, there has been a dialogue between leading disability theorists – such as

Oliver, Barnes and Finkelstein – about what, in Gramscian terms, could be called the role of 'organic intellectuals'. Journals, such as *Disability and Society* and *Disability Studies Quarterly* have published work by activists alongside that of academics. Courses such as the University of Leeds MA in Disability Studies in the UK, and the disability studies programmes at a number of prestigious universities in the USA and Australia, for example, have had an important role in this process. These courses have been more than instrumental in enabling disabled people to explore disability studies and to work more effectively towards progressive social change.

In spite of these significant developments, and the possibilities for partnership that they bring, tensions between the activist and academic wings of the disability community remain. New texts are audited for accessibility and for 'fit'; authors who use difficult language or introduce complex theoretical analyses are frequently castigated in the political press. The notion of emancipatory research suggests that social investigators need to place themselves at the service of disabled people's organizations, and conduct research according to political priorities. This is not always seen to be compatible with research that is based on intellectual interests or instincts and that has the intention of advancing the collective interests of disabled people, however they might be defined.

The danger of moving further into post-structuralist and postmodernist territory is that disabled activists may increasingly be left behind as disability is opened up to its own complexity. These new theories *are* often opaque, and expressed in language that is highly obscure. Moreover, analysis increasingly centres not on mainstream political issues, but on aspects of culture, identity and the body, which may seem secondary in the struggle to end the oppression of disabled people. Nevertheless, a look at the trajectory of other emancipatory struggles shows that it was after the working-class political defeats of the 1920s and 1930s that Western Marxism moved into its more theoretical and cultural phase, with the work of the Frankfurt school. Similarly, it was after the women's movement met blocks to further political success, and began to fragment in the 1980s, that feminist thought turned to exploration of the cultural and theoretical realm in the search for why this had happened and what could be learnt from it.

But more importantly, and despite these dangers, we feel that postmodern ideas can contribute an enormous amount *to the development of inclusive societies*, which is surely as important as the challenge to the hegemony of normativism. We therefore believe that disability studies has little choice but to engage with these ideas. As we hope the previous section has shown, postmodernism is no longer restricted to weighty theoretical discussions in elite circles of the academy. Nor is it necessarily politically disengaged, as the work of writers from feminism, queer theory and post-colonialism demonstrates. Post-structuralism and postmodernism did not invent complexity or inaccessibility; they have been a traditional hallmark of much academic thought, as consideration of the work of Kant, Hegel or indeed the Marxist tradition itself shows. What postmodern ideas have noted, however, is that people's lives are far more complex than modernism likes to believe and they choose to engage with this complexity. As Derrida wrote, with more than a passing reference to Einstein, 'one shouldn't complicate things for the pleasure of complicating, but one should also never simplify or pretend to be sure of such simplicity where there is none. If things were simple, word would have gotten around' (1988: 119). The challenge remains to express difficult ideas, and develop complex analyses, in ways that are adequate, meaningful and accessible.

We believe that existing theories of disability – both radical and mainstream – are no longer adequate. Both the medical model and the social model seek to explain disability universally, and end up creating totalizing, meta-historical narratives that exclude important dimensions of disabled people's lives and of their knowledge. The global experience of disabled people is too complex to be rendered within one unitary model or set of ideas. Considering the range of impairments under the disability umbrella; considering the different ways in which they impact on individuals and groups over their lifetime; considering the intersection of disability with other axes of inequality; and considering the challenge which impairment issues to notions of embodiment, we believe it could be argued that disability is the ultimate postmodern concept. However, the work of disability theorists may be significantly harder than the work of feminists or other theorists of oppression, and we will need all the conceptual tools we can get. We also need to remember that this work is not just about what mainstream theory can bring to disability studies, but also about the ways in which disability can inform or challenge theory itself.

The future challenge for disability studies is to benefit from the new theoretical toolbox, without losing its audience among disabled people, the poorest of the poor in every society, and without losing its radical edge. Theory has to be conceived as a means to an end, rather than an end in itself. The aim of this collection is not to contribute to the establishment of disability studies as another discipline within the Western academy, but to encourage disability studies to look outwards. But the goal remains the same: to contribute to the emancipation of disabled people, whoever they are, and whatever they decide that emancipation means, and to the development of inclusive societies. This, in our view, continues to mean 'thinking globally' and 'acting locally' *at the same time* – seeing and researching disabled lives as both constrained by social structures and as an active process of production which transforms social structures. Central to this must be ongoing empirical research, within the intellectual framework provided by post-structuralist and postmodern thought, and we are especially pleased by the many chapters in this volume that contain data from social research projects. Alongside empirical investigation must come an ongoing engagement with organizations of disabled people, with disabled people who are not members of these organizations and with the policy issues facing the disability community locally, nationally and internationally. Foucault's (1984) dream was of

> the intellectual who destroys evidence and generalities, the one who, in the intertias and constraints of the present time, locates and marks the weak points, the openings, the lines of force, who is incessantly on the move, doesn't know exactly where he is heading nor what he will think tomorrow for he is too attentive to the present; who, wherever he moves, contributes to posing the question of knowing whether the revolution is worth the trouble and what kind (I mean, what revolution and what trouble), it being understood that the question can be answered only by those who are willing to risk their lives to bring it about. (p. 124)

This, for very different reasons, is our dream also.

References

Derrida, J. (1988) *Limited Inc.* Evanston, IL: Northwestern University Press.
Foucault, M. (1984) 'The masked philosopher', trans. A. Sheridan, in L. D. Kritzman (ed.), *Michel Foucault: Politics, Philosophy, Culture: Interviews and Other Writings 1977–1984*. New York: Routledge.

Key source texts related to postmodern and post-structuralist theory

Baudrillard, J. (1988) *Selected Writings*, ed. Mark Poser. Cambridge: Polity Press.
Bauman, Z. (1992) *Intimations of Postmodernity*. London: Routledge.
Bhabha, H. K. (1994) *The Location of Culture*. London: Routledge.
Butler, J. (1993) *Bodies That Matter: On the Discursive Limits of Sex*. New York: Routledge.
Butler, J. (1999 [1990]) *Gender Trouble*, 2nd edn. New York: Routledge.
Derrida, J. (1978) *Writing and Difference*. Chicago: University of Chicago Press.
Derrida, J. (1993) *Memoirs of the Blind: The Self-Portrait and Other Ruins*. Chicago: University of Chicago Press.
Foucault, M. (1980) *Power/Knowledge: Selected Interviews and Other Writings (1977–1984)*, ed. Colin Gordon. Brighton: Harvester Press.
Foucault, M. (1989) *Madness and Civilization: A History of Insanity in the Age of Reason*, trans. Richard Howard. London: Routledge.
*Giddens, A. (1990) *The Consequences of Modernity*. Cambridge: Polity Press.
Haraway, D. (1991) *Simians, Cyborgs and Women: The Reinvention of Nature*. London: Free Association Books.

Hardt, M. and Weeks, K. (eds) (2000) *The Jameson Reader*. Boston: Blackwell.

*Lemert, C. (1997) *Postmodernism Is Not What You Think*. Oxford: Blackwell.

Lyotard, J.-F. (1984) *The Postmodern Condition: A Report on Knowledge*, trans. Geoff Bennington and Brian Massumi. Manchester: Manchester University Press.

*MacGuigan, J. (1999) *Modernity and Postmodern Culture*. Buckingham: Open University Press.

*Narayan, U. and Harding, S. (2000) *Decentering the Center: Philosophy for a Multicultural, Postcolonial and Feminist World*. Bloomington: Indiana University Press.

*Nicholson, L. J. (1990) *Feminism/Postmodernism*. New York: Routledge.

*Price, J. E. and Shildrick, M. (1999) *Feminist Theory and the Body: A Reader*. Edinburgh: Edinburgh University Press.

*Seidman, S. (1998) *Contested Knowledge: Social Theory in the Postmodern Era*, 2nd edn. Oxford: Blackwell.

Spivak, G. C. (1987) *In Other Worlds: Essays in Cultural Politics*. New York: Methuen.

Young, I. M. (1990) *Throwing Like a Girl*. Bloomington: Indiana University Press.

Note

* These texts are general texts that introduce and critically explore many of the key themes explored above.

2

A Journey around the Social Model

Carol Thomas and Mairian Corker

Introduction

This chapter is written from the experience of two disabled women with different impairments – one physical (Carol) and the other sensory (Mairian) – whose work has emerged from very different disciplinary backgrounds. Carol describes herself as a materialist feminist and sociologist, and Mairian as a 'post-structuralist feminist' and 'sociolinguist'. In our work, both of us, in different ways, have engaged with and/or problematized particular interpretations of the social model of disability. In this chapter, we aim to explore some of the tensions between modernity and postmodernity as they are implicated in creating and constructing disability as a social relation. To do this, each of us will attempt to engage with the other's position in a critical examination of a number of issues such as Marxism, identity, difference, discourse and materialism.

Positioning ourselves

Carol
For me, the great significance of the social model of disability, as encapsulated in the original UPIAS (Union of the Physically Impaired Against Segregation) (1976) formulation that disability is the active and purposive social exclusion and disadvantaging of people with impairment, resides in its redefinition of disability as a social relational as opposed to a biologically determined phenomenon. That is, disability becomes a product and oppressive quality of the social relationships that exist between people who are socially marked as having impairment and those who are marked as physically, sensorially and cognitively 'normal'. Defining disability as social relational poses a wide range of sociological questions, including: what sociocultural processes are involved in the construction of particular features of the body as constituting 'impairment', and in what times and places? What are the sociocultural mechanisms that shape the structural and interpersonal relationships in which disability is acted out – whether it be in the structural

exclusion of people with impairment from the mainstream education system or the labour force, or in the personal insult delivered to the wheelchair-using shopper by the store assistant who talks only to the wheelchair user's standing companion?

These are some of the sociological questions of interest to me. As stated in my book, *Female Forms* (1999), I particularly want to know how the social relationships which constitute disability are generated and sustained within social and cultural formations. I bring to this quest an already formulated understanding of the nature of social and cultural systems, one that draws on historical materialist premisses. This means that I am disposed to think that the disability, or disablism, we observe in our own society is fundamentally bound up with this society's capitalist social relations of production together with the cultural forms and ideological phenomena that are shaped by, and impact back upon, these economic foundations. Thus I am sympathetically drawn to the attempts by authors like Mike Oliver (1990, 1996a) and Brendan Gleeson (1999) to locate the foundations of present-day disablism in the historical emergence and developmental stages of capitalist relations of production. Apart from anything else, this approach assumes that other modes of production, past and future, are likely to generate different sets of social relationships between what *we identify* as impaired and non-impaired people. That is, disability and impairment are not universal, fixed, unchanging, transhistorical social phenomena.

I also bring feminist perspectives to bear in my study of disability. Feminism, in general, draws attention to the oppressive gender order within societies: to the fact that all social relationships carry the imprint of socially constructed gender difference. My empirical research has demonstrated that disability is fundamentally gendered (1997, 1998, 1999). This, in turn, makes one alert to the significance of other dimensions of social oppression associated with 'race', age, sexuality, class and so forth. This means that the study of disability should carefully consider the ways in which oppressive social relationships intersect, and the consequences that this has for lived experience. In my view, social modellists to date, with a few exceptions, have given insufficient attention to this task. In *Female Forms* (1999), I have also argued at length that disability studies can learn a great deal from feminist scholarship on the epistemological and political significance of taking the lived 'experiences' of disabled people seriously. In addition, I have advanced the view that the dominance of masculinist, anti-experiential perspectives in social modellist work has had the effect of privileging the 'restrictions on doing' dimensions of disability over its 'restrictions on being' dimensions. I have made a case for considering the psycho-emotional dimensions of disability alongside those disablist practices that restrict disabled people's activities in the world. In the light of these considerations, my adaptation of the UPIAS formulation of disability is as follows: disability is a form of social oppression involving the social imposition of restrictions of activity on people with impairments and the socially engendered undermining of their psycho-emotional well-being.

There is another dimension of 'difference' that requires attention in disability studies: those bodily, sensory and cognitive 'differences' that carry a variety of medical labels signifying impairment. Whilst impairments make up the material prerequisite, or substantive premiss, for the social enactment of disability, different forms of impairment are often associated with specific configurations or manifestations of disability. In their attempt to distance themselves completely from the 'impairment causes disability' stance of the individualistic or medical model of disability, most social modellists have paid insufficient attention to the ways in which different forms of impairment come to be associated with different forms or manifestations of disablism. In fact, I believe that the whole question of impairment should be much more centrally addressed in disability studies (but not at the expense of a core focus on the theorization and empirical research of disability). In particular, I have suggested that it is important to acknowledge the reality of what I have called *impairment effects*. These are the direct effects of impairment which differentiate bodily functioning from that which is socially construed to be normal or usual. In our society, these impairment effects generally, but not always, become the medium for the social relational enactment of disability: social exclusionary and discriminatory practices. The lives of people with impairment are profoundly shaped by the interaction of disability and impairment effects, and in lived experience these join together with other dimensions of individuals' social positioning (gender, 'race', age, class, sexuality).

Historical materialist, or Marxist, theory is often characterized as being crudely economic determinist, and of either ignoring or downplaying the importance of cultural and/or psychological processes in the shaping of social phenomena, whether disablism or anything else. The agency of the individual actor is also often thought to be denied. I do not accept these versions of materialist or Marxist theory. In my view, a materialist perspective has the potential to engage richly with the cultural, ideological and psychosocial (for example, identity). This is not to deny, in turn, the value of the insights gained through other theoretical perspectives, for example post-structuralism, postmodernism and psychoanalysis. However, it seems to me that the incompatibilities of the philosophical underpinnings of materialist and post-structuralist (and other) theory has to be acknowledged and understood – these perspectives cannot simply be brought together in any new synthesis.

Mairian

Not everyone has the same means of access to the same knowledge. *How* we access knowledge therefore has an important bearing on *what* we know and *how* we know it, and this knowledge can both inform and distort our interpretations of the social world. If we interpret the social world without opening ourselves to knowledge that is *not* of our experience, then the way we make theory and engage in practice inevitably limits the liberatory possibilities of both. Certainly, when I think about my experience of disability, it has little to do with being unable to hear, but being unable to hear does at the same time affect how I orientate myself in the world. It has *ontological* consequences, notably the dependence on vision and text, that interact in complex ways with the oppressive consequences of the social organization of language and communication in a world that privileges the strongest and most articulate voices. My allegiance with other disabled people makes me aware that the social organization of discourse – or language in use – impinges on *all* our lives. But this allegiance also throws our ontological differences into stark relief in ways that disguise full understanding of their social constitution. How we deal with these differences requires open, engaged dialogue, not silencing. It seems therefore that discourse is a significant dimension of both our experience of oppression and our political struggles for social transformation. The question for me then becomes one of whether disability theory in its present configuration, and the social model in particular, can adequately address this dimension of our struggles and, if it cannot, what alternatives are there?

The 'first wave' of disability theory is dominated by the fleshly concerns of neo-Marxism. It acknowledges the influence of critical Marxists such as Raymond Williams, in particular his attempts 'to bridge the gap between literary criticism and sociology' (Barnes *et al.*, 1999: 183–4). But there are ways in which it also fails to get to grips with Williams's (1977: 21) assertion that 'Marxism has contributed very little to thinking about language itself'. He continues:

> The result has been either that limited and undeveloped versions of language as a 'reflection' of 'reality' have been taken for granted, or that propositions about language, developed within or in the forms of other and often antagonistic systems of thought, have been synthesised with Marxist propositions about *other kinds of activity*, in ways that are not only ultimately untenable but, in our own time, radically limiting to the strength of the social propositions. (1977: 21, italics mine)

The first wave of disability theory has elements of both outcomes. For example, if we interpret 'other kinds of activity' to mean the 'fleshly concerns' referred to earlier, I would argue that the modernist proposition that 'the body' is a fixed, material reality is too often synthesized with a similar proposition about language, when language-in-action is anything but fixed. I feel that the neo-Marxist view of discourse in disability theory originates in two contrasting, though ultimately interlinked positions. First, it seeks to strengthen and reinforce the boundaries between particular concepts – namely the individual nature of impairment and the social nature of dis-ability – and this is achieved through the silencing of impairment and its abstraction from the social context (see also Chapter 3). Second, it stems from a suspicion of what is referred to as 'the postmodern' idea that 'the world is constructed through discourse alone', whilst failing to explain that there is no such thing as a unified postmodern theory, nor a unified position on what 'postmodern' actually means (Lemert, 1997).

It is for this reason that neo-Marxist perspectives place limits on *how* we can explain social relations, because they do not take an embodied view of language. Further, social systems that are exclusively built on systems of classification – *including both the socially created and the socially constructed classifications 'disability' and 'impairment'* – are generally undemocratic, oppressive and exclusionary (Young, 1990; Butler, 1993). However, when a pragmatic approach is taken to the analysis of everyday situated social prac-tice, it *is* difficult to say, for example, exactly where the sphere of the indi-vidual ends and the sphere of the collective begins. I do not deny that there are oppressive social and historical forces, the most important of which is capitalism, and this is why I do not subscribe to postmodern ontologies that conflate the social with discourse, nor with epistemologies that advocate a 'playful' position for theoretical practice. On the contrary, I see discourse as existing in a mutually constitutive relationship with other dimensions of social process such as power, social relations, material practice, institutions/rituals and beliefs/values desires, described by Harvey (1996). But as valued forms of capital diversify and change, a radical politics cannot and must not be confined to visible and collective opposition. We have to understand that the collective itself usually acts as a structuring device. To challenge this, it seems to be better to view collective organization in terms of the tensions and contradictions between difference – what we call social differentiation or diversity – and sameness – the social cohesion or structure that produces social meaning. Therefore, I tend to support the view of Fraser and Nicholson (1990) that a critical synthesis of the postmodern deconstruction of mono-liths and a feminist commitment to radical politics can provide the basis for a powerful social theory of disability that overcomes the limitations of the two. Such a critical synthesis indicates that the emancipatory project is based on active and engaged dialoguing across difference, not the suppression of difference.

Constructing a dialogue

Mairian

My initial response to your position statement is to say that I can find very little that I am in direct disagreement with. As might be expected, however, it is the *details* that trouble me – the *what* and the *how* – and I think this may in part be explained through the difference between social theory and sociological theory. On impairment, you make two key statements: 'impairments make up the material prerequisite or substantive premiss for the social enactment of disability' and 'different forms of impairment are often associated with specific configurations or manifestations of disability'. Gleeson (1999: 20) refers to these manifestations of disability as 'unique *social* realities', but attributes uniqueness to 'geographical and historical differences' whilst insisting 'the body' plays a foundational role in the constitution of human society. Both you and Gleeson therefore seem to presuppose that the relation between impairment and disability implies a culture or an agency of the social which acts upon nature, which is itself presupposed as a passive surface outside the social and yet its necessary counterpart. This reminds me of extensive feminist debates about the relationship between female and male and sex and gender (Ortner, 1974; Butler, 1997).

At the same time, you say that impairment (and therefore disability?) 'are not universal, fixed, unchanging, transhistorical social phenomena'. I agree with the latter point, but I have difficulty reconciling this with a 'foundational' view of impairment, especially one that places emphasis on the physical materiality of the body (Corker, 1999). The reason for my uneasiness, I think, is not so much to do with your interpretation, but with 'the dominance of masculinist, anti-experiential perspectives in social modellist work'. In particular, I am thinking of the arguments about whether impairment should be counted 'in' or 'out' (Barnes *et al.*, 1999: 92).

Although I recognize that disabled feminists such as Jenny Morris (1991), Liz Crow (1996) and yourself have been at the forefront of challenging this perspective, I am not convinced that these arguments resolve the problem because they seem to leave the malestream basis of the social model intact. In Jenny and Liz's work, especially, impairment is often conflated with personal experience and thus remains firmly located at the level of the individual. It is also seen to be without value. Thus disability and impairment continue to exist in the kind of social relation of privileging that I reject. The danger of privileging lies not through the naming of difference but in how difference is essentialized and performed in social practice. Following Butler (1993), I would therefore argue that, when the conceptual boundaries between disability and impairment are materialized in the social practice of a politics of identity, this turns against the constitutive historicity of disabled people's oppression. I think this is precisely why including impairment does not depoliticize theory. Indeed, if impairment is left out, what, then, is the 'material prerequisite' unless it is a fixed, passive surface? And if it is a fixed, passive surface it must be regarded as an unproblematized *collective* corporeality, which *cannot* then correspond to Gleeson's 'unique social realities'. This seems to be part of the process whereby accounts *of disability* become overly focused on 'structure' and 'the built environment' at the expense of 'agency' and 'social practice'.

To understand how you see these problems, I think I need to draw you out further on the issue of impairment and the meaning of social relation. I'd also like to ask you whether you see capitalism as 'universal, fixed, unchanging and transhistorical'.

Carol

It is interesting and telling that our conversation is inexorably drawn to the issue of impairment. In disability studies, impairment is increasingly at the centre of theoretical disagreement and discussion. I have always thought that those of us working with the social model of disability *have* to engage with impairment in order to get on with the main task – theorizing and exposing disability, and thus clarifying the political terrain for challenging disablism. I agree with you that impairment cannot be left aside or, worse, treated as an unproblematized 'biological' or naturalistic phenomenon. It has to be 'brought back in' in at least three senses. First, the personal experience of living with impairment and impairment effects has to be acknowledged and understood. Second, impairment should be theorized as a biosocial phenomenon. Third, there should be an analysis of the similarities and differences in disability experiences associated with the full range of impairments.

Let me say more on this third point. I think we are in agreement that people with impairments such as learning difficulty, cognitive difference and deafness confront some forms of disability which are common to all disabled people (employment discrimination, for example). But they also have specific kinds of encounters with disablism more closely bound up with the features of the impairment itself. This is not because the impairment is 'the cause' of that disablism (in a medical model sense) but because disablism (discrimination, exclusion, prejudice) often expresses itself in direct response to the features of impairment of the individual disabled person (or their perceived group). This is what I meant in my position statement when I said that 'impairments make up the material prerequisite or substantive premiss of the social enactment of disability'. But I certainly do not see impairment itself as outwith the social, as 'pre-social' or as a fixed, passive surface.

So, impairment does matter, and I agree with your statement that 'including impairment does not depoliticize theory'. It is certainly the case that the specific forms of disablism encountered by people with sensory impairment and learning difficulty have been relatively ignored by social modellists within disability studies until very recently.

To your question 'Do you see capitalism as "universal, fixed, unchanging and transhistorical"?' my answer is definitely 'no'. Capitalism is a mode of generalized commodity production that emerged through the dissolution of feudal social relations of production (sixteenth to eighteenth centuries in Britain). It is a dynamic system of production that has transformed and continues to transform the social and cultural landscape. The key theoretical question for me is: how did the development of capitalist relations of production change the relationships between people with and without impairments? Did a new form of social oppression arise? Yes – disablism. I like Oliver's (1990) and Gleeson's (1999) approach because they ask the same kind of questions. These are questions in search of 'root causes', an endeavour that has been rejected as a mistaken modernist preoccupation by post-structuralists and postmodernists. Does this kind of question have any significance for you? If not, why is that the case? I think we could learn a lot about our different approaches through discussion of this issue.

Mairian

I think this has happened because those who engage with post-structural methodologies and with postmodernity as a social condition see these 'root causes' as having been presented as some set of universal truths that, in the case of disabled people, divide the social world up into oppressor and oppressed. Such 'truths' cannot account for differences in socially situated knowledge and localized resistance, for example. In response to your specific question about 'root causes', I think I would first change the question to 'How *does* the development of capitalist relations of production change the relationships between people with and without impairments *in contemporary society*?' The reason is that I take the view that the power relations in contemporary society are primarily structured by the possession of and access to knowledge and information. Thus people who are holders of knowledge and information capital are the main commodity in such a society, and education becomes the primary process of production. I then ask how the global economy, with its transnational corporations, capital mobility, informationalization and international divisions of labour, has influenced and changed social hierarchies and the social configuration of impairment and disability. In answer to this question, I suggest that the boundaries between disability and impairment have been blurred in such a way that modernist distinctions between them are no longer tenable. Thus it is important to examine the space *between* disability and impairment, which you refer to in your writing, but do not actually elaborate on. There is an important political reason for this. It seems reasonable to suggest that, when holders of knowledge and information are regarded as a commodity, there is a risk of *increased* discursive colonization by an authority that claims to speak for disabled people, particularly those who are seen to be unable to speak for themselves. At the same time, though I acknowledge the role of structure and ideology in the process of colonization, and though macrosocial processes profoundly affect people's daily choices and concerns, they are nevertheless mostly invisible to people who have these concerns and are making these choices. Identifying 'root causes' is all well and good, but the specifics of their operation in disabled people's lived experience is a far more complex issue that needs a different kind of analytical tool.

Carol
Let us go back to impairment for a moment. Your sensory impairment means that both the impairment effects you experience and the disability (social exclusions) that you live with are quite different from those that I have experiential knowledge of. What I have learnt from you and other people with hearing impairment is that disability resides and presents itself fundamentally in the realms of communication and language. Of course, my experiences of disability are also mediated through language, but I do not see them as originating in language.

Mairian
So what we seem to be getting at here is that language and communication are implicated in both impairment and disability. This leads me to wonder if it is not also the case that your impairment originates in language, at least to the extent that it has been labelled within medical discourse and these labels, and the ideologies on which they are built, frequently determine how people have learnt to respond to your impairment – or disable you – in the social context.

Carol
I agree that language and communication are absolutely key dimensions of social relationships in any society and would certainly not share in the view that language is of secondary importance. On the other hand, I disagree with some postmodernists and post-structuralists who reduce *everything* to language in the final analysis (that is, the 'there is no social reality outside of language' position).

Mairian
But if impairment is also social, then how can this *not* be the case, since 'the social' is mediated through language and communication and, as such, 'the social' is constituted through language and communication? Of course, one could equally make the same claims about approaches that reduce everything to 'material reality', particularly those that rest on the presentist

assumptions of the 'visual' and the 'visceral'. It is to break down such assumptions that I emphasize the mutual constitution of the different elements of social process, and an opening up of the space between them.

Carol
That is one thing that puzzles me. Whilst a self-defined post-structuralist, here and elsewhere you state clearly that you do not adopt this discursive reductionist position (Corker, 1998; Corker and French, 1999), and I recognize that the theoretical designation 'post-structuralist' encompasses many variants of thought. I want to ask you, however, to clarify for me exactly what your understanding is of the relationship between language and dimensions of material life. At the same time, I agree with your observation that Marxists have not cracked this nut either (and I certainly do not have all the answers!) – but in my view there is no inherent reason why historical materialism cannot or should not theorize language and culture more broadly.

Mairian
First, I think it would have to be a radically different and perhaps unrecognizable historical materialism with a 'strong' feminist orientation. Gleeson's account, for example, though it positions itself as close to Williams's 'cultural materialism' (1999: 26), and refers to Harvey's (1996) work in the context of justice, studiously avoids discussion of these authors' work on discourse, knowledge and information. However, before I say how I understand the relationship between language and dimensions of material life, I think I would first want to address this issue of self-definition. You may have noticed that in spite of my 'self-definition' as a post-structuralist feminist, I quite readily draw on work that is *not* part of this tradition. This is because I am uncomfortable with locating myself exclusively within the 'authority' of a single epistemological tradition as, among other things, I see this to be profoundly anti-feminist.

As to your specific question about the relationship between language and the dimensions of material life, I think it must be emphasized again that I write from the ontological position of people with language and communication impairments in a social world that increasingly privileges information and communication capital. The fact that I talk a lot about language reflects this, but this does not represent the epistemological position of discursive reductionism because the language I describe is embodied, situated language. The reason I do this is because social theory currently has a 'body focus' that sometimes degenerates into a materialist essentialism. I think that the theorizing of the *communicating, sensory and sensual* body still has to struggle against these relations of privileging precisely because language leans naturally towards the complex, the uncertain and the unpredictable. In other words, attention to language does not produce easy answers. The way I approach this problem is very similar to the way that post-structuralist feminists, queer theorists and critical 'race' theorists have challenged the 'universal' body by opening up social theory to the multiplicity of ways of being and forms of knowledge.

For example, in my work, I seek to develop some notion of *deaf* consciousness that can trouble the oppressive signifiers and practices that produce the value-ridden concepts of Deaf and hearing. Historical materialist accounts of deafness (for example, see Davis, 1995) in my view simply reproduce dis-value and therefore oppression. I believe that the signifier 'hearing impairment' and the social category 'people with hearing impairments' are materialized and performed through their exclusion, erasure or what linguists call elision from Deaf *and* hearing. In other words, they are rendered invisible and unintelligible in the battles between hegemony and counter-hegemony, and, as markers of in-between spaces, they require the authority of *both* Deaf and hearing to exist.

However, given the drive towards policy and practice that ostensibly promotes social and educational inclusion, it seems increasingly important to understand the politics of interdependency rather than the politics of opposition. In seeking to articulate *deaf* consciousness, I am attempting to locate the narrative of *deafness* in the material reality of cross-cultural, cross-border processes that are characteristic of such a politics. I do this in order radically to reorganize and reconstruct experience so that its mutually constitutive nature is emphasized. I hope this will both avoid the 'robot' repetition of others' views of 'deaf lives' (see Harding, 1991: 291) – something I see to be broadly characteristic of the disability studies literature – and facilitate a more nuanced exploration of the relationship between deafness, disability and the hegemony of 'normalcy'. I think this emphasis locates me within the post-structuralist view that subjects are not the autonomous creators of themselves or their social worlds, but are embedded in a complex network of social relations that determine which subjects can appear, where and in what capacity. But I would also argue that modernist theories posit agents as the source of knowledge and action, whereas post-structuralist theories maintain that agents are effects of a specific social and cultural logic. I use the post-structuralist *tool* of deconstruction to contest and trouble particular forms of foundationalism.

Carol

I would certainly agree that an adequate social model of disability *must* be able to embrace a theoretical understanding of the relationship between impairment, modes of communication and forms of disablism, together with an understanding of the political implications of this for the disabled people's movement. I also agree that, whatever our impairments are, we are all 'constituted', that is, positioned and given meaning, through the discourses we live with in our cultures. And, yes, these teach us to think in unhelpful dualisms that need to be problematized. However, for me, these discourses are part of the ideological superstructure of the mode of production of our times, and are fundamentally bound up with it (but not mechanically produced by it). Politically, whilst I agree that we should all engage in a struggle to change oppressive discourses, this is not enough on its own because the roots of disablism go deeper – into the very social relations of production of our society. The position of people with impairments (of whatever kind) in the social relations of production and reproduction has to be addressed too.

Neo-Marxist social modellists (your positioning of authors like Barnes and Oliver) have failed to deal with the *social* character of impairment. In my view, developing a social theorization of impairment requires an understanding of human bodies (as physiological, sensory and cognitive entities in social space) and their historical *interaction* with forms of production and cultural practices. Thus, this is not purely a matter of dealing with the social and the cultural, but requires of social scientists that they engage with (what is culturally labelled to be) the biological – something that those working in the field of genetics are beginning to do (see, for example, Scully, Silvers, and Price and Shildrick, in this volume).

Mairian
I think it is fair to say that, on the evidence of what they have written, Oliver and Barnes position *themselves* within neo-Marxist frameworks (see, for example, Oliver and Barnes, 1998). Though they claim that discourse is part of the story of disability, they do not attempt to analyse it in the context of social relations. Oliver (1996b) has also expressed the belief that a social theory of impairment should be developed *separately from* a social theory of disability. My worry is that if the social theorization of impairment is carried out in this way, and is conducted within the modernist dichotomies of mind/body, individual/society and structure/culture, for example, what will happen is what, historically, has always happened. There will, given the current privileging of the physicality of the body in sociology and related disciplines, be a sidelining of cognitive impairments accompanied by the erasure of sensory impairments. There will continue to be a physicalist emphasis on 'restrictions of doing' and, in particular, a focus on the employment-related solutions to disability oppression criticized by Abberley (1998). And there will be a continued focus on ideological superstructures rather than on the socially situated knowledges of disabled people and how they are constituted in everyday social practice. I remain of the view that post-structural methodologies and theories are better suited to the 'deep' analysis of socially situated knowledges, including hegemonic knowledge, and to the ontological mapping of oppressed subjectivities, but I sense that you agree with this. I am less certain as to whether it is possible to *resolve* what you describe as the philosophical

differences between materialist and post-structuralist disability theory, but I do think, as suggested above, that they can exist in a critical synthesis with each other.

Concluding remarks

In this chapter we have sought, through dialogue, to examine the complex interplay between the modern and the postmodern in contemporary analyses of disability. This dialogue has been helpful in teasing out some of the different ways of thinking about disability, impairment and political struggle that arise from contrasting theoretical traditions and the variable biographies of the authors. There is certainly common ground: agreement on the necessity of feminist perspectives within disability studies; the requirement to engage analytically with impairment; the dangers of dualistic thinking; the importance of language, discourse and culture; and the continued dominance of capitalism in the twenty-first century. In these areas, we have perhaps identified some of the difficulties of constructing too stark an opposition between modernist and postmodernist perspectives on culture and society. However, in other areas we have struggled over the details of each other's meanings and to comprehend where the other is coming from. For example, Carol continues to struggle with Mairian's insistence that the constructed boundaries which constitute categories like 'impairment' and 'disability' need to be broken down so that the 'space between disability and impairment is addressed'. Mairian remains unconvinced that such categories are simply clarifying 'concepts'. She feels that the kind of social relations and politics they have increasingly come to signify, and the kind of theories they promote, retain all the worst elements of modernist thought, which, in some of its denominations, continues to be oppressive and exclusionary. One outcome of this, not so much in our dialogue, but certainly within disability studies, is that the voices on the margins are silenced rather than allowed to exist in a state of creative tension. Nevertheless, we hope this chapter has demonstrated that engaged and open dialogue can be a useful pragmatic tool in developing understanding of contested perspectives. We believe that disability studies can only benefit from the critical, reflexive exchange of ideas between those who bring different theoretical perspectives and different biographies to bear.

References

Abberley, P. (1998) 'The spectre at the feast: disabled people and social theory', in T. Shakespeare (ed.), *The Disability Reader: Social Science Perspectives*. London: Cassell.

Barnes, C., Mercer, G. and Shakespeare, T. (1999) *Exploring Disability*. Cambridge: Polity.

Butler, J. (1993) *Bodies That Matter: On the Discursive Limits of Sex*. New York: Routledge.

Butler, J. (1997) 'Against proper objects', in E. Weed and N. Schor (eds), *Feminism Meets Queer Theory*. Bloomington: Indiana University Press.

Corker, M. (1998) *Deaf and Disabled, or Deafness Disabled?* Buckingham: Open University Press.

Corker, M. (1999) 'Differences, conflations and foundations: the limits to the "accurate" theoretical representation of disabled people's experience', *Disability and Society*, 15(4): 627–42.

Corker, M. and French, S. (1999) 'Reclaiming discourse in disability studies', in M. Corker and S. French (eds), *Disability Discourse*. Buckingham: Open University Press.

Crow, L. (1996) 'Including all our lives: renewing the social model of disability', in C. Barnes and E. Mercer (eds), *Exploring the Divide: Illness and Disability*. Leeds: Disability Press.

Davis, L. J. (1995) *Enforcing Normalcy*. London: Verso.

Fraser, N. and Nicholson, L. J. (1990) 'Social criticism without philosophy: an encounter between feminism and postmodernism', in L. J. Nicholson (ed.), *Feminism/Postmodernism*. New York: Routledge.

Gleeson, B. (1999) *Geographies of Disability*. London: Routledge.

Harding, S. (1991) *Whose Science? Whose Knowledge?* Ithaca: Cornell University Press.

Harvey, D. A. (1996) *Justice, Nature and the Politics of Difference*. Oxford: Blackwell.

Lemert, C. (1997) *Postmodernism Is Not What You Think*. Malden, MA: Blackwell.

Morris, J. (1991) *Pride Against Prejudice*. London: Women's Press.

Oliver, M. (1990) *The Politics of Disablement*. Basingstoke: Macmillan.

Oliver, M. (1996a) *Understanding Disability*. Basingstoke: Macmillan.

Oliver, M. (1996b) 'Defining impairment and disability', in C. Barnes and G. Mercer (eds), *Exploring the Divide: Illness and Disability*. Leeds: Disability Press.

Oliver, M. and Barnes, C. (1998) *Disabled People and Social Policy*. London: Longman.

Ortner, S. (1974) 'Is female to male as nature is to culture?', in M. Rosaldo and L. Lamphere (eds), *Woman, Culture and Society*. Stanford: Stanford University Press, pp. 67–88.

Thomas, C. (1997) 'The baby and the bathwater: disabled women and motherhood in social context', *Sociology of Health and Illness*, 19(5): 622–43.

Thomas, C. (1998) 'Parents and family: disabled women's stories about their childhood experiences', in C. Robinson and K. Stalker (eds), *Growing up with Disability*. London: Jessica Kingsley.

Thomas, C. (1999) *Female Forms: Experiencing and Understanding Disability*. Buckingham: Open University Press.

Williams, R. (1977) *Marxism and Literature*. Oxford: Oxford University Press.

Young, I. M. (1990) *Justice and the Politics of Difference*. Princeton: Princeton University Press.

3

On the Subject of Impairment[1]

Shelley Tremain

Introduction: Foucault and disability studies

The starting point of this chapter is the observation that writers in disability studies have not availed themselves of the insights into modern power that the work of Michel Foucault offers them. This neglect of the ways in which Foucauldian analyses would enrich disability studies and expand the scope of its theoretical practices seems surprising, given the huge currency that Foucault's work has enjoyed in the domains of feminist studies, post-colonial studies, queer theory and other oppositional discourses. It seems especially surprising, given that the birth of modern perceptions of disease and the body (Foucault, 1973a), the social production of madness (Foucault, 1973b) and technologies of normalization (Foucault, 1980) were among the topics which Foucault closely inspected.

This apparent disregard for Foucault's work should be attributed in part to certain misunderstandings of that approach in addition to the general refusal of 'postmodernism' in the materialist theories of prominent 'social model-lists' (to use Carol Thomas's term) in the UK. In most of that materialist work, Foucault's nominalist analyses (along with an array of other diverse, and even competing, theories) are subsumed under the banner of 'social constructionism', are identified as 'idealist', and are claimed to 'lack explanatory power'. Mark Priestley argues, for example, that although nominalist and other 'social constructionist' approaches to disability are instructive with respect to identifying the ideological and cultural processes that constitute 'disablism', they 'do not necessarily account for *why* these processes occur in particular historical contexts' (Priestley, 1998: 77–83, 87–8; see also Barnes, 1996: 48–9; Thomas, 1998: 60; cf. Hacking, 1999, on nominalism).

Most of the materialist analyses in disability studies assume a realist ontology, in whose terms 'real' objects with transhistorical and transcultural identities exist in Nature apart from any contingent signifying practice. By contrast, theorists and researchers who use Foucault's nominalist approach hold that there are no phenomena or states of affairs that exist independently of the historically and culturally specific language-games in which we understand them and with which we represent them. Thus, those who use

Foucault's approach think inquiry is misguided which aims to account for 'why' allegedly timeless processes constitutive of an allegedly timeless problem (say, disablism) occur in some socio-historical contexts and not in others. On Foucault's approach, the more appropriate, and important, question that social theorists should seek to answer is rather this one: What were the historical conditions of possibility for this problem in the present? Foucault's later works on the birth of the modern penal institution (1977), the history of sexuality (1978), the use of pleasure (1984) and the care of the self (1985) comprise a set of genealogies ('histories of the present') that trace the conditions of possibility for several ontologies and the historically contingent practices that have given form to them.

Theorists and researchers in disability studies should adopt this sort of genealogical approach to their work. For the conceptual framework within which an increasing number of theorists and researchers in the field conduct their work – the social model of disability – precludes analysis of the mechanisms of power/knowledge that Foucault has identified. Developed to counter individual (or medical) models of disability which construe that state of affairs as the detrimental consequences of an intrinsic deficit or personal flaw, the social model has two terms of reference, which are taken to be mutually exclusive. They are *impairment* and *disability* (Oliver, 1990: 4–11). As the formalized articulation of a set of principles generated by the Union of the Physically Impaired Against Segregation (UPIAS), the social model defines *impairment* as 'the lack of a limb or part thereof or a defect of a limb, organ or mechanism of the body'; in addition, *disability* is defined as 'a form of disadvantage which is imposed on top of one's impairment, that is, the disadvantage or restriction of activity caused by a contemporary social organization that takes little or no account of people with physical impairments' (UPIAS, 1976, in Oliver, 1996: 22).

Responding to one medical sociologist's claim that the UK disability movement (informed by the social model) discusses disability 'as if it had nothing to do with the physical body', Michael Oliver insists that, while disablement *is* nothing to do with the body, impairment is nothing less than a description of the physical body (Oliver, 1996: 35; emphasis in the original). Several interlocutors within disability studies have variously argued, however, that because proponents of the social model have forced a strict separation between the categories of impairment and disability in this way, the former category has remained untheorized (e.g., Shakespeare and Watson, 1995; Hughes and Paterson, 1997; Corker, 1999). Bill Hughes and Kevin Paterson have pointed out, for example, that although the impairment-disability distinction demedicalizes disability, it renders the impaired body the exclusive jurisdiction of medical interpretation (Hughes and Paterson, 1997: 330). I contend that this amounts to a failure to analyse how the sort of biomedical practices in whose analysis Foucault specialized have been complicit in the historical emergence of the category of impairment and contribute to its persistence.

Because much of the past work in disability studies has assumed a realist ontology, impairment has for the most part circulated in disability discourse as some objective, transhistorical and transcultural entity which biomedicine accurately represents. Foucault's historical approach could enable us to show, however, that this allegedly 'real' entity is in fact an historically contingent effect of modern power.

Hughes and Paterson allow that a Foucauldian approach to disability would be a worthwhile way to map the constitution of impairment and examine how regimes of truth about disabled bodies have been central to their governance and control (Hughes and Paterson, 1997: 332). They claim nonetheless that the approach I recommend ultimately entails the 'theoretical elimination of the material body' (*ibid.*, p. 34; see also Shakespeare and Watson, 1995). Notice that this argument begs the question, however; for the materiality of the 'impaired body' is precisely that which ought to be contested. In the words of Judith Butler, 'there is no reference to a pure body which is not at the same time a further formation of that body' (Butler, 1993: 10). Furthermore, Foucault does not deny the materiality of the body; rather, Foucault's argument is that the materiality of the body cannot be dissociated from the historically contingent practices that bring it into being, that is, *objectivize* it (cf. Hughes and Paterson, 1997: 333–4). Indeed, it seems politically naïve to suggest that the term 'impairment' is value-neutral, that is, 'merely descriptive', as if there could ever be a description which was not also a *prescription* for the formulation of that to which it is claimed innocently to refer. Truth-discourses which purport to describe phenomena contribute to the construction of their objects.

Contrary to Oliver, therefore, I want to argue that impairment and its materiality are naturalized *effects* of disciplinary knowledge/power. In what follows, I take what might seem to be a circuitous route to arrive at this thesis. First, I introduce some pertinent arguments in Foucault, which provide an historical context for the emergence of impairment as an object of knowledge/power. Readers should note I draw attention to the simultaneous historical emergence of *natural impairment* and *natural sex* as discursive objects. For in order to show how the form of power which Foucault identifies naturalizes and materializes its objects, I trace a genealogy of practices in various disciplinary domains (biology, clinical psychology, medico-surgical and feminist) which produce two 'natural' sexes. In turn, I apply these analyses to my argument that the foundational premise of the social model (impairment) is an historical artefact of this regime of knowledge/power.

Both 'natural sex' and 'natural impairment' have circulated in discursive and concrete practices as non-historical (biological) matter of the body, which is moulded by time and class, is culturally shaped or *on which* culture is imprinted. The matter of sex and of impairment itself has remained a prediscursive, that is, politically neutral, given. When we recognize that matter is an *effect* of historical conditions and contingent relations of power, however, we can begin to identify and resist the ones that have material-*ized* it.

Biopower and the juridical subject

The historical conditions that shaped modern perceptions of the body did not emerge until the late eighteenth century. In that historical context, the modern body was created as the effect and object of medical examination, which could be used, abused, transformed and subjugated. The doctor's patient had come to be treated in a way that had at one time been conceivable only with cadavers. The passivity of this object resulted from the procedure of clinical examination, where the investigative gaze fixed and crystallized as 'the body' that which it perceived. Clinical descriptions elaborated in the course of these examinations constituted new objects of knowledge and information, created new realities and introduced new, inescapable rituals into daily life, rituals whose participants became epistemologically dependent on the newly created objects (Foucault, 1973a, in Duden, 1991). Foucault argued that this objectification of the body in eighteenth-century clinical discourse was one pole around which a new regime of power – biopower – coalesced (Foucault, 1978). Foucault's concept of biopower refers to the strategic tendency of relatively recent forms of power/knowledge to work toward an increasingly comprehensive management of life: both the life of the individual and the life of the species (Allen, 1999).

In *The Birth of the Clinic* (1973a), Foucault demonstrates how the treatment of the body as a thing paralleled, and worked in concert with, the 'dividing practices' (Foucault, 1983 [1982]: 212) which were instituted in the nineteenth-century clinic's spatial, temporal and social compartmentalization. Foucault uses the term 'dividing practices' to refer to those modes of manipulation through which a science (or pseudo-science) is combined with practices of segregation and social exclusion: dividing practices categorize, distribute and manipulate subjects who are initially drawn from a rather undifferentiated mass of people (Rabinow, 1984). It is important that the Foucauldian *subject* is not confused with modern philosophy's *cogito*, autonomous self, or rational moral agent. For Foucault, to be a subject is to be subject to someone else by control and dependence and tied to one's own identity by a conscience or self-knowledge. In both cases, one is subjugated and made subject to. By a process of division either within themselves or from others, subjects are *objectivized* as (for instance) mad or sane, sick or healthy, criminal or good and, as a consequence, come to understand themselves scientifically (Foucault, 1983 [1982]). In short, through these objectifying procedures of division, classification and ordering, subjects become attached to a personal and social identity (Rabinow, 1984).

From the eighteenth century, a new set of procedures and operations – 'technologies' – came together around the objectification of the body. These technologies did not cause the rise of capitalism, but they were preconditions for its success (Rabinow, 1984; Gordon, 1991). Foucault refers to one of these technologies as 'discipline'. Not to be identified with a structure or institution, discipline 'is a type of power, a modality for its exercise, comprising a whole set of instruments, techniques, procedures, levels of application, targets; it is a "physics" or an "anatomy" of power, a technology' (Foucault, 1977: 215). Disciplinary technology is designed to produce a body which is 'docile', that is, one which can be subjected, used, transformed and improved (1997: 136). It is essential to understand, however, that disciplinary practices presuppose agency on the part of the subject: they enable subjects to act in order to constrain them (cf. Hughes and Paterson, 1997: 334). For juridical power *is* power, as opposed to mere physical force or violence, only if and when it is addressed to individuals who are free to act in one way or another. Although power appears to be fundamentally repressive, the 'essence' of power consists in 'acting upon an acting subject by virtue of their acting or being capable of action' (Foucault, 1983 [1982]: 220–1). The exercise of power consists in guiding the possibilities of conduct and putting in order the possible outcomes. In addition, the production of these practices, these *limits* of possible conduct, is a concealing. Concealment of these practices allows the naturalization and legitimation of the discursive formation in which they circulate (Butler, 1999 [1990]: 2). To put it another way, the production of seeming acts of choice on the everyday level of the subject makes possible hegemonic power structures.

Foucault regarded 'normalization' as the central component of the regime of biopower. In the first volume of *The History of Sexuality* (1978), Foucault explains the rationale behind normalizing technologies in this way:

> [A] power whose task is to take charge of life needs continuous regulatory and corrective mechanisms . . . Such a power has to qualify, measure, appraise, and hierarchize, rather than display itself in its murderous splendor; it does not have to draw the line that separates the enemies of the sovereign from his obedient subjects; it effects distributions around the norm . . . [T]he law operates more and more as a norm, and . . . the juridical institution is increasingly incorporated into a continuum of apparatuses (medical, administrative, and so on) whose functions are for the most part regulatory. (1978: 144)

Technologies of normalization are instrumental to the systematic creation, classification and control of 'anomalies' in the social body. Foucault argued that the function of these techniques is to isolate so-called anomalies, which can in turn be normalized through the therapeutic and corrective strategies of other, associated technologies (Rabinow, 1984). Because some normalizing technologies (such as practices of rehabilitation, breast reconstruction, psycho-analysis and confession) require a given subject to engage with an external authority or institution, they can easily be recognized as the disciplinary mechanisms that they are. Other normalizing technologies (such as self-help groups, assertiveness-training programmes, weight-loss regimens and fitness programmes) perform their disciplinary functions so effectively, however, precisely because the self-surveillance which induction in them requires seems for all intents and purposes to be expressive of a subject's personal desires and individuality. Indeed, an especially insidious aspect of normal-izing technologies is that the power of the state to produce an ever-expanding and increasingly totalizing web of social control is inextricably intertwined with, and dependent upon, its capacity to generate an increasing specification of individuality in this very way (Rabinow, 1984). Put directly, 'the great complex idea of normality' has become the means through which to identify subjects and make them identify themselves in ways that make them governable (Rajchman, 1991: 104).

The discipline of biology has served a key role in the expansion of this individuating form of power. Anne Fausto-Sterling (2000) remarks that, as biology emerged as an organized discipline during the late eighteenth and early nineteenth centuries, it accumulated increasing authority over bodies which were regarded as 'anomolous' or ambiguous in some way. For example, Isidore Geoffroy Saint-Hilaire founded a new science – *teratology* – for the study and classification of unusual births, including those of 'hermaphro-dites' and people with what have come to be referred to as 'birth defects', or 'congenital impairments'. While in the past unusual bodies had been regarded as unnatural and freakish, the new field of teratology offered a *natural* explanation for the birth of people with 'extraordinary bodies'. Nevertheless, in so far as teratology redefined such bodies as 'pathological', or 'unhealthy conditions' in need of a cure through the use of increased medical knowledge, scientific understanding operated as a tool to discipline precisely the wonders it had cast its gaze upon. By the middle of the twentieth century, medical technology had in fact 'progressed' to a point where, in the name of 'correcting nature's mistakes', it could make bodies that might at one time have been objects of awe and astonishment disappear from view completely (Fausto-Sterling, 2000: 36–7; see also Thomson, 1997: 75).

UNIVERSITY OF WINCHESTER
LIBRARY

Subjects of sex and gender

It was in the context of research on intersex, for example by Money and his colleagues, that the term 'gender' was initially used to refer to the psychosocial aspects of sex identity. Researchers who at the time aimed to develop protocols for the treatment of intersexuality required a theory of identity that would enable them to determine which of two 'sexes' to assign to their clinical subjects. They deemed the concept of *gender* (construed as the psychosocial dimensions of 'sex') as that which would enable them to make these designations (Hausman, 1995). In addition, they claimed that 'gender identity theory' allowed medical authorities to understand the experience of a given subject who was manifestly one 'sex', but who wished to be its ostensible other. In the terms of this sex-gender paradigm, 'normal' development was defined as that in which one's 'gender identity' is congruent with one's 'sexual anatomy' (*ibid.*, p. 7). The restrictive character of the paradigm might seem surprising, given the conclusion of these studies with intersexed people that sexual behaviour and orientation as 'male' or 'female' do not have an innate, or instinctive, basis. However, these researchers never questioned the fundamental assumption that there are only two sexes, because they studied intersexuality in order to gain a better understanding of 'normal' development. In their view, intersexuality resulted from fundamentally *abnormal* processes; thus, their patients required immediate treatment because they *ought* to have become *either* a male *or* a female (Fausto-Sterling, 2000).

Despite the prescriptive residue of the sex-gender formation, it appealed to early second-wave feminists because it assumed that everyone has a 'gender identity' which is detachable from each one's so-called 'sex' (Hausman, 1995: 7). Without questioning the realm of anatomical or biological sex, feminists took up the sex-gender paradigm in order to account for the culturally specific forms of an allegedly universal oppression of women. The distinction between sex and gender articulated through an appropriation of structuralist anthropology and Lacanian psychoanalysis (Rubin, 1975) has arguably been the most influential one in feminist discourse. By drawing on Lévi-Strauss's nature–culture distinction, Gayle Rubin cast *sex* as a natural (that is, prediscursive) property (attribute) of bodies and *gender* as its culturally specific configuration: 'Every society has a sex-gender system – a set of arrangements by which the biological raw material of human sex and procreation is shaped by human, social intervention and satisfied in a conventional manner' (Rubin, 1975: 165). For Rubin, in other words, sex is a product of nature and gender is a product of culture.

The structuralist nature–culture distinction on which this distinction relies was putatively invented to facilitate cross-cultural anthropological analyses; however, the universalizing framework of structuralism obscures the multiplicity of cultural configurations of 'nature' (Butler, 1999 [1990]). In fact, the distinction, as a theoretical device, is already circumscribed in a culturally specific epistemological frame. As Sandra Harding points out in a critical discussion of the sex-gender distinction, the way in which contemporary Western society draws the borders between culture and nature is both modern and culture bound. For the culture–nature dichotomy is interdependent on a field of binary oppositions (such as reason–emotion, mind–body, objectivity–subjectivity and male–female) which have structured Western modes of thought. In this dichotomous thinking, the former term of each respective pair is privileged and the latter term of each pair is discounted; moreover, the first term of each respective pair is assumed to provide the *form* for the second term of the pair. Indeed, within the terms of binary thinking, the very recognition of each respective latter term is held to depend upon, that is, *require*, the transparent and stable existence of the former term of the pair (Harding, 1989: 31).

Further, Donna Haraway has remarked that these oppositions have a certain socio-political history in colonialist Western discourse. In particular, this discourse structures the 'world' as an object of knowledge in terms of the cultural expropriation of the 'resources' of nature (Haraway, 1991). From the end of the eighteenth century, 'nature' emerged as a new organizing category of thought. For the Scientific Revolution produced a new concept that became central to social-scientific thinking of the nineteenth century: a Nature that is passive, subduable, inherently inert and obedient. In short, Nature could be appropriated and exploited (Duden, 1991).

Though early second-wave feminists criticized the nature–culture distinction and identified binary discourse as a dimension of the domination of those who inhabit 'natural' categories (women, people of colour, animals and the non-human environment), these critiques did not extend to the sex-gender distinction (see, for example, Harding, 1986). As Haraway explains it, this oversight was because it was too useful a tool with which to combat arguments for biological determinism in 'sex difference' political struggles (1991: 134). By conceding the territory of physical sex, however, feminists inadvertently opened themselves to massive resistance and renewed attack on the grounds of biological difference from the domains of biology, medicine and significant components of social science (Fausto-Sterling, 2000). In short, the political and explanatory power of the category of gender depends precisely upon relativizing and historicizing the category of sex, as well as the categories of biology, race, body and nature (Haraway, 1991). Indeed, the explanatory power of the sex-gender system has been criticized politically as part of the ethnocentric and imperialist tendencies of European and American feminists (see Tremain, 2000a, for a fuller account of these critiques)

Foucault makes remarks in another context that cast further ~
how the construct of 'nature' operates within the terms o.
distinction. Although 'sex' is generally taken to be a self-evide1

and biology, Foucault contends that 'sex is the most speculative, most ideal, and most internal element in a deployment of sexuality organized by power in its grip on bodies and their materiality, their forces, energies, sensations, and pleasures' (1978: 155). For Foucault, the materialization and naturalization of 'sex' was integral to the operations of biopower. In the final chapter of *The History of Sexuality*, *Volume 1*, Foucault explains that the category of 'sex' is actually a phantasmatic *effect* of hegemonic power that comes to pass as the *cause* of a naturalized heterosexual human desire.

It might seem counter-intuitive to claim, as Foucault does, that there is no such thing as 'sex' prior to its circulation in discourse; for 'sex' is generally taken to be the most fundamental, most value-neutral aspect of an individual. Thus, one could argue that even a diehard anti-realist must admit that there are certain sexually differentiated parts, functions, capacities and hormonal and chromosomal differences that exist for human bodies in advance of any discursive construction. Yet, sexual difference is never merely a function of material differences that are not marked and formed in some respect by discursive practices. On the contrary, when one concedes that 'sex', or its 'materiality', is undeniable, one always concedes to *some version* of 'sex', that is, a *certain formation* of its 'materiality' (Butler, 1993: 2, 10). Indeed, any description of the materiality of 'sex' is a candidate for the formulation of that materiality. For what counts as 'sex' is formed through a series of contestations over the criteria used to distinguish between two natural sexes, which are alleged to be mutually exclusive. Thus, an array of scientific, medical and social discourses must be continuously generated to reinforce these supposedly definitive criteria. Of course, dominant beliefs about gender infect these discourses, conditioning what kinds of knowledge scientists endeavour to produce about sex in the first place.

As the work on intersexuality referred to above shows, however, the regulatory force of knowledge/power about the category of sex is none the less threatened by the birth of infants whose bodies do not conform to normative ideals of sexual dimorphism, that is, infants which are neither clearly 'male' nor clearly 'female'. In fact, the clinical literature produced by those upon whom authority is conferred to make such pronouncements is replete with references to the birth, or expected birth, of an intersexed infant as 'emergenc(ies)' and 'devastating problem(s)' (Fausto-Sterling, 2000: 275–6, n. 1). Since this is the almost universal reaction of medical practitioners, 'technologies of normalization' – for example genetic manipulation, surgical mutilation and chemical control – are mobilized to 'correct' these so-called *unfortunate errors of nature* (see Fausto-Sterling, *passim*; see also Chase, 1998; Dreger, 1998; Tremain, 1998; Tremain, 2000a). In so far as these technologies circulate as remedial measures performed on the basis of spurious projections about the future best interests of a given infant, their disciplinary character is depoliticized; in addition, the role they play in naturalizing the binary sex-gender and upholding heterosexual normativity remains disguised.

If the category of sex is itself considered a *gendered* category – that is, politically invested and naturalized, but not natural – then there really is no *ontological* distinction between sex and gender. 'Sex' cannot be thought as prior to gender as the sex-gender distinction assumes, since gender is required in order to think 'sex' at all (Butler, 1999 [1990]: 143). Thus, gender is not the product of culture, nor is sex the product of nature, as Rubin's distinction implies. Gender is instead the means through which 'sexed nature' is produced and established *as natural*, as *prior* to culture and as a politically neutral surface *on which* culture acts (Butler, 1999 [1990]: 10–11). Moreover, rather than the manifestation of some residing essence or substrate, 'gender identity' is simply the stylized *performance* of gender, that is, the sum total of acts which it is believed to produce as its 'expression'.

Butler's claim that relations of power produce sex as the naturalized foundation of gender draws upon Foucault's argument that juridical systems of power generate the subjects they subsequently come to represent. This was illustrated above in the discussion of how juridical notions of power seem to work through the contingent and deniable operation of choice that form, define and reproduce subjects in particular ways. That the practices of gender performance, when construed as the cultural interpretation of a 'natural sex', seem to be dictated by individual choice conceals the fact that complicated networks of power have already limited the possible interpretations of that performance. For only those genders that conform to highly regulated norms of cultural intelligibility may be lived without risk of reprisal (Tremain, 2000a).

Disciplining disability

Returning to the earlier arguments about UK disability theory's move to break the causal link between 'our bodies' (impairment) and 'our social situation' (disability) (Shakespeare, 1992: 40), we can perhaps begin to articulate its striking similarity to the sex-gender distinction in genealogical terms. For example, it was noted that the social model was intended to counter individual models of disability that conceptualized that state of affairs as the unfortunate consequences of a personal attribute or characteristic. In the terms of the social model, impairment neither equals, nor causes, disability; rather, disability is a form of social disadvantage, which is imposed on top of one's impairment.

Proponents of the social model explicitly argue first, that disablement is not a necessary consequence of impairment, and, second, that impairment is not a sufficient condition for disability. Nevertheless, an unstated premiss of the model is that impairment is a necessary condition for disability. Proponents of the model do not argue that people who are excluded, or discriminated against on the basis of, for example, skin colour, are by virtue of *that* fact disabled, nor do they argue that racism is a form of disability. On the contrary, only people who *have*, or are *presumed to have*, an impairment are counted as disabled. Thus, the strict division between the categories of impairment and disability which the social model is claimed to institute is in fact a chimera.

If we combine the foundational premiss of the social model (impairment) with Foucault's argument that modern relations of power produce the subjects they subsequently come to represent, then it seems that subjects are produced who 'have' impairments because this identity meets certain requirements of contemporary political arrangements. Further, if the identity of the subject of the social model – people with impairments – is actually produced *in accordance with* requirements of the political configuration which that model was designed to contest, then a political movement which grounds its claims to entitlement in that identity will inadvertently *extend* those relations of power.

Inasmuch as the 'impairments' alleged to underlie disability are actually constituted in order to sustain, and even augment, current social arrangements, they must no longer be theorized as essential, biological characteristics of a 'real' body upon which recognizably disabling conditions are imposed. Instead, those allegedly 'real' impairments must now be identified as the incorporated constructs of disciplinary knowledge/power that they are. As *effects* of an historically specific political discourse – biopower – impairments are materialized as unitary and universal attributes of subjects through the iteration and reiteration of rather culturally specific regulatory norms and ideals about human function and structure, competency, intelligence and ability (see Amundson, 2000). As universalized attributes of subjects, furthermore, impairments are naturalized as an interior identity or essence *on which* culture acts in order to camouflage the historically contingent power relations that materialized them *as* natural (cf. Abberley, 1987; Thomas, 1999).

In short, impairment has been disability all along. Disciplinary practices in which the subject is inducted and divided from others produce the illusion of impairment as their 'prediscursive' antecedent in order to multiply, divide and expand their regulatory effects. The testimonials, acts and enactments of the disabled subject are *performative* in so far as the 'prediscursive' impairment which they are purported to disclose or manifest has no existence prior to, or apart from, those very constitutive performances. That the discursive object called impairment is claimed to be the embodiment of natural deficit, or lack, furthermore obscures the fact that the constitutive power relations which define and circumscribe it have already delimited the dimensions of its reification. Thus, it would seem that, in so far as proponents of the social model claim that disablement is not an inevitable consequence of impairment, they misunderstand the productive constraints of modern power. For it would seem that the category of impairment emerged and in part persists in order to legitimize the disciplinary regime that generated it in the first place.

The management and administration, both public and private, of impairment contribute to its objectivization. In one of the few detailed appropriations of Foucauldian analyses for disability studies, Margrit Shildrick and Janet Price (1996) demonstrate how impairment is naturalized and materialized in the context of a particular piece of welfare policy, relating to the UK's Disability Living Allowance (DLA). This policy is designed to distribute resources to those who need assistance with 'personal care' and 'getting around'. The official rationale for the policy is to ensure that the particularity of certain individuals does not cause them to experience undue hardship that the welfare state could ameliorate. However, the questionnaire that prospective recipients must administer to themselves abstracts from the heterogeneity of *their own* bodies to produce a regulatory category – impairment – that operates as a homogeneous entity in the *social* body (Shildrick and Price, 1996: 101). The definitional parameters of the questionnaire, and indeed the motivation behind the policy itself, posit an allegedly pre-existing and stable entity (impairment) on the basis of regulatory norms and ideals about (for example) function, utility and independence. By virtue of responses given to the assortment of questions posed on the form, the subject/recipient is compelled to engage in self-surveillance ('the more you can tell us, the easier it is for us to get a clear picture of the type of help you need') in order to elaborate the specifications of this entity (*ibid.*, p. 102). To produce the full and transparent report that government officials demand, the most minute experiences of pain, disruptions of one's menstrual cycle, lapses of fatigue and difficulty in operating household appliances must be documented, and associated in some way with this abstraction.

Thus, through a performance of textual confession, the potential recipient is made a subject of impairment, in addition to being made a subject of the state, and is rendered docile. For despite the fact that the questions on the DLA form seem intended to extract very idiosyncratic detail from potential recipient/subjects, the differences that they produce are actually highly co-ordinated and managed ones. In fact, the innumerable questions and subdivisions of questions posed on the form establish a system of differentiation and individuation whose totalizing effect is to grossly restrict individuality (*ibid.*, pp. 101–2). As Foucault repeatedly pointed out, the more individualizing is the nature of the state's identification of us, the further is the reach of its normalizing disciplinary apparatus in the administration of our lives (see Rajchman, 1991).

Because Foucault maintained that there is no outside of power, that power is everywhere, that it comes from everywhere (Foucault, 1978: 93), some writers in disability studies have suggested that his approach is nihilistic, and offers little incentive to the disabled people's movement (see, for example, Thomas, 1999). However, this conclusion ignores Foucault's dictum that 'there is no power without potential refusal or revolt' (Foucault, 1988: 84). As I have shown, Foucault maintained that the disciplinary apparatus of the state, which puts in place the limits of possible conduct by materializing discursive objects through the repetition of regulatory norms, also, by virtue of that repetitive process, brings into discourse the very conditions for subverting that apparatus itself. The disabled people's movement is a case in point; for the disciplinary relations of power that produce subjects have, as a consequence, spawned a defiant movement whose organizing tool, the social model of disability, has politicized its subject.

Nevertheless, in so far as the identity of that subject (people with impairments) is a naturalized construct of the relations of power which the model was designed to subvert, the subversive potential of claims which are grounded in it will actually be limited. For the current state of disability politics typifies what Foucault calls the 'polymorphism' of liberalism, which is its capacity continually to refashion itself in a practice of auto-critique. As various critics of liberalism have noted, the governmental rationality of the modern liberal state *presumes* that particular social groups will make claims to entitlement on the basis of a singular and injured identity. These writers have pointed out, furthermore, that the liberal state actually depends upon such claims for its own expansion (Brown, 1995; Weir, 1996).

The polymorphic character of liberalism gives rise to the paradox of identity politics in the contemporary social world, a paradox with which disability studies and the disabled people's movement must soon come to terms. Many feminists have long since realized that a political movement whose organizing tools are identity-based shall inevitably be contested as exclusionary and internally hierarchical. A disability movement that grounds its claims to entitlement in the identity of its subject can expect to face similar criticisms from an ever-increasing number of constituencies that feel excluded from, and refuse to identify with, those demands for rights and recognition. In addition, minorities internal to the movement will predictably pose challenges to it, the upshot of which is that those hegemonic descriptions eclipse their respective particularities (Tremain, 2000b). My argument, therefore, is that disability activists and writers must develop strategies for advancing claims that make no appeal to the very identity upon which that subjection relies.

The agenda for a *critical* disability studies should be to expose the disciplinary character of that identity. That is, it should expose the way that disability has been naturalized *as* impairment by identifying the 'constitutive mechanisms of truth and knowledge' within scientific and social discourses, policy and medico-legal practice which produce it and sustain it. Shildrick and Price's analysis of the DLA suggests one way in which this might be done. An interdisciplinary study of 'natural impairment' and 'natural sex' which examines how the disciplinary boundaries of disability studies and gender studies operate to naturalize their own respective 'objects', *and* each other's, might be another way to do this.

Of course those of us involved in disability studies and the disabled people's movement must continue to expand discursive space by articulating our lived experiences, including our experiences of corporeality. But if we continue to animate the regulatory fictions of 'impairment' and 'people with impairments', however, the Disabled People's International (DPI) slogan, 'the right to live and be different', will only translate as 'the right to live and be the same'.

Acknowledgements

My thanks to Barry Allen, who made suggestions on an earlier draft of this chapter and to Ron Amundson, with whom I discussed one of its arguments.

Note

1. A revised and expanded version of portions of this chapter appears in my essay 'On the government of disability', published in *Social Theory and Practice*, 24(4) (October 2001).

References

Abberley, P. (1987) 'The concept of oppression and the development of a social theory of disability', *Disability, Handicap and Society*, 2(1): 5–19.
Allen, B. (1999) 'Disabling knowledge', in G. Madison and M. Fairbairn (eds), *The Ethics of Postmodernity*. Evanston: Northwestern University Press.
Amundson, R. (2000) 'Against normal function', *Studies in History and Philosophy of Biological and Biomedical Sciences*, 31c: 33–53.
Barnes, Colin (1996) *Theories of Disability and the Origins of the Oppression of Disabled People in Western Society*. Harlow: Longman.
Brown, W. (1995) *States of Injury: Power and Freedom in Late Modernity*. Princeton: Princeton University Press.
Butler, J. (1993) *Bodies That Matter: On the Discursive Limits of 'Sex'*. New York: Routledge.

Butler, J. (1999 [1990]) *Gender Trouble: Feminism and the Subversion of Identity*, 10th anniversary edition. New York: Routledge.

Chase, C. (1998) 'Affronting reason', in D. Atkins (ed.), *Looking Queer: Body Image and Identity in Lesbian, Bisexual, Gay, and Transgender Communities*. New York: The Harrington Park Press.

Corker, M. (1999) 'Differences, conflations and foundations: the limits to the "accurate" theoretical representation of disabled people's experience', *Disability and Society*, 14(4): 627–42.

Dreger, A. D. (1998) *Hermaphrodites and the Medical Invention of Sex*. Cambridge: Harvard University Press.

Duden, B. (1991) *The Woman Beneath the Skin: A Doctor's Patients in Eighteenth Century Germany*, trans. Thomas Dunlap. Cambridge: Harvard University Press.

Fausto-Sterling, A. (2000) *Sexing the Body: Gender Politics and the Construction of Sexuality*. New York: Basic Books.

Foucault, M. (1973a) *The Birth of the Clinic: An Archaeology of Medical Perception*, trans. A. M. Sheridan. New York: Pantheon Books.

Foucault, M. (1973b) *Madness and Civilization: A History of Insanity in the Age of Reason*, trans. R. Howard. New York: Vintage/Random House.

Foucault, M. (1977) *Discipline and Punish: The Birth of the Prison*, trans. Alan Sheridan. New York: Pantheon Books.

Foucault, M. (1978) *The History of Sexuality, Vol. 1: An Introduction*, trans. Robert Hurley. New York: Random House.

Foucault, M. (1980) 'Two lectures', in C. Gordon (ed.), *Power/Knowledge: Selected Interviews and Other Writings 1972–1977*. New York: Pantheon Books.

Foucault, M. (1983 [1982]) 'The subject and power', in H. Dreyfus and P. Rabinow (eds), *Michel Foucault: Beyond Structuralism and Hermeneutics*, 2nd edn. Chicago: University of Chicago Press.

Foucault, M. (1984) *The Use of Pleasure*, trans. Robert Hurley. New York: Random House.

Foucault, M. (1985) *The Care of the Self*, trans. Robert Hurley. New York: Pantheon Books.

Foucault, M. (1988) 'Power and sex', in L. D. Kritzman (ed.), *Politics, Philosophy, Culture: Interviews and Other Writings (1977–1984)*. London: Routledge.

Foucault, M. (1991), 'Governmentality', in G. Burchell, C. Gordon and P. Miller (eds), *The Foucault Effect: Studies in Governmentality*. Chicago: University of Chicago Press.

Gordon, C. (1991) 'Governmental rationality: an introduction', in G. Burchell, C. Gordon and P. Miller (eds), *The Foucault Effect: Studies in Governmentality*. Chicago: University of Chicago Press.

Hacking, I. (1999) *The Social Construction of What?* Cambridge: Harvard University Press.

Haraway, D. J. (1991) *Simians, Cyborgs, and Women: The Reinvention of Nature*. New York: Routledge.

Harding, S. (1986) *The Science Question in Feminism*. Ithaca: Cornell University Press.

Harding, S. (1989) 'The instability of the analytical categories of feminist theory', in M. R. Malson (ed.), *Feminist Theory in Practice and Process*. Chicago: University of Chicago Press.

Hausman, B. L. (1995) *Changing Sex: Transsexualism, Technology, and the Idea of Gender*. London: Duke University Press.

Hughes, B. and Paterson, P. (1997) 'The social model of disability and the disappearing body: towards a sociology of impairment', *Disability and Society*, 12(3): 325–40.

Oliver, M. (1990) *The Politics of Disablement*. Basingstoke: Macmillan.

Oliver, M. (1996) *Understanding Disability: From Theory to Practice*. Basingstoke: Macmillan.

Priestley, M. (1998) 'Constructions and creations: idealism, materialism, and disability theory', *Disability and Society*, 13(1): 75–94.

Rabinow, P. (ed.) (1984) *The Foucault Reader*. New York: Pantheon Books.

Rajchman, J. (1991) *Truth and Eros: Foucault, Lacan, and the Question of Ethics*. New York: Routledge.

Rubin, G. (1975) 'The traffic in women: notes on the "political economy" of sex', in R. R. Reiter (ed.), *Toward an Anthropology of Women*. New York: Monthly Review.

Shakespeare, T. (1992) 'A response to Liz Crow', *Coalition* (September).

Shakespeare, T. and Watson, N. (1995) 'Habeamus corpus? Sociology of the body and the issues of impairment', Aberdeen, Quincentennial Conference on the History of Medicine.

Shildrick, M. and Price, J. (1996) 'Breaking the boundaries of the broken body', *Body and Society*, 2(4): 93–113.

Thomas, C. (1999) *Female Forms: Experiencing and Understanding Disability*. Buckingham and Philadelphia: Open University Press.

Thomson, R. G. (1997) *Extraordinary Bodies: Figuring Physical Disability in American Culture and Literature*. New York: Columbia University Press.

Tremain, S. (1998) 'Review of D. Atkins (ed.), *Looking Queer: Body Image and Identity in Lesbian, Bisexual, Gay and Transgender Communities DSQ*, *Disability Studies Quarterly*, 18(3): 198–9.

Tremain, S. (2000a) 'Queering disabled sexuality studies', *Journal of Sexuality and Disability*, 18(4), Winter.

Tremain, S. (2000b) 'Review article of C. Thomas, *Female Forms: Experiencing and Understanding Disability*', *Disability and Society*, 15(5).

UPIAS (1976) *Fundamental Principles of Disability*. London: Union of the Physically Impaired Against Segregation.

Weir, L. (1996) 'Recent developments in the government of pregnancy', *Economy and Society*, 25(3): 372–92.

4

A Postmodern Disorder: Moral Encounters with Molecular Models of Disability

Jackie Leach Scully

Introduction

> We need to maintain medical 'modernity' as a port and haven in the post-modern storm. (Charlton, 1993)

Medicine is the business of reconstituting normality and health; and although concepts of normality and health sometimes appear self-evident, even a cursory look at the history of medicine shows that these ideas evolve over time, even over relatively short time-spans. For example, hip fractures, spinal deformities and loss of height used to be thought of as 'normal' events in the late stage in the human life cycle. But, since 1994, the World Health Organization has classified osteoporosis as a disease that can be diagnosed, prevented and treated; and this has significant consequences for the image of the healthy older woman, and for health insurance reimbursement of the costs of diagnosis and treatment. Concepts of 'normality' and 'abnormality' are not delivered in an unmediated form by biology. The biological data with which we are presented are interpreted through existing understandings of the body and in accordance with cultural standards.

It is not just our vision of what normality and health look like that undergoes change. Models of disease and disability – *how* we devise their aetiology – also evolve, reflecting changing perceptions of the relationship between individual physiology, environment and society. In the twentieth century, medicine underwent a transformation in the foundational model used to comprehend deviations from health and to provide explanations for the occurrence of abnormality – a transformation that gave rise to the 'molecular model' of disease. In this chapter, I want to look at this new foundational model, its relationship to postmodern thought, how it influences the encounter between medicine and the disabled person and what the consequences for medical ethics might be.

Medical concepts of disability: the molecular model

The history of disease models is fascinating and complex – too complex to detail here, but it is particularly worth noting that until relatively recently there would have been little discrepancy between the 'lay' model of abnormality and that of the professional practitioner. In ancient Greek or medieval medicine, for example, both practitioner and patient shared a common ground in a discourse about the balance of the bodily humours; the practitioner was distinguished by his or her experience in knowing what to use as an appropriate intervention. This lay/professional parity began to disappear with the emergence, in the seventeenth century, of the Cartesian view of the body as a machine. As the workings of the human body were reduced to a set of biomechanical and biochemical problems, understanding its abnormal function required a grasp of the underlying, and increasingly complex, basic sciences. By opting to see 'the human body as a vast, elaborate and sometimes mysterious machine' (Elliott, 1999: 64), modern medicine committed itself to conceptual models that could only be used with confidence by experts, and which excluded the sick or disabled person's own comprehension of his/her state.

A distinguishing mark of modern medicine is the replacement of subjective self-reporting of disease with objective, preferably quantitative, data (Feinstein, 1975; Engelhardt, 1986; Helman, 1990; Kleinman, 1995). Further, in modern medicine, abnormality is *defined* in terms of deviation from the normal state. Consequently, in medical practice the problematic of 'normality' has been reduced to agreeing on the *magnitude of deviation* from certain numerical 'normal' ranges outside of which a person should be considered ill or disabled. It is not concerned with the question of whether a norm can be, or why it should be, defined at all. The referral to 'normal' ranges is itself a reflection of:

- the increased technical ability to quantify physiological and biochemical parameters;
- the expanded repertoire of diagnostic tools, particularly in diagnosis of conditions that are essentially asymptomatic, at least in their early stages (a good example is hypertension), and that have been redefined in terms of the size of measurable deviation from a normal range (in the case of hypertension, the range of acceptable diastolic and systolic blood pressure).

Genetic medicine is the current focus of scrutiny for deviation. Today's medical headlines are made by the 'breakthroughs' in genetic medicine that claim to locate the 'aberrant' gene for 'abnormal' states or behaviours such as alcoholism, familial breast cancer or shyness (see, for example, Gayther *et al.*,

1998; Nielsen *et al.*, 1998; Plon, 1998; Crabbe *et al.*, 1999; Foroud and Li, 1999; Peterson *et al.*, 1999; Osher *et al.*, 2000). The genetic model sees abnormality as largely or wholly caused by genes, whether through mutations (alterations in the gene) that lead directly to an aberrant function of the protein produced by the gene, as in the classic single gene disorders like achondroplasia (dwarfism), or through genetic variation that more subtly influences the individual's predispositions and vulnerabilities to other factors that are generally classed as environmental or behavioural, such as viral infection. The genetic model is attractive for a number of reasons, not least because its essentials are easy to grasp, and this attraction is apparent in the enthusiasm with which genetic modes of thought have been adopted by medicine. A concrete demonstration of this can be found on the contents pages of recent medical textbooks. Twenty years ago, it would have been incomprehensible to launch students into a text on the basic principles of medicine with a chapter entitled 'The molecular and cellular basis of disease' (Haslett *et al.*, 1999); today, it forms the standard introduction. Even within the subdiscipline of psychiatry, with its non-materialist background, the current power of the genetic model means that, for example, anxiety neurosis may now be described *first* by a confident statement of the hereditary factors involved ('Anxiety neurosis occurs in 15 per cent of relatives of affected patients compared with 3 per cent of the general population'), followed by a substantially more reserved claim about non-genetic aetiologies: 'Psychodynamic theory . . . is a *theoretical* explanation that *suggests* that anxiety neurosis reflects . . . difficulties in the child–parent relationship in early childhood or *even* at birth' (Kumar and Clark, 1994: 977, italics added).

The dominance of this model obscures the fact that genetics is only a part of a larger framework, the molecular model, which is the real *meta-narrative* of today's medical science. Conceptual models have made the 'molecular turn', using the vocabulary of the biochemical components of the body (proteins, nucleic acids, carbohydrates, fats, sugars and other molecules), and how they act and interact, to explain states of medical interest. Medical science (and to a lesser extent, as we shall see, medical practice) has so far adopted molecular biology as its organizing principle. '[T]he goal of molecular medicine [becomes the generation of] new therapies for disease to accompany the goals of a basic molecular biology directed towards the understanding of biological processes and disease' (Haslett *et al.*, 1999: 49). The molecular model is a far more radical reduction of the whole concept of disease than that proposed by genetics. In its purest form, the genetic model claims only that a variation in the DNA sequence is the prime cause of a pathology, but makes no statements about exactly how the path from gene to physical manifestation – the phenotype of the organism – is followed. The way is left open for a variety of ideas about how genes function in development and disease, including approaches that hold no single component – whether genes, cellular morphology, biochemistry, environment – to be 'the bearer of ultimate causal control' (Rehmann-Sutter, 2001, in press). By contrast, the molecular model attempts a description of the entire disease process, using the theoretical and practical techniques of molecular biology to elucidate the molecular pathway from genetic lesion to pathology. The production of abnormality, the complete pathological process, can be successfully explained by molecular interactions without invoking any other factors. The belief that this approach to medical science can be extrapolated unproblematically to medical practice is exemplified by the introduction to one medical textbook, which thanks 'many of our contributors [who] pursue basic research in the diseases they describe and are able to give an exciting appreciation – from the gene to the bedside' (Haslett *et al.*, 1999: v).

Postmodern medicine

So, firmly grounded in the Enlightenment, the medicine with which we are familiar is a product of a modernist faith in the ability of reason and rationality to drive continued technological and social advancement. For twentieth-century medicine, progress was symbiotic with modernist scientific practices and modes of thought. What is interesting is the way that the contemporary molecular meta-narrative of medicine runs directly counter to the postmodern trend in other areas of thought. Although postmodernism is complex, the different versions share certain common aspects. For example, they recognize a diversity of knowledges rather than any ultimate grand truths, or meta-narratives; they see meaning as constructed and constantly negotiated; they replace the authority of a single autonomous subject with a diversity of subject standpoints; they recognize that these subject standpoints are inseparable from the social processes that create them; and they pay close attention to the way things are constructed in and through discourse (see also introductory chapter). Against this background, medical science takes what has been described as the anomalous position of 'an island of rationalist modernity floating in a shifting sea of subjective post-modernity – a castle of objectivity besieged by the forces of relativistic cynicism . . .' (Charlton, 1993: 497). The confrontation is particularly acute at the point where contemporary molecular medicine's epistemological assumption that modernist science provides objective knowledge about 'how the body really is' runs into the postmodernist claim that all forms of knowledge, including knowledge about and of the body, are subjectively situated and discursively produced.

But we must be careful not to confuse the models of disease used predominantly or exclusively by medical science with the way either doctors or patients engage with these models in practice. For one thing, in conventional modernist science, models are used as heuristic devices: they provide a way of manipulating a problem, not a description of 'how it really is'. They help because they provide a way of thinking towards the truth, not to be confused with the truth itself. The charge levied by Charlton against postmodern medicine that '[b]elief, for the post-modern citizen, can only be ironic, bracketed, provisional, subject to the possibility of future revision' (1993: 497), is paradoxically equally applicable to modernist medical science. Of course there is a difference, in that post-Enlightenment science sees progress in the construction of continually refined and improved models, which therefore draw ever closer to the 'objective' truth. Postmodernism, on the other hand, would not allow any final universal truth. Even if there were to be such a thing, it would doubt that it could be known in a way that takes account of our historically and culturally situated selves. Despite this difference, both procedures should be able to choose between different available models with differential utility in different situations, without ideological commitment to a particular theory. They should be capable of accepting that every model is likely to be limited, and therefore provisional in anticipation of acquiring new data that force it to be modified or abandoned in favour of a different one.

It is thus possible to use the molecular model of abnormality within a postmodern framework. Although the model is embedded in a modernist context and praxis, *in itself* the molecular model is neither modernist nor postmodernist: it does not say anything about subjectivity, progress, diversity or truth. Medicine is, moreover, a pragmatic art. Ultimately, its practitioners are simply asked to do things that are helpful in particular instances of sickness, before they are required to produce any theoretical rationale for their actions. In a sense, there should be a natural affinity between postmodernism and medical practice, as two forms of pragmatic scepticism. Wiesing argues that an epistemological change in the direction of pragmatism in medical *practice* could be detected in the twentieth century, and that this has had to contend with 'the obstinate tendency to see medical science only with the eyes of natural science' (Wiesing, 1994: 282). But it can also be argued that within medical *science* the epistemological 'turn' has been more towards an alliance with molecular biology, and from this perspective it is the traditionally eclectic art of medical practice that is under threat.

Postmodern medicine and the body

If there is a potential affinity between medical practice and the stance of postmodernism towards epistemologies, it must be acknowledged that the medical engagement with certain aspects of postmodernism, especially with the postmodern idea of the body and its variations, is fraught. The molecular model of disease generates a particular view of the body, and of the way in which abnormality is expressed by it. It sees the body as a unit constructed and maintained through a network of interior molecular processes, complex but finite; the 'normal' body as explicable in terms of interactions between molecules; and deviations from the 'norm' as comprehensively described by the language of biochemistry.

Biomedical science profoundly shapes our assumptions about what a normal body is, how it should behave, when a bodily change is threatening and what the natural limitations of the body are. The dominance of biomedicine obscures the way that 'the' body can be interpreted in a multiplicity of ways. And here lies a problem: when the medical and non-medical worlds meet, what are we to do when there is disagreement even over what, precisely, the body is? 'Biomedical practitioners . . . see themselves as practising on nature's human representative – the human body' (Gordon, 1988: 24), but the exact nature of the representation is elusive. To medical research, the body is the material object of biomedical enquiry; to the practitioner, it is the fleshly site of biomedical intervention, and the task of medicine is simply to intervene and put matters right when the material goes awry. To those who would say, on the other hand, that '[t]he body is the vehicle of being in the world . . . [and we are] conscious of the world through the medium of [the] body' (Merleau-Ponty, 1962: 82), medicine's job could be described as restoring a particular consciousness of the world whenever this is disrupted; while if the body is 'literally ourselves expressed' (Schenk, 1986: 46), then medicine must help restage an act of self-expression rather than repair a malfunctioning mechanism. And the extreme discursive claim that '[t]he body is an effect of the extant, culturally contingent forms of discourse within which medicine operates and which also find expression in the contemporaneous political forms' (Komessaroff, 1995: 15), would be close to meaningless to the majority of practising clinicians or molecular medics.

Biomedicine not only promotes a distinctive way of describing what a body is and investigating how it does what it does; it also accords special status to certain forms of embodiment and certain ways of knowing embodiment. First, the belief that disease and disability are 'deviations' from a set of 'normal' somatic parameters (Foss, 1989) rests on the assumption that there is only one, or a very limited number, of 'valid' embodiments – embodiments that can be referred to as the normal/healthy body, and can be defined by these parameters. A multiplicity of reference points would be seen to render the whole system useless. While accepting that some differences between bodies (for example in sex, age or ethnicity) are compatible with health, the repertoire of 'normal' variation is actually quite restricted. The repertoire of pathological embodiments, however, is very large, and expands as our ability to identify and make fine distinctions grows. This is particularly apparent for the collection of conditions unearthed by genomic medicine. Thus cystic fibrosis, once considered a single disease entity, is now a collection of distinct genetic variations that can lead phenotypically to cystic fibrosis. Similarly, the disease known as Fanconi anaemia is now subdivided according to which of several gene loci is involved. The expansion in collected deviations need not challenge the acceptability of the 'norm', because as long as there is a single or limited number of reference points, the accumulation of exceptions serves only to define and hence reinforce them (Scully and Rehmann-Sutter, 2001, in press).

Second, biomedicine also presumes there is only one way of knowing the body. At a pinch, objectivist medical knowledge can cope with the idea of diverse bodily forms. It recognizes that these variations occur, even if they must be placed in a hierarchy of validity according to how normal or how healthy they are. What it cannot acknowledge is that there may be more than one system of bodily knowledge, nor that other ways of knowing the body can flatten or dissolve distinctions between kinds of bodies – particularly between 'normal' and 'abnormal' bodies – that seem to be very clear from strictly biomedical perspectives. Some postmodernist interpretations suggest that bodies are discursive entities (what exists materially is constructed and interpreted through language) as well as material ones (there is something material that exists, to be interpreted). Bodies, *in the way we understand them,* are not pre-given in some objective reality but are specific, variable and historically contingent constructions. If this is so then different constructs will be more or less valid, according to need and circumstances. The biomedical body is the one that medical science takes as 'the' body, but at other times it will be the genomic body, the fantasized body, the erotic body, the ritualized body, the developing body or the body in pain, that we find most relevant.

A corollary of biomedicine's dependence on molecularity as meta-narrative rather than model – a meta-narrative in which deviation from a molecular norm is synonymous with disease and disability – is that the prime goal of medicine becomes the control of these deviations. No space is left for an exploration of how variation, even when experienced as disability or disease, can be understood not in terms of suffering and deficit, but as a dynamic, sometimes satisfying, engagement with corporeal difference.

If we could allow that there are many different kinds of body, and many different ways of living an embodiment, how would medical practice cope? One possibility would be for healthcare to incorporate all the different body knowledges that might be active within the practitioner–patient encounter. Beyond the practical difficulty of extending an already overstuffed medical curriculum to train medical students to do this, we would also have to ask to what extent it is actually *desirable* for other forms of body knowledge to become subsumed within the medical domain. Medicine has already encroached upon a number of areas of life that until recently had little or nothing to do with health or disease, such as family life, sexual behaviour or employment practices. It may not be beneficial to confer on medicine even more extensive authority.

An alternative strategy would be for medicine consciously to restrict itself to a *limited range* of body knowledges that are collectively agreed to fall within its remit. In practice, this is what already happens, but the difference would lie in the *conscious* acknowledgement that the area of medical relevance is limited, that only a subset of possible approaches is being used, and that many others, equally useful to the comprehension of disability, lie outside its boundaries. The difficulty would lie in maintaining this awareness within medicine as it is currently practised. Even if we assume that the medical encounter takes place because the disabled person feels the need for some kind of help – therapeutic, rehabilitative, hermeneutic or whatever – a medical practice that deliberately limits itself *only* to those supportive interactions that are congruent with the molecular model, the disabled person is required to find other kinds of practitioners to invoke other body knowledges. This would need a radical reappraisal of the kind of help available, the dynamics of discipline and authority in each encounter and the role of the disabled person in choosing what kind of support is needed at any time.

Postmodern medical ethics?

Within the practice of medicine it is possible to envisage ways in which what might be called a postmodern approach can be taken, in a consciously pragmatic fashion. For this to happen, however, there must be a complementary shift in medical ethics, which has evolved to fit the demands of the profession as it currently exists. If postmodernism is problematic for the molecular medical approach to disability, it also poses severe problems for medical ethics, which has only just started to grapple with issues within disability at all. To understand this, we might imagine a hypothetical medical practice in which the molecular model was used as one of many approaches to the issues at hand. As we have seen, models of abnormality try to organize the disorderly nature of individual being, and so they are fundamentally connected to metaphysical issues of human identity and the ontological and ethical significance of persons. How and why we think abnormality occurs shapes our concepts of identity and thus our concept of a moral agent, along with all the associated issues of responsibility, autonomy and relationship. The Enlightenment ideal of reason drew on Kantian notions of what constitutes a person, where autonomy and rationality become the key objective standards for the assignment of personhood, to decide what makes someone a subject, and how a subject behaves as a moral agent. Only the autonomous, rational, self-aware subject is capable of making reasoned moral choices that are coherent with the framework of the accepted system of values. In this view of subjectivity the core virtue, reason, 'was . . . exercised by an isolated, monadic subject whose connection with society and *embodied form* [my italics] were secondary characteristics' (Komessaroff, 1995: 6).

Recent trends in ethical thought, however, have taken a more sceptical look at the *validity* of this picture of the normative moral agent; and also at the *value* of it, in a world increasingly conscious of diversity and the inter-dependence of its human, and non-human, components. Embodied form may have *overtly* been a 'secondary characteristic', but in practice the qualities held to confer rationality were possessed only by a very restricted set of embodiments (male, white and able-bodied). Feminists, in particular, have recognized the consequences that women's embodiment has had for their status as moral agents. As Shildrick writes, 'the inescapable and distinctive embodiment of those persons deemed to be in less than normative health [i.e. women] becomes a determinant of their being treated as less than full sub-jects, as less than capable of independent moral agency' (Shildrick, 1997: 169). If this is true for women's bodies, it is even more the case for disabled persons, who are 'deemed to be' of less than normative structure or function. The biological phenomenon of not hearing the same range of frequencies as most people do, for example, when seen as a pathological state, pathologizes the identity of persons embodying that state. It renders it in need of restora-tion if their claim to moral agency is to be equivalent to that of 'normal' people. If, on the other hand, deafness is interpreted as 'membership of a linguistic minority', it has a very different ontological significance and con-sequences for the conferral of individual autonomy and agency. The treat-ment of disabled people as less than full subjects, incapable of genuine moral agency, is manifest in the taken-for-granted processes of social exclusion and oppression.

Through taking the standpoint of women seriously, feminist ethics has developed alternative models in which moral agency is transactional and is formed in connection with others. Both traditional and feminist ethics would agree that morality is connected with ontology, because being cannot be separated from the moral context in which being occurs. But many feminist ethicists would argue for the moral context as *necessarily* one of self in relation, rather than one in which isolated individuals reinforce and somehow validate their selfhood through moral conflicts with others.

Medical ethics is founded on traditional views of moral agency, and so far is almost untouched by the new moves in various branches of ethics. Far from incorporating ideas about relationality, or discourse, medical ethics has been almost exclusively concerned with the (mis)behaviour of medical professionals. Its chief function has been to provide guidelines for appropriate medical and moral actions. If the medical practitioner acts in accordance with the guidelines, not a lot – it is felt – can go wrong in ethical terms. This has meant there was only one ethically active partner in the medical encounter, the practitioner. In ethics, as in medical practice, '[t]he real dualism . . . is between the physician as (active) knower and patient as (passive) known' (Kirmayer, 1988: 59). There has been less interest in the ethical positions of any of the other participants, even the 'other' who (one would have thought) gives the whole business its *raison d'être*: the patient.

A postmodern approach specifically acknowledges the moral agency of subjects other than those validated within a traditional Enlightenment model. It pays serious attention to the claims and desires of the more obviously dependent participant, though I leave open here the question of just how we notice and evaluate different kinds of dependency. And by allowing agency on the part of the patient the moral context is transformed into one of relationship. But this involves a restructuring of the location of authority within the encounter, and a careful reconsideration of the whole notion of what 'medical authority' means. Medicine is a profession of knowers, of experts. Its internal leitmotiv is the face-to-face meeting of two persons, one of whom, it is assumed, knows more than the other *about* the other. The postmodern dismantling of absolute authority, its openness to a plurality of local authorities none of which provides 'the' truth, does not sit comfortably with this.

Another question is how medical ethics would cope with a postmodern approach to the body and corporeal variation. Writing of psychoanalysis, Adam Phillips asks, 'What would [it] be like . . . if we were to attend not only to the patient's personal dream idiom, but also to the idiosyncratic function of his dreaming? We would no longer be asking: what do this patient's dreams mean? But, what does *this particular person* use dreaming for, use dreaming to do?' (Phillips, 1995: 75). Conventional ethics has relied on the chivalrous use of necessary pretences, among them that there is such a thing as 'the' patient (and also 'the' physician), and that there are characteristics of the patient and her or his 'problem' that can be universalized. These pretences are necessary, because no situation can be approached without some extrapolation from precedent. The difference that postmodernism brings is a severe reduction in the extent of universalization. Consciously turning towards the situatedness of the individual, and of the individual's style of comprehending his or her body, medical ethics cannot simply ask, 'How should the patient be treated ethically?' Rather, the question becomes 'What does this particular subject, in this particular context, use the body – use hearing or childbearing or eating – for, and, *given this specificity*, what is the ethical thing to do?'

Consequences

It is important not to fall into the trap of seeing postmodernism, with its openness to diverse subjectivities and its collapsing of hierarchical authority, as being necessarily more conducive to the good of disabled people within the medical or any other context. Any aspect of the postmodern view could be used to make things worse rather than better. For example, a formulation of subjectivity as discursively constructed rather than a manifestation of an essential self, tends to remove much of the grounds for individual autonomy – and this is already a too-familiar position for the disabled person. Activists have been claiming for many years that disabled people are the experts on the experience of living with their particular disability. But the postmodern absence of a single, authoritative discourse – if this is taken to apply to the intersubjective world, the encounter with others, as well as to the individual's own subjectivity – is equally applicable to the experience of the disabled person. No standpoint can claim any special authority, whether by virtue of being disabled or of having medical or other expertise. This aspect of post-modernist thought has been criticized by other marginalized groups, most notably feminists, who point out the ironic coincidence (which may not be a coincidence) of an intellectual movement that erases authority, arising just at the historical moment when women are being included within the circle of authority. Other liberatory movements also criticize the political impotence that follows from the inability to state unequivocally that a particular behaviour or belief is better than another. All of this tends to leave the disabled person, concretely situated in the doctor's office, in pretty much the same position as before: powerless to claim any kind of authority from within the experience of their lives over the medical control of the disabled body.

Some resolution of these difficulties may be provided by a model of *hermeneutic dialogue*. Hermeneutics – or what philosophers call the art of interpretation – is not normally considered a key pillar of postmodernism. Nevertheless, I think the preceding discussion indicates that a medical practice influenced by postmodernity, and retaining any respect for the patient, cannot ignore it. Genuine dialogue entails that each participant is acknowledged as speaking from his or her own unique position, and a hermeneutic approach requires at least an attempt to understand the other participant's words and actions. In dialogue, a medical understanding – although informed by the interpretive models doctors are trained to use – remains open to the new light brought by the dialogue partner. The biomedical approach and its models, including the molecular model, would be one of several gazes turned towards the issues presented by the disabled person. It would not be privileged as providing a more objective or more fundamental account of disability, but neither would the subjective understanding of the disabled person: both would be brought to this meeting. I want to emphasize that hermeneutic dialogue means more than simply improving verbal communication. The medical message can be conveyed from practitioner to patient with *clarity*, but may nevertheless be sent from such a different standpoint as to be without *meaning* to the recipient. In the traditional medical encounter as monologue, the physician has never been actively required to engage in any kind of interpretive venture within the horizon of the disabled person's world (although good doctors have always done so). The patient, by contrast, as the less powerful partner – the supplicant – has always had to step a little inside the medical world in an effort to comprehend the message being sent.

This does not mean that the patient has always been a passive recipient of the 'truth' conveyed by the medical professional. There is empirical evidence that patients engage creatively, even subversively, with the biomedical explanation given to them, modifying it 'as they try to make the explanation liveable' (Blaxter, 1983: 952; see also Hunt *et al.*, 1989). This is important for a new practice of communication between professional and patient, since it implies that, even if physicians restrict themselves to delivering the molecular, or any other meta-narrative, patient(s) would in any case modify it until it made sense on their terms. These terms would in turn be modified by the engagement with new information. The difference is that, in this tradition, the physician–patient encounter is enacted as a kind of mutually agreed misunderstanding. It seems more sensible, more *honest*, to position the interpretive exercise not as a flaw or an optional extra, but as a cornerstone.

If postmodernism is to influence medicine at all, it is likely to begin with the appreciation of diversity and of situated subjectivity. In practice this will require participants in a medical encounter to enter into another life world, and the turn towards interpretation becomes central. While the molecular model sees abnormality as the outcome of a decontextualized biochemical mechanism, with no intrinsic significance or moral value, a hermeneutic approach interprets abnormality by relocating it within the experiential life world of the patient, and within the context of the meanings and values conferred on it. A postmodern medical practice therefore needs a parallel ethics that does not simply regulate the acts of one participant in his or her attempts to return the other to 'normality'. It recognizes the medical encounter as an intrinsically ethical process in which both professional practitioner and disabled person reflect on the sort of life they find worth living and how they can best be enabled to live it.

Acknowledgements

I thank Dr Christoph Rehmann-Sutter for very helpful comments on an earlier version of this paper. The research project *Perceptions of Healing Needs: Somatic Gene Therapy, Disability and Identity* is supported by the Swiss National Science Foundation grant 4037–053073.

References

Blaxter, M. (1983) 'The causes of disease: women talking', *Social Science and Medicine*, 17: 59–69.

Charlton, B. G. (1993) 'Medicine and post-modernity', *Journal of the Royal Society of Medicine*, 86: 497–9.

Crabbe, J. C., Phillips, T. J., Buck, K. J., Cunningham, C. L. and Belknap, J. K. (1999) 'Identifying genes for alcohol and drug sensitivity: recent progress and future directions', *Trends in Neurosciences*, 22: 173–9.

Elliott, C. (1999) *A Philosophical Disease: Bioethics, Culture and Identity*. London: Routledge.

Engelhardt, E. T. (1986) *The Foundations of Bioethics*. Oxford: Oxford University Press.

Feinstein, A. R. (1975) 'Science, clinical medicine and the spectrum of disease', in P. B. Beeson and W. McDermott (eds), *Textbook of Medicine*. Philadelphia: Saunders, pp. 3–6.

Foroud, T. and Li, T. K. (1999) 'Genetics of alcoholism: a review of recent studies in human and animal models', *American Journal of Addiction*, 8: 261–78.

Foss, F. (1989) 'The challenge to medicine: a foundations perspective', *Journal of Medical Philosophy*, 14: 165–91.

Gayther, S. A., Pharoah, P. D. and Ponder, B. A. (1998) 'The genetics of inherited breast cancer', *Journal of Mammary Gland Biology and Neoplasia*, 3: 365–76.

Gordon, D. R. (1988) 'Tenacious assumptions in Western medicine', in M. Lock and D. Gordon (eds), *Biomedicine Examined*. Dordrecht: Kluwer, pp. 19–56.

Haslett, C., Chilvers, E. R., Hunter, J. A. A. and Boon, N. A. (eds) (1999) *Davidson's Principles and Practice of Medicine*, 18th edn. London: Churchill Livingstone.

Helman, C. (1990) *Culture, Health and Illness: An Introduction for Health Professionals*. London: Wright.

Hunt, L. M., Jordan, B. and Irwin, S. (1989) 'Views of what's wrong: diagnosis and patients' concepts of illness', *Social Science and Medicine*, 9: 945–56.

Kirmayer, L. J. (1988) 'Mind and body as metaphors: hidden values in biomedicine', in M. Lock and D. R. Gordon (eds), *Biomedicine Examined*. Dordrecht: Kluwer, pp. 57–93.

Kleinman, A. (1995) *Writing at the Margin*. Berkeley: University of California Press.

Komessaroff, P. A. (ed.) (1995) *Troubled Bodies: Critical Perspectives on Postmodernism, Medical Ethics and the Body*. Durham, NC: Duke University Press.

Kumar, P. and Clark, M. (1994) *Clinical Medicine*, 3rd edn. London: Saunders.

Merleau-Ponty, M. (1962) *Phenomenology of Perception*. London: Routledge.

Nielsen, D. A., Virkkunen, M., Lappalainen, J., Eggert, M., Brown, G. L., Long, J. C., Goldman, D. and Linnoila, M. (1998) 'A tryptophan hydroxylase gene marker for suicidality and alcoholism', *Archives of General Psychiatry*, 55: 593–602.

Osher, Y., Hamer, D. and Benjamin, J. (2000) 'Association and linkage of anxiety-related traits with a functional polymorphism of the serotonin transporter gene regulatory region in Israeli sibling pairs', *Molecular Psychiatry*, 5: 216–19.

Peterson, L. E., Barmholtz, J. S., Page, G. P., King, T. M., de Andrade, M. and Amos, C. I. (1999) 'A genome-wide search for susceptibility genes linked to alcohol dependence', *Genetic Epidemiology*, 17: Supplement 1, pp. S295–300.

Phillips, A. (1995) *Terrors and Experts*. London: Faber and Faber.

Plon, S. E. (1998) 'Screening and clinical implications for BRVA1 and BRCA2 mutation carriers', *Journal of Mammary Gland Biology and Neoplasia*, 3: 377–87.

Rehmann-Sutter, C. (2001, in press) 'Genes, embodiment and identity', in A. Grunwald, M. Gutmann and E. M. Neumann-Held (eds), *Anthropology – Biological and Philosophical Foundations*. New York: Springer.

Schenk, D. (1986) 'The texture of embodiment: foundation for medical ethics', *Human Studies*, 9: 43–54.

Scully, J. L. and Rehmann-Sutter, C. (2001, in press) 'When norms normalize: the case of gene therapy', *Human Gene Therapy*.

Shildrick, M. (1997) *Leaky Bodies and Boundaries: Feminism, Postmodernism and (Bio)ethics*. London: Routledge.

Wiesing, U. (1994) 'Style and responsibility: medicine in postmodernity', *Theoretical Medicine*, 15: 277–90.

5

Bodies Together: Touch, Ethics and Disability

Janet Price and Margrit Shildrick

The plaint that theorizations of postmodernism ignore the embodied conditions of varied physical disabilities, and equally that disability studies have
little or no time for the insights of postmodernism, is well-founded, but
ultimately self-defeating for both. In this chapter, we will pick up the challenge to bring the two fields together, and in doing so – as one writer who fits
into the category of disability and the other who does not – we will question
the very notion that such clear-cut distinctions can be drawn. If it is not
apparent at any given point which of us is speaking, then that is intended.
This is not because we wish to mask our identity or wilfully confuse readers,
but because we believe firmly that it is in an acknowledgement of the permeability between bodies and between embodied subjects that disability studies
might move forward. Against an ingrained tendency for disability activists
and scholars to claim a clear set of identities *as* disabled people, the trajectory
within postmodernism has been to fragment the concept of identity in general and to substitute a fluid, shifting notion of a process of becoming that
defines neither its own corporeal boundaries nor a fixed context. In suggesting such a radically different approach, our purpose in part is to open up the
ethical agenda to encompass not just the liberal humanist pursuit of rights,
interests or even individual moral flourishing – all of which presuppose identity – but the post-conventional concerns with encounter, with relationship
and becoming-in-the-world-with-others.

Addressing disability from the perspective of the embodied subject has
been especially contentious within disability studies. In countering the medical model of disability, which focuses on the failure of the body to achieve
normative standards of appearance or comportment/behaviour, disability
activists have advocated a social model. Carol Thomas suggests that, rather
than offering a unified approach to the understanding of disability, the social
model has developed into two distinct approaches. The first focuses on
unequal social relationships between those with impairments and those who
approximate the norm, 'which manifests itself through exclusionary and
oppressive practices', while the second focuses on disability as the property of
the individual, as the restriction of activity she faces due to social factors
(Thomas, 1999: 40). Both models have tended to deny the relevance of the

body as such to *disability* – in contrast to *impairment*, which is firmly situated in the body. Moreover, neither acknowledges the constitutive relationship between the embodied subject and the world, the notion that our subjectivity consists in a becoming in a world of others. In these social models, the disabled subject occupies a socio-material world that is always already there, which acts upon her or upon which she can act, to produce respectively the effects of disability, and of resistance to it. Identity here relies upon a separation between self and other which is deployed as powerfully by disabled people in their struggle for rights as it is by non-disabled people in their rejection of those who fall outside the boundaries of embodied norms. For both, the body is a given, a source of pleasure and pain, of activity and, for some, of what have been termed 'impairment effects'. Ultimately, however, it plays no part in subjectivity, but is merely the flesh-and-blood material basis from which the subject can express herself.

In contrast, postmodern writers, and in particular feminist critics, have challenged this exclusionary model, proposing in its place a notion of embodied subjectivity, which is actively and continuously produced through social interactions with other body-subjects. Moreover, the body is materialized *through* discourse – which we understand as both text and practice – and it becomes present to us not as a stable entity but as something that is always in process. Given that its boundaries are insecure, the act of claiming and defining identity is one of shoring up the inevitable and necessary slippages in our embodied subjectivity. This disruption of the notion of a unified, self-present individual brings more clearly into focus the question of our relationships with others as they are enacted, not simply through social relations, but through the interactions of our bodies and their mutually constitutive effects one on another. From such a perspective, disability clearly cannot be conceptualized as the property of an/y individual. But it is also much more than the result of unequal power relations. For, rather than focusing solely on the competing rights and interests of individuals that are a familiar part of the modernist paradigm, the post-conventional perspective demands recognition that our sense of self, and how we orientate ourselves to the world, is irrevocably tied up with the bodies of those around us.

Given the interest of postmodernism in deconstructing the usual binary division between the self and the other, it might seem readily apparent that writing largely without that division – as we try to do – would be highly relevant to the task of reconceiving relationship. One way of moving forward might be to write together where the question of unique authorship – and thus of authority to speak – is suspended. None the less most work on disability studies, even that which would claim to be at least loosely within the ambit of postmodernism, remains single-authored – as is the case in most academic disciplines – and is often self-identified as that of someone with disabilities or not. It goes without saying that work written within the medical model effectively others those with disabilities. Interestingly, the editors of this volume state in their initial call for papers that they 'want disabled authors to set the agenda', and indeed we recognize that it is precisely the voices of disabled people themselves that have been so often silenced in the past and which need to be recovered. What we reject, however, is the suggestion that disability is not an issue for non-disabled people, and that there is some privileged standpoint from which disabled people alone can speak – as though theirs is the only 'authentic' understanding of the specific embodiments in question. Nonetheless, in our writing together as one disabled and one non-disabled woman, our intention has been precisely to resist the separation of the primary and marked terms of embodiment.[1]

Our experience, however, has been that many readers, conference-goers, academic critics and even editors have failed to grasp the necessity – as we see it – of writing *together*. It is as though there is a reluctance to acknowledge that someone without evident disabilities could have anything useful to say, or that at most her role would be strictly subsidiary. So we want to ask what is going on here, and why is it relevant to the whole question of how disability studies and postmodernism might forge a more fruitful relationship? We would want to draw a parallel between approaches to race and to disability, where for the former it is finally being recognized that the importance of addressing how the concept of *whiteness* is constructed is crucial to the understanding of racial otherness. In a similar way, we believe that disability studies must encompass how 'disabled' and 'non-disabled/able-bodied' are constructed in mutual relation. Clearly the task should not be the prerogative of one group alone.

As we understand it, postmodernism disrupts not only the singular identity, but any unified voice, or body, and any claim to authenticity as such. It is not that those things are entirely discarded, as some misunderstandings of postmodernist theory seem to suggest, but that they are put into question, taken apart and sometimes reassembled in new and surprising forms that are themselves open to the same critical process, and thus never more than provisional. Margrit/and/Janet choose to write together – not as one, and not as two either – but as a process of fluid encounter that expresses, we hope, the nature of the ever-changing relationship between, not just us, but all those who want to get away from the straitjacket of unified identities. The very fact that we are very differently embodied at this point in time encourages us to explore not only those aspects that cannot be assimilated one in the other – the radical differences that no amount of disavowal, or rights or empathy can veil – but also the ways in which we are mutually constituted, mutually dependent for any sense of self. Put very simply, as one of us changes, so does the other, and although there are many asymmetries within the relationship, they need not be hierarchies. The significance is not that we think there is anything extraordinary about our particular interaction, but that the coming together of anomalous and normative embodiment can stand for a limit case for all relationships between self and other. Where less obvious differences may simply be glossed over in the security of sameness – those just like ourselves, those we recognize, rarely make us uncomfortable – radical difference, provided it is not pushed out of sight altogether, lays bare what is at stake in *every* encounter.

In further explanation of the decision to write in collaboration as an ethico-political point in itself, the inevitable result of resisting the comfortable familiarity of attributive naming is that one avoids a hierarchy of utterances. It is certainly not the case that our experiences are the same, but nor are they isolated and unified 'events'. In so far as we spend time together, both professionally and in friendship, the past, present and future effects of that relationship cannot be recounted as singular narratives. In place of unified stories with clearly delineated boundaries around the 'I', with divergent categories of embodied being, and with fixed points of view, we want to emphasize the multiple points of interchange, the blurring of categorical boundaries and the discontinuities that make up experience before narrative is imposed on it. Instead of the condition of being, with its ready-made certainties, expectations and capacity for calculation, what matters is the risky process of becoming with others. When this process is transposed to the sphere of writing it results in an open multiplicity in the text itself. Speaking of his own joint work with Guattari, Deleuze summarizes the effects:

> We were only two, but what was important for us was less our working together than this strange fact of working between the two of us. We stopped being 'author'. And these 'between-the-twos' referred back to other people, who were different on one side from on the other . . . This had nothing to do with . . . processes of recognition, but much to do with encounters. (1987: 17)

The question is how these particular insights into the process of collaboration have relevance to a reconfiguration of the way in which disability can be understood. What we want to emphasize is that the willingness to give up ownership of the text parallels the willingness to give up ownership of 'my' body, which in each case opens up new social and ethical possibilities.

The story of the disabled (body) is a familiar one in autobiographical writings, covering both the experience of bodily restrictions, discomfort and limitations, and of the physical and social barriers that disabled people face. These reveal themselves not just in terms of the lack of access provisions, such as ramps or interpreters, but in social and interactional dimensions, which uncover/demonstrate prejudice, intolerance, dismissal and patronage. In the representation of these experiences, Mitchell and Snyder suggest:

[a]utobiographical narratives demand that the disabled subject develop a voice that privileges the agency of a bona fide perspective of disability . . . what motivates these stories is the pressing need for true-life verification that disability provides a specific and distinct perspective of its own. (1997: 11)

In discussing people's reaction to her disability with a friend, Lois Keith, for example, remarks on '[m]y feeling that she had to accept my definition and understanding of the world. I lived it' (1994: 68). In common with other standpoint approaches, the assumption is that what counts is the experience of the disabled person alone.

The problem, which is well illustrated in a recent book by Albert Robillard (1999), in which he explores his experience of living with motor neurone disease, is that there may seem to be an abdication of responsibility for others.[2] In claiming rights for himself, Robillard gives no indication of how they might be balanced against, or interact with, the rights of others such as his wife and the nurses who care for him in hospital. Without denying the anger and frustration that Robillard feels as a result of the failures of his attempted communications with carers and colleagues, we need to problematize throughout the histories and the embodied experiences of *all* of the subjects in carefully described interchanges, and to open up the complex power dynamics that must surely exist. Rather than accepting the reduction of those dynamics to the opposition between Robillard as disabled and with limited physical control, and his assistants or carer as mobile, verbal and powerful, there are crucial questions to ask about what is happening on both sides of the interactions.[3] If meaning is constituted through the encounter with others, what do those who fail to communicate with Robillard feel, and how do their joint actions combine to constitute his silencing? Our point is that, for all Robillard's experiences of changed mobility and communication patterns in ways that disadvantage him, he remains – as a white, male, university professor – a potentially powerful figure holding a position of authority. The ambivalence of power and vulnerability is not investigated in that he sees his vulnerability as a special case rather than the condition of us all. Without wanting to take away from the specificity of Robillard's experience, what seems to be missing is an ethical dimension that moves beyond a simple recognition of vulnerability in the self, to that of recognition of difference and vulnerability in others.

Whether in telling the story through a description that invokes the distressing corporeality of disablement, as does Nancy Mairs (1986), or in exploring the social responses to, and the socio-physical barriers of, disabled living, as in some of the essays in anthologies such as *With Wings* (Saxon and Howe, 1988) and *Mustn't Grumble* (Keith, 1994), such narratives encourage the reader to see the person with disabilities as distinctly other in her corporeal specificity, whilst at the same time striving to attain standards of normativity. The issue of bodily difference – read as impairment – is positioned as a 'problem' for her alone, and the engagement of others, whether read as assistance or interference and control, is distanced. It is almost as though the body were simply a more or less troublesome possession that had little to do with one's own sense of self, still less played any part in the instantiation of other selves. In disability politics, and to a large extent in theory, that putative split between mind and body has been perpetuated to the extent that the body is seen simply as the focus of discriminatory practices on the part of wider society which limit the possibilities open to its owner. This denial of the body has been more recently challenged by feminist dis-abled writers, such as Jenny Morris (1996) and Liz Crow (1996), who demand an acknowledgement of the bodyliness associated with disability, of the pain, tiredness and limitations that affect individuals. However, the fear of the medical model, with its corrosive approach to disabled people, and its denial of their subjectivity and almost exclusive focus on the possibilities of 'mending broken bodies', is so great that the distinction drawn in the social model between bodily impairment and socially constructed disabling effects still holds powerful sway.

For those who perceive themselves as matching the norm, there is a drive to mastery of the other. Within disability, this is clearly seen in the actions of medical staff as they encourage disabled people to achieve ways of being, of moving, that in the name of rehabilitation approximate more closely to the bodily actions and practices of 'able-bodied' people. And where 'nature' does not suffice, technology can be recruited to produce the effects or appearance of normality. As Mary Duffy writes:

'bionic' limbs arrive when i am five years old.
they are big heavy hooks
powered by gas cylinders (1994: 25)

The intention to substitute for and 'improve' upon the actions of the limbs with which Mary Duffy was born aptly illustrates what Foucault has termed disciplinary practices of power/knowledge. Given that the truth of the body is not predetermined, but rather is constituted through the ways in which bodies are talked about and managed, biomedicine – with its claims to scientific expertise – plays a pre-eminent role in producing the disabled body as a universalized other. Therapeutic practices such as rehabilitation serve to reduce the sense of corporeal difference, of strangeness, and thus normalize the disabled body. However, whilst it may be normalized, it is emphatically not 'normal'. At the same time, moreover, such practices separate out those whose bodies are non-recuperable to the norm, and – as a part of the struggle to preserve the purity of the 'healthy' body – position them as radically different.

The regulation of the body, however, is not just imposed externally. Through self-surveillance, the individual monitors her own actions, comportment and ways of being to produce herself as a subject. It is in such practices of self-maintenance that we are offered an illusion of mastery that serves to establish a sense of bounded identity and autonomy. The fantasy of self-mastery, however, applies as much to disabled as to non-disabled people as they too become complicit in the process of constituting themselves as embodied subjects, their identity established against that of the non-disabled through the deployment of regulatory norms (Shildrick and Price, 1996). Thus, the notion of self-mastery is not a denial of the power that disabled people experience in their encounters with doctors, carers or social workers. But it does suggest that the opposing locations of victim or hero, which are often offered as the only options for disabled people, are more complicated. Foucault (1980) argues that, wherever there is power, there is always resistance exercised through the body's refusal as much as through the conscious will. Mary Duffy's poem finishes by saying of her 'bionic' limbs:

and you send them back after two weeks.
with them go all attempts
to make my body conform.

Nonetheless, both the cycle of recurrent resistance which is met always by new forms of power, and our identification as disabled or non-disabled only through a constant reiteration of the norms that hold in place the contested boundaries of self/other, speak to a radical instability. Because those norms can never fully encompass the body-subject, the closure of embodied identity is always just beyond grasp. The imperative to control and maintain fixed boundaries is inevitably doomed to failure.

We have written elsewhere (Shildrick and Price, 1996) about the performativity of the body, and of the constant need for reiterative behaviours that seek to stabilize a solid sense of the embodied self, which remains, nevertheless, always at risk of disruption. Such a situation is common to all bodies, regardless of their (dis)ability status, but the ever-present potential of disorganization is perhaps clearest in those conditions where the materiality of the body resists not just conscious control but predictability. The characteristic markers of a postmodernist approach to the embodied subject, and to corporeality itself, are fragmentation, provisionality, disarticulation and instability, and they are equally descriptive of the effects of the MS with which Janet has been diagnosed. The very slipperiness of the terms indicates a breakdown of normative certainty, a failure to hold in place the boundaries that are usually so well practised that we can take them for granted. But if the precariously embodied subject experiences an unsettling phenomenological transformation in her sense of self, then she does not do so in isolation. On the contrary, all those in relationship with her may, according to the strength of their investments in a phantasmatic unity, be brought face to face with their own originary body 'in bits and pieces'.

To relate the 'autobiographical' factors of Janet's condition would be always to speak of encounters: encounters not simply as they occur in any life as discrete events, but as they shape the substance of that life. In using personal material as illustrative, we are following the widespread feminist practice of breaking down the division between objective and subjective views, and of finding in specificity not universal rules, but an indication of which mechanisms might be at play. As Susan Brison has put it: 'To be epistemologically useful, first-person narratives must be scrutinized critically' (1999: 214), and although the experiences are our own, we hope they will serve to open up a particular way of thinking.

Although there is a multiplicity of other directions – or 'lines of flight', as Deleuze would call them – that might be explored, we shall look specifically, though briefly, at how the medically deteriorating condition of one of us has uncovered the disunity at the heart of all human beings and disrupted both the illusion of corporeal and psychic wholeness, and the sense of bodily separation. Friends, casual acquaintances and healthcare professionals alike may in consequence experience an uncomfortable sense of uncertainty in the company of a disabled person. Like many others who have MS, Janet has decreased sensation across large areas of her body. Whilst it is often highly distressing for those experiencing such changes, the symptom does not make itself visible and thus can be largely brushed out of the picture, and ignored by the medical profession as much as by others. In contrast, changes in the ability to walk, the need to use a wheelchair, partial facial paralysis or the inability to grasp objects, which are some of the more visible symptoms of MS, provoke dis-ease even amongst doctors and a desire to attempt to control the sense of otherness, of the 'patient' as irreducibly different. What is at stake in the biomedical encounter is a complex mix of emotion and sensation not reducible to clinical pertinence.

Much has been written in broadly phenomenological literature about how our sense of touch is every bit as important as, if not more important than, sight in mapping out the morphology of our bodies and of the spaces in which we move. Between sentient beings, touch, unlike sight, is quintessentially an interactive sensation in which the moment of touching is indivisible from being touched. There is never a point at which we can fail to reverse the sensation, nor at which we can distinguish clearly between the active and passive mode. Again, unlike sight, touch frustrates hierarchy, and crosses boundaries rather than creates distance. According to developmental psychologists (Montagu, 1971; Anzieu, 1989), touch is the primal sense which operates from the foetal stage, is paramount during early infancy and only becomes less acceptable when, as adults, we accede to an understanding of ourselves as essentially singular, unified and bounded. In adult years we are extremely cautious about whom we may touch, precisely because an unwelcome touch seems to threaten the integrity and ontological separation of the other. In view of both these positive and negative aspects of our relation to tactility, it is scarcely surprising that the disruption of our expectations of touch in many disabling conditions is highly significant. What occurs – if there are problems of mobility for example – is that the disabled person may find herself being touched by others in ways that far exceed normative contact, especially between strangers; or if she is deaf or vision-impaired, she equally may need to touch others to gain attention or for orientation and recognition. The clinical encounter itself is a paradigmatic site illustrating the power relation between physicians and disabled people, where – possibly even more than the medical gaze – it is the touch of the doctor that represents the exercise of a power that disrupts all the standard practices of intimacy.

Where Foucault's analysis of biopower suggests that the patient can be seen as a 'docile body', controlled and maintained by disciplinary practices (Foucault, 1979), his account of the inevitable resistance to such totalizing moves to categorical constraint is frustratingly scanty. We have suggested elsewhere some ways in which resistance to normalization might operate for disabled people: through their rejection of normative expectations of career or leisure activities; through direct protest, or a refusal to be classified by the myriad state-sponsored forms which structure a standardized notion of disability; and through challenges to approaches to rehabilitation (Shildrick and Price, 1996; Price and Shildrick, 1998; Moss, 1999). But these accounts of power and resistance, while offering ways to think about the disruption of unitary and normative identities, focus primarily upon the body of the disabled person or, in the clinical encounter, of the patient. What has been underplayed is that any encounter is, as Ros Diprose puts it, 'an encounter between at least two bodies'. Whilst the setting of the doctor's office, and the tools and symbols that support the professional status and role, may suggest that 'only one body examines the other, the examination is in fact contiguous and therefore ambiguous: bodies that touch are also touched. For every eye or hand on skin, there is skin on hand or eye' (1998: 37). The significance of this acknowledgement is that it disrupts the usual notion of subject/object that is used to analyse the relationship between doctor/patient, or assistant/disabled person. The point is that every subject who can touch and see can also be touched and seen by others. The body of the doctor, of the assistant or carer, is not closed, self-contained, independent of the process of examination or of assisting, but is itself 'open to a world of the other and immersed within it . . . rendering the encounter indeterminate and ambiguous' (*ibid.*, p. 38).

Although power operates within such relationships, what a phenomeno-logical approach suggests is that the mastery can never be complete, that it is, in fact, self-defeating. Nor should the ambiguity of the bodily encounter be taken to suspend responsibility. On the contrary, as Diprose notes, ethics demands the recognition of alterity (*ibid.*, p. 41).

Within care/assistance relations, the very fact that the usual rules of behaviour are being broken can be a potent source of anxiety in a society in which it is separation rather than contact that figures the adult self. The difficult relations between carers and those they assist, the discomfort not only of the disabled self, but of external others drawn into unwonted tactile proximity and the resultant avoidance of contact – effectively an insistence on keeping a 'safe' distance from the dangerous possibility of touch – are all consequences of a dominant modernist discourse of separation that devalues our most basic sensation. It is a discourse that both structures and is structured by everything from psychodynamic processes to socio-political power. And it in turn devalues those who have little option but to transgress normative boundaries of bodily self-sufficiency and closure. In order to appreciate the needs of a different body, one must in some degree open oneself to it, which in turn serves as further source of anxiety. In touching, we become more exposed to each other, immersed in each other, opening up the possibility of facing similar experience which could arouse fear and discomfort. What can be read in the uneasiness of carers, both professional and lay, is the thought that 'this could be me'. In consequence, far from conveying support and recognition, touching may attempt to distance the anomalous other – at best in the guise of professional but aloof competence, at worst as an inadequate fumbling and embarrassment. This is not a plea for sympathy or even empathy with the disabled person, but an assertion of the importance of acknowledging irreducible difference, of recognizing that, although bodily boundaries are shifting and permeable, they should not be trangressed at will in disregard of the feelings of security or ease for both assistant and disabled person.

There is a qualitative difference that I, Janet, experience in assistance from friends as opposed to care workers, however competent they might be. Security with friends grows from the prior knowledge of what the embodied experiences of self and other have in common: hands held, coffees drunk together, dances and hugs, the afternoons in the sauna or spa pool, the mutual touches of friendship, of comfort, of joy, of sadness translated into the moves and actions needed to lift me, to help me transfer, to climbing in the bath with me to help me bathe. These friends do not experience my body as it is now for me, but our mutual histories offer an ease through these moments. The difference, the discomfort emerges in the touches that seem unfamiliar, that have no history in the friendships upon which we can draw, such as helping with toilet needs, or with changing my tampons. In a period of acute disability, these were things that I could not accept from friends, but that my lover or respectful/sensitive care workers could do, for the differing dimensions of sameness and difference, of closeness and separation, in these relationships, allowed for those moments of contact to be negotiated. Given that such negotiations occur within modernist discourse, I – like everyone else – feel compelled to enact them under the constraints of normative separation, but it could be otherwise. It is clear that any alternative ethic of relationality, of mutuality, that did not rely on the strictly autonomous agency of the singular, detached self would go at least some way towards forestalling the anxiety, and even hostility, evoked by proximity. It means taking seriously the notion of becoming-in-the-world-with-others.

As a result of Janet's overtly fluctuating sense of touch, in which her personal body map was clearly undergoing unpredictable changes, I (Margrit) also was unsettled in the context of tactile interaction. Lacking a clear sense of Janet's own corporeal boundaries, I found it difficult to know at any given moment whether a greeting hug was still experienced as a sign of affection, given and returned, an unfelt and therefore meaningless gesture or even a more or less painful assault. Although at that time I was familiar and confident with the procedures of helping Janet wash, eat or dress, for example, those could all be done with a certain distancing efficiency which deferred a recognition of the mutuality of touch. Where feeling and emotion are to the fore, however, the experience of uncertainty spreads to our understanding of our own bodies. What does it mean to hold a hand that has temporarily lost sensation, that cannot press back in return? Why does your own hand suddenly feel so clumsy in its gestures? Those things which we habitually take for granted become open to question, the interactive bodily skills that seem constant and unremarkable are revealed as reliant as much on response as on personal agency. In other words, what was uncovered during that acute period of Janet's illness was that, through the mutuality and reversibility of touch, we are in a continual process of mutual reconstitution of our embodied selves. Moreover, the instability of the disabled body is but an extreme instance of the instability of all bodies. It is not just that any body can 'break down' in illness or as the result of accident, but that, for all, the 'bits and pieces' are held together in contingent ways. Final integration is never achieved.

In the light of the foregoing analysis of the precarious nature of bodies and of embodied subjectivity, it might appear that the conventional moral parameters that regulate the relationship between self and other are to be welcomed in their sidestepping of uncertainty. Even though the subjects to whom they refer are not in fact assimilable to a standard of sameness, even though bodies are not simply personal property subject to our conscious wills and even though the institution of self and other may be processes of mutual and transformatory becoming, is it not better to accede to a model of equal, autonomous and fully self-contained subjects? If the disabled person is accorded all the same general rights and duties as others, and additional benefits that reflect her specific interests in order to minimize disadvantage, is that not a morally appropriate response? Clearly the advances made by disability activists in terms of specifically targeted benefits and of equal rights to employment, access, housing and so on are very valuable, but what they do not address is the more fundamental disavowal of difference that characterizes modernist society. Our argument is not that there is no place for practical concerns, but that what is morally expeditious falls short of ethical responsibility in relationship. The adoption of pragmatics alone, as though it closes the question of ethics, speaks to a denial rather than radical recognition of difference, a difference that is both multiple and irreducible. Once it is accepted that the embodied subject is always a figure of undecidability, and that the distinctions between self and other are never firm or final, then adherence to a delimited set of moral rules and codes cannot answer to the call for response/ibility.

Postmodernism has been attacked for many perceived shortcomings, but perhaps the most damaging criticism has been that, even if its deconstruction of conventional models of morality is well-founded, it is unable to deliver an alternative ethics. By implication, it has nothing to say of consequence to those who are in any way morally dispossessed, including people with disabilities. Against such a view, Jacques Derrida in particular has been insistent that ethics itself must be rethought. It must move away from a closed system of rules that can be calculated in advance of application – precisely because of the misplaced assumption that one knows what kind of being a subject is. Instead, ethical engagement – what he sees as the moment of decision between self and other – can only claim that name if it opens itself to radical difference and undecidability. It is in the uncertainty and risk of response to the unknowable other that real responsibility lies. As he puts it:

> I believe there is no responsibility, no ethico-political decision, that must not pass through the proofs of the incalculable or the undecidable. Otherwise everything would be reducible to calculation, program, causality . . . (Derrida, 1991: 108)

In other words, what Derrida advocates, and what is adequate to the implications of the deconstruction of normative bodies and subjects, is an ethics without formal limits.

In contrast to the desire to pin down identity into nameable categories that interact only across the predictable space of boundaries and codes, the move of postmodernism is one that opens up the positivity of transformatory possibilities. Moreover, if we fully accept both the phenomenological notion of the inseparability of bodyliness and being-in-the-world, and the postmodernist contention that not only the subject but the body itself is discursively constituted and maintained, then it is necessary to rethink what would actually make a difference to those with physical disabilities. The disintegrity and permeability of bodies, the fluctuations and reversibility of touch, the inconsistency of spatial and morphological awareness, the uncertainty of the future, are all features that may be experienced with particular force in the disabled body, but they are by no means unique to it. If disability studies can benefit from the epistemological and ethical framework that postmodernist theory provides, then it is no less the case that postmodernism itself might gain from opening itself, and advancing its explanatory force by listening, to the experiences of those with disabilities. What we – Janet/and/Margrit – are proposing is not a *programme* for change, but a step in thinking together and otherwise.

Notes

1. In mainstream discourse, the primary term would refer to normative embodiment, with disability as the marked term. In disability theory, the relationship is reversed but does not deconstruct the implicit hierarchy between primary and marked terms.
2. See Price (2000) for a fuller critical review of Robillard (1999).
3. The language used to describe personal assistance for disabled people is a fraught one, including, as it does, terms such as assistant, carer and care worker. These carry with them different intimations of professionalism, intimacy and in/dependence that no one term seems to encompass fully. We have chosen to interchange them, depending upon the context.

References

Anzieu, D. (1989) *The Skin Ego*. New Haven: Yale University Press.

Brison, S. (1999) 'The uses of narrative in the aftermath of violence', in Claudia Card (ed.), *On Feminist Ethics and Politics*. Lawrence: University Press of Kansas.

Crow, L. (1996) 'Including all our lives: renewing the social model of disability', in J. Morris (ed.), *Encounters with Strangers: Feminism and Disability*. London: Women's Press.

Deleuze, G. with Parnet, C. (1987) *Dialogues*, trans. Hugh Tomlinson and Barbara Habberjam. New York: Columbia University Press.

Derrida, J. (1991) '"Eating well", or the calculation of the subject: an interview with Jacques Derrida', in Eduardo Cadava, Peter Connor and Jean-Luc Nancy (eds), *Who Comes after the Subject?* London: Routledge.

Diprose, R. (1998) 'Sexuality and the clinical encounter', in M. Shildrick and J. Price (eds), *Vital Signs: Feminist Reconfigurations of the Bio/logical Body*. Edinburgh: Edinburgh University Press.

Duffy, M. (1994) 'Making choices', in L. Keith (ed.), *Mustn't Grumble: Writing by Disabled Women*. London: Women's Press.

Foucault, M. (1979) *The History of Sexuality, Vol. 1*, trans. R. Hurley. London: Allen Lane.

Foucault, M. (1980) 'Body/power', in *Power/Knowledge: Selected Interviews and Other Writings, 1972–1977*, trans. Colin Gordon. Brighton: Harvester Press.

Keith, L. (ed.) (1994) *Mustn't Grumble: Writing by Disabled Women*. London: Women's Press.

Mairs, N. (1986) *Plaintext: Deciphering a Woman's Life*. New York: Perennial Library.

Mitchell, D. T. and Snyder, S. (eds) (1997) *The Body and Physical Difference*. Michigan: University of Michigan Press.

Montagu, A. (1971) *Touching: The Human Significance of the Skin*. New York: Columbia University Press.

Morris, J. (ed.) (1996) *Encounters with Strangers: Feminism and Disability*. London: Women's Press.

Moss, P. (1999) 'Autobiographical notes on chronic illness', in R. Butler and H. Parr (eds), *Mind and Body Spaces: Geographies of Illness, Impairment and Disability*. London: Routledge.

Price, J. (2000) 'Review symposium. Meaning of a disability', *Body and Society*, 6(2): 87–93.

Price, J. and Shildrick, M. (1998) 'Uncertain thoughts on the dis/abled body', in Margrit Shildrick and Janet Price (eds), *Vital Signs: Feminist Reconfigurations of the Bio/logical Body*. Edinburgh: Edinburgh University Press.

Robillard, A. B. (1999) *Meaning of a Disability: The Lived Experience of Paralysis*. Philadelphia: Temple University Press.

Saxon, M. and Howe, F. (eds) (1988) *With Wings: An Anthology of Literature by Women with Disabilities*. London: Virago Press.

Shildrick, M. and Price, J. (1996) 'Breaking the boundaries of the broken body', *Body and Society*, 2(4): 93–113.

Thomas, C. (1999) *Female Forms: Experiencing and Understanding Disability*. Buckingham: Open University Press.

6

The Body as Embodiment: An Investigation of the Body by Merleau-Ponty

Miho Iwakuma

Introduction

The French phenomenologist, Maurice Merleau-Ponty, has greatly influenced the paradigm of the body, and his most important work, *Phenomenology of Perception* (1962), has been considered to be one of the most valuable works of research about the body (Stewart and Mickunas, 1990). Phenomenologists deal with any phenomenon with which consciousness is involved. Phenomenological research on the body has enjoyed particular attention, which seems to be logical, since the body is where consciousness resides (Behnke, 1994; Toombs, 1992). Both phenomenology and postmodernism are philosophical movements that are interconnected due to the fact that '[p]henomenology is not *of* but *in* postmodernity' (Jung, 1997: 558; emphases in original). Likewise, phenomenologists and postmodernists retort that Cartesian dualism has given birth to such alienations as nature/culture, subject/object, substance/extended substance and body/soul. Both postmodernists and phenomenologists, including Merleau-Ponty, therefore, attempt to transcend these dualisms and to comprehend a phenomenon as 'total parts' (Madison, 1988: 67). This chapter outlines Merleau-Ponty's contribution, which intersects with research on the body, postmodernity and disability.

The Cartesian dualism and philosophy of Merleau-Ponty

While Merleau-Ponty was enlightened by Gestalt psychology, he was clearly opposed to the domination of modern philosophy by the Cartesians (Madison, 1988; Spiegelberg, 1982). The philosophy of Descartes (1596–1650) cannot be fully comprehended without understanding his era. The period of the seventeenth century was a time when people became fascinated by automation, electricity and mathematics: their world-view was a 'mechanical world of lifeless matter, incessant local motion, and random collision' (Lindberg, 1992: 362). The dominance of metaphysics in this era undoubtedly influenced Descartes, who likened the body to a constitution of mechanical components.[1]

The German scholar, Gebser (1991), relates the rise of dualism in the seventeenth century to the advent of ideas about the perspectival world. Along with this conscious mutation at the end of the Middle Ages, human beings began to perceive such dualities as subject–object, nature–culture and, most importantly, body–soul. This transition was possible due to the realization of space and the self ('I') of humans, concepts which had not existed in the previous era, the unperspectival world. Since the beginning of the dualistic perspectival world, the 'contemporary state of narrow specialization' in the sciences has become prominent, and human beings have perceived the body as an entity dissociated from the soul (Gebser, 1991: 23).

Since the dawn of the Renaissance, Western science has created the notion of mutual exclusiveness – if something is A, it cannot be B at the same time (Gebser, 1991). This marked the beginning of empiricism and rationalism (Stewart and Mickunas, 1990). The 'new scientists', such as Newton, Galileo and Descartes, rejected Aristotelian metaphysics, and 'new science' has departed from philosophy since then (Lindberg, 1992: 361). From that time, Western science has been fragmented, discontinued and specialized in order to compensate for our ignorance and our inability to study a phenomenon as a whole. The most prominent example of the fragmentation of Western science may be seen in the field of medicine. Since medical science divided the body artificially into manageable pieces, numerous medical specializations have emerged to deal with illness. Likewise, human existence has been split between the soul and the body since the seventeenth century.

Merleau-Ponty's works, including *Phenomenology of Perception* (1962), are an attempt to exemplify how this dualistic standpoint is inadequate to explain human existence. Merleau-Ponty shows that neither rationalism nor empiricism is capable of handling 'unobservable' phenomena. For example, scientists cannot explain why a doctor can treat a patient's symptoms, such as a cold or headache, that cannot be seen or touched by the doctor. The phenomenon of imaginary pregnancy cannot be explained as long as the body is perceived as a separate entity from the mind. It illustrates the mysterious power of the mind. A female so desperately longs to have a child that her body goes through *physical* changes, such as a rise in temperature, termination of menstruation and/or changing food preferences, as if she is physically pregnant. Cartesian dualism is insufficient to unlock the mystery of these phenomena. In order to explain these, Merleau-Ponty (1962) elaborated the paradigm of embodiment.

It is evident that Gestalt psychology influenced Merleau-Ponty's philosophy. He asserts that 'an initial perception independent of any background is inconceivable. Every perception presupposes . . . a certain past, and the abstract function of perception, as a coming together of objects, implies some more occult acts by which we elaborate our environment' (Merleau-Ponty, 1962: 281). Some find two faces, while others perceive a vase in the famous Gestalt picture. Therefore, it is impossible to isolate the vase from the two faces because the vase needs the two faces to exist as the front, and vice versa. Both the faces and vase are complementary, and which picture comes to the fore depends on one's focus.

However, for Merleau-Ponty, Gestalt psychology represented merely a beginning, since he was not satisfied by its inability to embrace the notion of the 'form' which emerges not in the physical reality, but with one's consciousness (Merleau-Ponty, 1962; Madison, 1981). Without consciousness, one would never be able to notice a form, just as a person fails to see his or her friend coming in a crowd until the person's consciousness is directed at the friend. Until that moment, the friend, a form, would be blended into the background. Nevertheless, with the rise of the person's consciousness, the presence of the friend suddenly comes forward, the rest remains as the background and the background contrasts with the form, the friend. Merleau-Ponty (1962) attempts to go beyond Gestalt by stating that the 'form' does not exist, unless consciousness is directed at it.

The body as embodiment

Merleau-Ponty's work uses a phenomenological perspective to investigate the body. One of his foremost notions is 'embodiment', which alludes to interconnectedness, and Merleau-Ponty (1962) calls the body a 'grouping of lived-through meanings which moves towards its equilibrium' (p. 153). Furthermore, he introduces the innovative idea that the body 'extends' an object, for example a cane for the blind, so that it literally becomes a part of the body.[2] This 'extension of the bodily synthesis' is a process of embodiment (Merleau-Ponty, 1962: 152), and this search for equilibrium also seems to be the core of adjustment by a person to his or her impairment, which will be discussed hereafter.

A pianist with a visual impairment comments that 'the piano is *a part of my body* that cannot be separated from me' (*http://www.zakzak.co.jp/geino/nws3204.html*; my translation). In order to understand this phenomenon, one must go beyond empiricism and the Cartesians. His assertion is not just figurative or metaphoric speech: the piano *is* an extension of his body. He has embodied the piano as a part of his identity and, without it, he would lose who he is. His identity or wholeness cannot be completed without this instrument. In a like fashion, when a lover of a person in a wheelchair touches the chair, s/he shivers as if the flesh of the person were caressed. In a sense, the person *was* touched: the lover touched the wheelchair as an extension of the person. For a person with a visual impairment, a cane is not a mere object, but has become his or her tactile organ. Through stimuli from the cane (and from beneath the shoes s/he is wearing), the person with a visual impairment can tell if s/he is walking on concrete or on grass. The skilled blind person with a cane, therefore, is capable of manoeuvring himself or herself without relying on visual data, due to the embodiment of the object. Using von Uexkull's term, the object is absorbed with one's *umwelt* (a literal translation in English would be 'environment') (1957).

On the other hand, a newly blind person who refuses to use a cane and stumbles over obstacles has not reorganized his/her *umwelt* according to his/her new condition (Merleau-Ponty, 1962). This love–hate relationship between people with disabilities and their aids, such as a wheelchair or cane, is quite prominent, particularly for newly disabled individuals. Such people tend to hold on to their familiar *umwelt*, the world of the able-bodied, without perceiving that it has been altered by their disabilities. For example, an amputee, whom the author interviewed, was obsessed with the length of his artificial legs. He hoped that he would be able to wear prosthetics to make his height equivalent to what it used to be. At the same time, he reluctantly admitted that using a wheelchair in daily life would be far more efficient and safer than prosthetics. The anthropologist Robert Murphy (1990) consciously avoided using a wheelchair because it was the 'symbol of disability' (p. 61), and insisted on using a walker. These people's peculiarities, obsessions and mixed feelings towards their aids cannot be explained satisfactorily if they are seen as mere instruments. In fact, newly disabled individuals are ashamed of their aids *because they have started embodying objects as a part of themselves*. Their instruments are embodied as aids while they are symbols of these individuals' stigma. Interestingly, newly disabled people's mixed feelings towards aiding instruments contrast sharply with the congenitally disabled person's emotions toward them. Murata (1996), who has had polio for most of his life, felt uplifted when he received his first wheelchair; at the same time, he felt nothing but 'fear' about walking with prosthetic legs. Likewise, Asaka (1997) was enlightened when she started using a wheelchair instead of walking with the aid of crutches. The marked differences in the attitudes of newly disabled people and those born with impairments towards adaptive aids deserve more detailed investigation and analysis.

As a process of embodiment, an object becomes a part of the identity of the person to whom it belongs. When the author visited a competitive wheelchair basketball team in Japan, she observed that the players were spending considerable time adjusting the basketball wheelchairs before the practice. They seemed fetishistic and particular about the chairs. A choice of colours, from dark blue to vivid pink, and various models is available, and each person customizes his or her chair to his/her fashion and identity. The players mended the chairs just as one combs hair in a specific way. According to them, the slightest change, say, the tightness of a single nut, would create a whole new sphere, as if they were in a different chair. Their obsession makes perfect sense because they have embodied their chairs. Yet these instruments are, unlike legs, adjustable and creative: these players engineer their legs. As Haraway (1988) observes, 'embodiment is [a] significant prosthesis' (p. 588). Both Haraway's notion of the 'cyborg' and Merleau-Ponty's 'extension of the body' through aids overlap in terms of the body's 'quasi-technicality' (Casey, 1998: 213).

The interviews conducted by the author showed that the notion of walking is not merely a physical matter, but about *lebenswelt*, the life world, itself. Not being able to walk does not simply alter one's physical condition, but family life, interpersonal relationships with others, self-image, the world-view and even the sense of temporality (Iwakuma, 2001). Murphy (1990) contends that his *lebenswelt* and the self were shaken most by his spinal cord tumour. He states that 'From the time my tumor was first diagnosed through my entry into wheelchair life, I had an increasing apprehension that I had lost much more than the full use of my legs. I had also lost a part of my self . . . I felt differently toward myself. I had changed in my own mind, in my self-image, and in the basic conditions of my existence' (p. 85). Accordingly, many of the interviewees commented that 'I had no idea there was this kind of *world* (the one of the "disabled") until I had my disability' (my translation; emphasis added). In a sense, it is accurate to describe their transformation since their 'old' life world was changed, and a new hermeneutic horizon has opened from a different angle. Colloquially, 'opening horizon' refers to a positive experience. However, in phenomenology, 'horizon' constitutes an 'encompassing frame of reference, without which any account of even single perception would be incomplete' (Spiegelberg, 1982: 146). Thus, phenomenologically speaking, one expands his or her 'horizon' even through a traumatic experience, such as one of paralysis.

If a cane represents a mere object for a person with visual impairment, as the Cartesians or empiricists would insist, the skilful use of the cane by the blind would not be possible since a foreign object (a cane) and the body cannot be mingled together. However, in reality this is not the case. As a newly disabled person broadens his or her horizon from the viewpoint of paralysis, s/he embodies the wheelchair and his or her experiences with it into his/her *umwelt*. It is possible that, through embodiment, a person using a wheelchair, for example, will be able to calculate instantly whether a space ahead is wide enough to pass through. The reason why a newly disabled person in a wheelchair keeps bumping into objects is that his or her sense of space is still that of a standing person. The same process of embodiment can be observed when a person who used to drive a small car and now drives a van has to learn the boundaries of the new vehicle since it provides a different horizon for the driver. This process is much more complex and creative than just 'getting the hang of it'. Both a person who has started using a wheelchair and the van driver embody their new proximity, a sense of space, along with a new body image, which Merleau-Ponty (1962) defines as a 'total awareness of my posture in the intersensory world' (p. 100). Regarding the notion of 'body image', this author recalls that, during a medical examination, a doctor once asked her to keep both arms at the level of her shoulders *while her eyes were closed*. When she was told to open her eyes, she found that her right, paralysed, arm had gone down without her knowing. The non-disabled would have no difficulty in maintaining the same posture because of their body image, which enables them to know unconsciously where their arms are. The examination was meant to test whether the author's arms were included as a part of her body image. Nevertheless, for the author, her paralysed right arm is sometimes out of the 'total awareness' of her 'intersensory world' without a conscious effort. Accordingly, her 'awkward' posture of the right arm is often noticed by others.

For newly disabled people, embodiment cannot be completed without holding a 'healthy' body image of themselves. An interviewee who was a recent amputee, having lost his legs less than a year ago, was experiencing a phantom limb. For an amputee, a phantom limb signifies that the person's body image has not matched the actual body situation (Merleau-Ponty, 1962), and it occurs due to the 'habit-body' (p. 82) 'which cannot decide to recede into the past' (p. 85). In contrast, 'Diane', who was born without limbs, never experienced phantom pain because her body image is already complete without limbs (Frank, 1986). She embodies her *umwelt* with deformed limbs, and her proxemics (such as her 'reach') is established according to her body image.[3] This is similar to, say, a lady who is wearing a long hat bowing deeper than usual when coming out from a car in order not to crush the hat (Merleau-Ponty, 1962). Embodiment means, thus, taking one's body image into account unconsciously. Embodiment means, conversely, making one's *umwelt* transparent. Embodiment cannot be completed as long as s/he is conscious of, for example, pushing a wheelchair for transportation or is making an effort to flip a page while using a prosthetic arm.

Merleau-Ponty (1962) examined the case of 'Schneider', who was his patient. Although 'Schneider' had no difficulty in doing 'practical' activities, such as blowing his nose with a handkerchief or lighting a match, he could not follow directions to carry out such 'abstract' movements as pointing to his nose or stretching his arms. Based on his study of 'Schneider', Merleau-Ponty proves that 'Schneider's' problems cannot be fully explained in terms of a visionary function. Like Merleau-Ponty's argument, recent studies show that the visual sense, an ability to see, is different from reading comprehension or recognition as seen in children (or people) with learning disabilities

(LD) (Wingert and Kantrowitz, 1997). Learning disability has recently begun to be recognized, yet it is still confusing for parents and teachers since people with learning disabilities or autism have the capacity to see (Wingert and Kantrowitz, 1997). This is because people hold a close connection between vision and recognition. Most autistic people also live with symptoms of LD, such as hyperlexia. Although 'Schneider' was not autistic, his problems were quite similar to those of people with autism.

An autistic female on the Internet commented that she cannot determine whether someone is a male or a female at first glance without a detailed observation. She also asserts that many autistic people cannot 'read' what is usually taken for granted, facial expressions or nuances in the voice.[4] For them, interpersonal communication is similar to, according to the woman, 'following only the captions without having the picture or sound when watching the movies'. This autistic woman recalls her childhood as being 'obsessed with the alphabet'. She memorized the numbers and English alphabet by the age of one and learned the Japanese alphabet when she was two. However, like Schneider's case, she was not able to understand the meaning of the story she was reading or the emotional nuances of the characters in the story. Following a line of the alphabet and comprehension are separate entities. The latter, comprehension, requires the synthesization of the meaning: embodiment.

A friend of the author, who teaches children with autism, related an interesting story about a child who was being taught that touching a stove is dangerous through the use of direct tactile experience. However, the child learned only that touching *that specific* stove was dangerous. She could not perceive the stove as representative of stoves in general. Instead, the stove she touched was fixed and independent. Likewise, she could not expand and generalize her experience of danger to other contexts involving other stoves, a phenomenon that Merleau-Ponty calls 'projection' or 'summoning' (1962: 112). In order to teach this child that touching a stove is dangerous, it would theoretically be necessary for her to touch every stove in the world.

Both the child with autism mentioned above and 'Schneider' in Merleau-Ponty's book lack a 'flow of experiences' (Merleau-Ponty, 1962: 281), or an ability to synthesize different facets of perspective into a recognizable whole. People without this function cannot participate in role-playing or simulation, shed tears when reading a novel, nor can they understand a metaphor. They literally do not understand the concept of 'being in another's shoes'. This function of the 'flow of experiences' enables people to sympathize with another's feelings. A person sheds tears or experiences fatigue after reading a long novel due to this capacity. For the autistic child and 'Schneider', every experience is discontinued and fragmented from others and they can learn only through their own experience. These people cannot 'get used to' anything because each experience is as vivid as the first time. Further-more, based on the arguments above, the author speculates that people without the function of a flow of experiences would not hold any 'ism' such as racism, ageism or sexism since, for example, they would not gen-eralize a negative experience with one Japanese to other Japanese. All 'isms' take the notion of 'knowing ten by seeing one' (Japanese proverb) into account.

In his later work, Merleau-Ponty's attempt at transcending dualism used the notion of 'flesh' which is 'the undivided Being existing before the consciousness-object split' (Madison, 1988: 64). As his famous metaphor illustrates, grasping hands are both the touched and touching; they are object as well as subject. So is the flesh which is 'the visible-seer, the audible-hearer, the tangible-touch – the sensitive-sensible' (Lanigan, 1991: 131). Due to this 'reversibility' of the flesh, 'the subject and the world . . . have no existence in themselves, independent of one another, but rather constitute one single *system* and are *correlates* of each other' (Madison, 1981: 169, emphases in original).

Merleau-Ponty (1962) further suggests that the body is the centre of the temporal and spatial matrixes. When one perceives an object, perception 'occupies' the person while consciousness is directed at the object and, as the result of it, the self, or the body, becomes transparent. Just as a light-house cannot direct a ray of light at its building, the body stays as unconsciousness since it is the centre of one's perception, unless there is something 'wrong' with it. An experience of having a headache provides an explanation of this from the opposite side. Until you perceive a headache, you are unaware of having a head, even though you know of the existence of the head from past experiences. A pounding pain makes one's consciousness focus on the head and, suddenly, the head, which usually remains in the background, comes forward, just as the eye focusing on the Gestalt picture determines the existence of either the vase or faces as apparent. Murphy (1990) observed the progress of his own spinal cord tumour as 'The body no longer can be taken for granted, implicit and axiomatic, for it has become a problem. It no longer is the subject of unconscious assumption, but the object of conscious thought' (p. 12). Moreover, one's consciousness, as triggered by a headache, delineates the shape of the head, and conscious-ness makes the person able to locate the precise spot of the headache on the head. Conversely, it may be stated that experience of a pain or disturbance proves one's existence. The zoologist, Morris (1969), introduces an example of caged animals which hurt or masturbate themselves until they bleed. This self-abusing act may be explained as their attempt to reconfirm the existence of the body, which is imprisoned, by experiencing pain. For Merleau-Ponty, perception comes first, then an object: as he puts it, 'our perception ends in objects'.

It is known that the body embodies time. Embodiment of time ties each temporality as a stream of time, the past, present and future (Merleau-Ponty, 1962). Without this function, the author assumes, a person cannot expect the next occurring phenomenon based on what s/he has just seen, and s/he would wait until a moment of reality comes to her/him. Without this, there are no regrets for the past, and no worries and expectations for the future.

Time is experienced by the body; therefore, it is subjective (Merleau-Ponty, 1962). Some people with disabilities perceive a different time flow as a result of their disability experiences (Iwakuma, 2001). This subjective time is what Husserl (1962) calls the 'phenomenological time' (p. 215). Toombs (1992) asserts that often people with illness or pain cannot communicate successfully with their doctors because the patients have to use objective time in order to explain their phenomenological (or inner) time and these are quite different from each other. In similar fashion, von Uexkull (1957) demonstrates that different species have different time-frames based on their *umwelten*. A major premiss of *umwelt* theory reads that any animal, including human beings, embodies 'unique worlds with equal completeness', which are derived from the temporal and spatial frames peculiar to the species (von Uexkull, 1957: 11). Von Uexkull's phenomenological theory seems to be in accordance with findings in physics. Einstein (1961) notes in his general theory of relativity that 'every reference body has its own particular time' (p. 26). Moreover, Hall (1983) asserts that people in different cultures are living in different time flows. He compares time between those in the West and East, and he terms the Western time-frame as Monochronic and the other, the Eastern time-frame, as Polychronic. Hall (1983) also notes that, as a species, human beings experience 'dragging or flying' time based on their psychological state, which seems to be similar to Einstein's idea of 'bending or stretching' time. Merleau-Ponty (1962) suggests that the body 'takes possession of time; it brings into existence a past and a future for a present; it . . . creates time instead of submitting to it' (p. 240). Therefore, without the body, there would not be time or space – the body sets its own position in history and it gives an identity, 'who I am'.

Closing remarks

As long as the body is a focal point of perception, 'objective' truth represents the most shared agreements among humans, which is nothing but 'subjective'. A study a researcher is engaged in undeniably changes the person, as s/he studies according to a constantly opening horizon. Therefore, this researcher agrees particularly with Behnke's statement that 'the more open I can be in respectfully attending to the phenomenon, just as it presents itself, the more liable it is to change in response to the awareness I bring to it' (Behnke, 1994: 307). At the same time, it should be noted that any 'objective' research is originated based on the ever-changing perception of the researcher. This is why Husserl called for 'Zu den Sachen selbest' ('to the phenomenon itself'), letting a phenomenon speak by itself.

At the core of Merleau-Ponty's work, including *Phenomenology of Perception*, is the attempt to overcome Cartesian dualism. Instead of saying, 'I have my body', therefore, Merleau-Ponty (1962) declares that 'I am my body' (p. 198). A phenomenological inquiry is ultimately a quest for a fusion of subjectivity and objectivity (Madison, 1988; Stewart and Mickunas, 1990), and so indeed was Merleau-Ponty's. This search is well in accordance with this postmodernist era which perceives that '[t]hings of physical nature not only respond to the web they are caught in, they also make the web respond to what it has caught' (Deely, 1994: 181). Thus, Madison (1988) thinks of Merleau-Ponty as 'indeed postmodern' (p. 72). Returning to the disability discourse based on this premiss, there is no distinction between an adapter, a person who has a disability, or an adaptee, the rest of the world. The person with a disability does not 'adapt to' the static environment or to his or her disabled physical condition. The rest of the world, surrounding people and environment, alters as the individuals with disabilities transform, as Merleau-Ponty's notions of 'embodiment' or 'flesh' indicate, amounting to monism – any theory that denies the duality of mind or body. As discussed in this chapter, Merleau-Ponty's work helps us to comprehend disability experiences, especially in terms of the process of becoming a 'fully fledged' person with a disability. It is further expected that his work will be valuable for such disability studies as the emergence of disability consciousness, the (re)habilitation of individuals with disabilities, technological evolution and people with disabilities or body politics in the postmodern era.

Notes

1. Nevertheless, it seems unfair to criticize Descartes for his ignorance with regard to the body when considering the period in which he lived. Philosophy, as well as science, is undeniably under the influence of temporality and spatiality, which means that 'truth' changes according to perceptions of them. Therefore, the author agrees with Lindberg (1992) who asserts that 'we must forgive medieval scholars for being medieval and cease to castigate them for not being modern. If we are lucky, future generations will do us a similar favor' (p. 363).

2. Like Merleau-Ponty, McLuhan (1964) and E. T. Hall (1983) also discuss an intertwined relationship between humans and objects from the perspectives of mass communication and of anthropology. Hall's conception of extension transference (ET), as well as McLuhan's, however, discusses objects with the amplified

functions of human organs, such as wheels for the legs and telephones for the voice.

3. However, 'Diane's' embodiment of the body was in conflict with American aesthetics; therefore, she had to wear 'fake legs' for a cosmetic reason. Her prostheses represent her compromise, somewhat dissociated from her embodiment, in order to live in the able-bodied-centred world. Similarly, it is well known that children missing a body part often refuse to wear a prosthesis because of embodiment: adding a foreign object to the body is not natural and is 'more of a hassle than a help' (Frank, 1986: 202). It is only the able-bodied's perception that missing a limb is 'not healthy'. This pervasive perception in society undoubtedly influences newly disabled individuals, such as is apparent in the amputee mentioned earlier, who is obsessed with prostheses designed to make him 'look better'.

4. She further discusses the advancement of the computer and its effect on autistic people. Today's advanced computer age has undeniably opened great possibilities for people with disabilities, whether physical or not. This is because computer-mediated communication (CMC) enables people with autism to relate to others without 'reading between lines', such as using facial expressions or the tone of the voice, which for autistic people are hard to read. She calls the Internet a 'lifeline' for people with autism. The literature of CMC has been booming in communication studies while, as far as the author notices, CMC studies of people with non-physical disabilities, such as autism, remain severely limited.

References

Asaka, Y. (1997) *Iyashi no sekushi torippu [A Journey of My Sexuality]*. Tokyo: Taro-Jiro Press.

Behnke, E. (1994) 'The study project in phenomenology of the body', *Humanistic Psychologist*, 22: 296–317.

Casey, E. (1998) 'The ghost of embodiment', in D. Welton (ed.), *Body and Flesh*. Malden, MA: Blackwell.

Deely, J. (1994) *New Beginnings: Early Modern Philosophy and Postmodern Thought*. Toronto: University of Toronto Press.

Einstein, E. (1961) *Relativity: The Special and the General Theory*, trans. R. W. Lawson. New York: Crown Press.

Frank, G. (1986) 'On embodiment: a case study of congenital limb deficiency in American culture', *Culture, Medicine and Psychiatry*, 10: 189–219.

Gebser, J. (1991) *The Ever Present Origin*, trans. N. Barstad and A. Mickunas. Athens: Ohio University Press.

Hall, E. T. (1983) *The Dance of Life: The Other Dimensions of Time*. Garden City, NY: Anchor Books.

Haraway, D. (1988) 'Situated knowledges: the science question in feminism and the privilege of partial perspective', *Feminist Studies*, 14: 575–9.

Husserl, E. (1962) *Ideas: General Introduction to Pure Phenomenology*, trans. W. B. B. Gibson. New York: Collier Macmillan Publishers.

Iwakuma, M. (2001) 'Aging with disabilities in Japan', in M. Priestley (ed.), *Disability and the Life Course*. Cambridge: Cambridge University Press.

Jung, H. Y. (1997) 'Post-modernism', in L. Embree, E. A. Behnke, D. Carr, J. C. Evans, J. Huertas-Jourda, J. J. Kockelmans, W. R. McKenna, A. Mickunas, J. N. Mohanty, T. M. Seebohm and R. Zaner (eds), *Encyclopedia of Phenomenology*. Dordrecht: Kluwer Academic Publishers, pp. 558–62.

Lanigan, R. (1991) *Speaking and Semiology*. Berlin: Mouton de Gruyter.

Lindberg, D. C. (1992) *The Beginnings of Western Science*. Chicago: The University of Chicago Press.

McLuhan, M. (1964) *Understanding Media: The Extensions of Man*. New York: McGraw-Hill.

Madison, G. B. (1981) *The Phenomenology of Merleau-Ponty*. Athens: Ohio University Press.

Madison, G. B. (1988) *The Hermeneutics of Postmodernity*. Bloomington and Indianapolis: Indiana University Press.

Merleau-Ponty, M. (1962) *Phenomenology of Perception*. New York: Routledge.

Morris, D. (1969) *The Human Zoo*. London: Dell Books.

Murphy, R. (1990) *Body Silent*. New York: Norton Press.

Murata, M. (1996) *Kurumaisu kara mita machi [The View from My Wheelchair]*. Tokyo: Iwanami Junior Bunko.

Spiegelberg, H. (1982) *The Phenomenological Movement*. Hingham, MA: Kluwer Boston.

Stewart, D. and Mickunas, A. (1990) *Exploring Phenomenology*. Athens: Ohio University Press.

Toombs, S. K. (1992) *The Meaning of Illness: A Phenomenological Account of the Different Perspectives of Physicians and Patient*. Dordrecht: Kluwer Academic Publisher.

Uexkull, J. von (1957) 'A stroll through the worlds of animals and men', in C. H. Schiller (ed. and trans.), *Instinctive Behavior: The Development of a Modern Concept*. New York: International Universities Press.

Wingert, P. and Kantrowitz, R. (1997) 'Why Andy couldn't read', *Newsweek*, 27 October, pp. 56–64.

UNIVERSITY OF WINCHESTER
LIBRARY

7

Disability in the Indian Context: Post-colonial Perspectives

Anita Ghai

Introduction

Within the Indian subcontinent awareness about the issues and concerns of lives touched with disabilities is a fairly recent phenomenon. It was only in the forty-ninth year of independence from colonial oppression that the first legislation advocating equal rights for disabled people became a living reality. While the discourse in the developed world has progressed from the issues of service delivery and rehabilitation to an engagement with the multiple nuances/meanings of disabled existence, the developing world continues to agonize over the very basic of survival needs. For this process of negotiation to acquire authenticity, an attempt has to be made to understand the context in which meaning is being ascribed to a life condition such as disability. This query is critical in a country like India where social theorizing has generally excluded the realities of disability even when it has sought active engagement with marginal realities such as gender, caste or poverty, to name a few. The present chapter delves into the possibility of understanding disability in the Indian situation with the insights offered by post-colonialism.

Why post-colonialism?

Even though it is difficult to posit a clear answer to this question, I take recourse to Appiah (1992: 142), who maintains that in many domains, such as poetry, architecture, film, rock and philosophy, there is an antecedent practice that laid claim to a certain exclusivity of insight. In each of these domains postmodernism is a name for the rejection of that claim to exclusivity, a rejection that is always more playful – though not necessarily less serious – than the practice it aims to replace. That exclusivity cannot suffice, as a definition of postmodernism follows from the fact that, in each domain of inquiry, the rejection of exclusivity takes up a specific form, one that reflects the specificities of its setting. The attraction towards diverse writings, ranging from literary criticism to social inquiries, and generally termed postmodern, is thus understandable, because they reject stories that claim to encompass all human history. To quote Lyotard (1984), postmodernism designates a general condition in which 'grand narratives of legitimation' are no longer credible. All modern forms of knowledge, he claims, be they positivist, hermeneutical or Marxist, legitimate themselves by making explicit appeals to some type of universal standard. He argues that recent developments in social sciences and politics have undermined these claims, producing what he calls an 'incredulity towards grand narratives'. Postmodern society is thus defined in terms of a radical heterogeneity characterized by a decline of ideological hegemony in politics and social life as well as an abundance of creative discoveries in arts and science. In this sense, very few of us can deny that postmodernism has had profound consequences for contemporary social life.

Within the context of disability, Corker (1998: 232) delineates the viability of postmodernism in highlighting the relationship between individual and society, as opposed to a focus on the grand narrative of either. She suggests that postmodernism, or more specifically post-structuralism, encourages us to question the oppositional character of discourses on social reality. The dominant ideologies in Indian culture have continued to operate paradoxically in characterizing the binaries that define social realities. While in principle they might be postulated as complementary, their actual meaning/working is oppositional. Thus there is a strong cultural belief that, while the female is opposed to male, she is at the same time encompassed in male. This is symbolized in the figure of Lord Shiva entitled *Aard Nareshewar*, where the left side is depicted as female and the right side as male. Similarly, *Pursha* (man)/*Prakriti* (nature), touchable/untouchable, represent the same paradox. The binary of disability/ability, however, does not figure, as disability represents horror and tragedy. That the impaired body is unwanted in Indian culture is evident from the reluctance of people to part with their body organs even after death. All binaries, according to Rutherford (1990: 22):

> operate in the same way as splitting and projection: the centre expels its anxieties, contradictions and irrationalities onto the subordinate term, filling it with the antithesis of its own identity; the other in its very alienness simply mirrors this and represents what is deeply familiar to the centre, but projected outside of itself. It is in these very processes and representations of marginality that the antagonisms and aversions which are at the core of dominant discourses and identities become manifest racism, and class contempt as the products of this frontier.

In the Indian context the position of the disabled is reflective of such representation. Before undertaking a detailed analysis of the possibility of postmodernist thought as contributing to an understanding of disability and the

Indian situation, it is essential to conceptualize disability in India. This is definitely not a pedantic requirement, for at the root are larger questions about the meaning and nature of disability itself.

The Indian scenario

India, often described as the emerging superpower, has a population of one billion, out of which approximately 70 million are characterized as disabled. The word approximate is a pointer towards the reality of disability in India. The estimation of numbers is on the basis of national sample surveys, the last being conducted in 1991. The initial unwillingness of the government to include the domain of disability in the census of 2001 to obtain a conclusive idea about prevalence reflects the attitudinal barriers in acknowledging the disabled identity. A concerted protest by the disability activists eventually made it mandatory for the census of 2001 to include the issue of disability.

However, before this countrywide protest, the issue found no space in the political agenda of the country. Thus, the dominant political discourse is concerned neither with the absolute number of disabled people nor with disability categories and their social relevance and validity. Disability is even missing from the most forward-looking social movements since the post-independence period, be they focused on political issues, exploitation of labour, feminist agendas or issues of environment. Historically, disabled people have been invisible, both physically and metaphorically. This invisibility can be seen to parallel the invisibility experienced by the radicalized protagonist of Ralph Ellison's novel, *Invisible Man*, when he explains,

> I am invisible, understand, simply because people refuse to see me. Like the bodiless heads you see sometimes in the circus sideshows, it is as though I have been surrounded by mirrors of hard distorting glass. When they approach me they see only my surroundings, themselves, or figments of their imagination. Indeed everything and anything except me. (Ellison, 1952: 3)

Consequently, within the dominant Indian cultural ethos, labels such as 'disability', 'handicap', 'crippled', 'blind' and 'deaf' are used synonymously. The assumption of the label's naturalness is unquestioned. The roots of this assumption lie in the ideology that conceives of disability as inherent in the mind or body. This leads to a conception which associates lack, deficit and inability with disability. In a culture that valorizes perfection, all deviations from the perfect body signify abnormality, defect and distortion. Conveying feelings of inability and uselessness, disability epitomizes 'failure', and gets conceived of as a personal tragedy. Labels such as *Bechara* (poor thing) accentuate the victim status for the disabled person, and the roots of such attitudes lie in the cultural conception that views an impaired body as resulting from the wrath of fate, and thus beyond redemption. Destiny is seen as the culprit, and disabled people are the victims. The common perception views disability as a retribution for past karmas (actions) from which there can be no reprieve. The dominant cultural construction in India therefore looks at disability as an essential characteristic of the individual that has to be endured to pay back for all the sins committed in the past. The popular images in mythology attest to extreme negativity associated with disability in India (Ghai, 2001, in press). In a culture in which there is widespread female infanticide, killing imperfect children will not even count as a crime. Historically, treatment of those who have survived was sought mostly from shamans and mystics. That remittance has to be made for past sins was unambiguous. The general response of the non-disabled world ranges from pity and charity to hostility, anger, banter and ridicule. Very rarely has the public response been positive.

It is not as if individuals and their families have not challenged these dominant constructions. However, their resolve to fight their destinies is met with implicitly and explicitly negative messages from the community, which signify the futility of their efforts. Although it is reported that it was as early as 1880 that educational and rehabilitative services were started (Chauhan, 1998: 46), it was not until 1992 that a statutory body called the Rehabilitation Council of India started functioning to recognize the need for systemic efforts in the rehabilitation of 'the disabled'. The intervening period saw sporadic attempts aimed at rehabilitation both by disabled people and by nongovernmental organizations. It was with the declaration of the year 1981 as the International Year of the Disabled Persons that renewed efforts to rehabilitate disability gained impetus. However, the general understanding then and today does not differentiate between impairment, disability or handicap and uses the terms synonymously, with a firm cultural grounding in destiny.

A paradigmatic shift in disability and related issues came in the form of medical explanations. However, it continued to replicate the narrow vision of its predecessor, destiny, by recognizing disability as a 'disease'. Medical constructions encouraged cure/overcoming theories. The naturalness of disability thus gained further sanction from the overarching medical model. The influence of global agencies, such as the World Health Organization and the United Nations, was influential in bringing about the change in terminology used to define disabling conditions. As a result, terms such as 'mentally challenged', 'visually impaired' and 'physically impaired' came to replace the more trite, negative usages such as 'retarded', 'crippled' or 'lame'. Indian writings in the rehabilitation field came to include this change in congruence with international standards (Sen, 1988; Ghai and Sen, 1996).

In spite of the change in language, the social and cultural perception of society did not undergo change. Charity and philanthropy remained the predominant response to the predicament of disability. Even today many institutions are regular recipients of food, old clothes and money from wider society, which makes these charitable gestures not out of a sense of commitment to the issue, but as a response to a cultural expectation to do one's *dharmic* (religious) duty towards the needy in the same spirit as one would give alms to beggars. The altruistic paradigm is reflected in governmental policies, which until very recently looked at disability as a welfare issue. Even now most of their efforts are targeted at strengthening the non-governmental organizations without making any direct interventions. The question 'Who is disabled?' is not a part of the dominant discourse of agencies whose primary aim is service delivery. In this situation, the experience of oppression is an integral and internal part of the psyche of the 'affected', and is seen to be without any social or political ramifications. The consequence is the exclusion of most disabled people from participation in everyday activities of life. The experience of disability in a world where organization is based on particular conceptions of normality impedes functioning in every walk of life. Widespread inaccessibility in buildings, non-representation in education, rampant unemployment, unavailability of satisfying personal relationships and a general unacceptance in society adds to an already marginalized existence.

Within this pessimistic situation, a silver lining comes in the form of disabled people themselves, and their struggles to resist the system. Along with their families, their strivings to chart out a different destiny saw the first legislation for equal opportunities being passed in 1996. The expectation that legislation will be able to alter their life remains a pipe dream, however. Even if the likelihood of proper implementation is accepted in principle, a number of issues still need to be contended with. Many impairment categories, such as autism, learning difficulties and haemophilia, do not find space in the definition of disability. As the recognition of a category depends on its inclusion in the legislative scriptures, this is a serious lacuna. Further, the legislation demands that the disabled prove the degree of their disability to gain any benefits, where degree is determined by the proportion of physical and bodily impairment without acknowledging the social, psychological or political impact, and therefore adds to individual disability. For instance, disabled children must produce a medical certificate proving their disability to seek admission in government schools and take advantage of the very meagre facilities in educational institutions. As the provisions of the state are contingent on a medical certificate indicating the percentage of impairment decided by the state-constituted board, the queries of who is disabled and to what degree they are 'disabled' are extremely significant. These stipulations have to be read as supporting traditional conceptions of dependency. The medical recognition of disability only shifts the agency of oppression. It does not challenge the perception that continues to look at disabled people as passive clients and victims of their own destiny. The 'benefits' that accrue are seen to be in terms of social welfare rather than as their rights as members of a minority group, because disability has only recently been constructed as a marginal issue, necessitating political concerns.

That recognition of disability is absent from the wider educational discourse is evident from the historical practices within the educational systems that continue to marginalize the issue of disability by maintaining two separate education systems – one for disabled students and one for everyone else. In a country where half the children in the age group of 5–14 are out of school (Sadgopal, 2000: 251), how can there be space for children with disabilities, especially if a segregated schooling is being advocated for them? Even if the legislation optimistically tries to make education available to every disabled child, parents in a village do not see this as instrumental in achieving any autonomy for their disabled child. What they would prefer is perhaps a better way of fetching water from the well and improved agricultural facilities. Similarly, parents in an urban slum expect education to be related to a world of work that would enhance their child's basic quality of life. And in the area of employment a reservation of jobs is there for three categories of disabled, that is, 'orthopaedically impaired', 'visually impaired' and 'hearing impaired'. That educational facilities are different for each of these categories is not very well recognized and, apart from the first two categories, disabled people do not manage to obtain education.

Inability to have the privilege of education results in the continued unemployability of disabled people, reproducing the serious conditions of poverty in which they find themselves. A reservation of jobs (3 per cent) in the government sector is hardly a solution, particularly when the statistics clearly indicate that barely 1 per cent of about 35 million children with disabilities are being educated (Ghai, 1999). The assumption that the job contender would have a basic level of education and vocational competence has no basis in reality.

Notwithstanding the different realities of education and employment, my contention is that the discourse of disability activism in India itself constitutes a meta-narrative that universalizes disability. The leaders of the movement are middle-class urban men who have been educated in public schools and are representative of an 'elite' background. Their fight for 'disability rights' is borrowed from their Western counterparts without any clear analysis of the inherent biases. Whereas the West can focus on male-centric concepts of autonomous and independent individuals without any notion of collective responsibility, Indian society is not in a position to do so, not only because of a lack of resources and insight, but also because of the cultural construction of social realities along patriarchal lines. Consequently, the imported packages of 'nothing for us without us', while perfectly appropriate in some contexts, are universal solutions that ignore the specifics of the Indian dilemma. Sign language programmes taught in most metropolitan cities are borrowed from the West. Their applicability is not judged before introducing them into the curriculum. Similarly, aids for augmentative communication are available only for the English language spoken by the urban educated, who constitute only approximately 25 per cent of India's population. This ignores the multilingual character of society in India, and the scale of linguistic impoverishment.

Academic and social reflection on whether these programmes borrowed from the West have the potentiality for understanding and responding to the diversity of Indian culture is non-existent within disability activism. Consequently, the fight for rights thus ends up giving lip service to the needs of diverse groups, whereas in actuality the agenda remains dictated by the understanding/needs of the leaders. The question, however, is not really whether the programmes are useful or flawed. What is important is whether the disability movement in India is raising pertinent issues about power, discourse and context in the construction and use of the term 'disabled', and whether Western symbols and ideas can explain the intricate patterns of rural and urban culture, considering that 75 per cent of India's population still lives in rural India. In the midst of these harsh and disabling realities, whether and how other marginalizing aspects of caste, gender and class play a significant role is not even questioned. For instance, when one is contending with recurring issues of poverty and disability, that gender would define accessibility is not considered.

India has been particularly slow to engage in discourse where questions about the nature of disability and understanding of a 'disabled self' are raised. What role impairment plays in the life of individuals, or what signs and symbols of an apparently normal/able culture apply, is slowly being questioned. Theories borrowed from the West are not in a position to answer these questions, because they lack the cultural grounding needed for understanding the Indian perspective and perception. It therefore becomes important to ask if and how postmodernism, which is also a Western idea, can make the understanding of disability in the Indian context possible. One answer I believe lies in the deconstructive capacity of post-colonial theories. As Spivak (1990: 104) puts it, 'A deconstructive approach teaches us to look at limits and questions. Further deconstruction suggests that there is no absolute justification of any position.'

Post-colonialism and disability in India

The preceding arguments construe an image of a disabled person within the Indian cultural ethos as an incomplete entity. Carrying a sense of shame, most find that their voices are silenced as they are always looked upon as the 'other'. The deterministic framework of destiny/fate allows very few to escape the erosion of agency, thus creating a situation where a person with disability is not accorded expert status either on his/her own life, or that of the dominant group. As Smith (1995: 169) argues:

> hegemony does not take the form of brute domination; it entails instead the delimitations of the intelligible . . . To fail to achieve an adequate fit within an officially recognised position is to be de-authorised – to be denied recognition as an author of the text and to have one's text dismissed from the start as incoherent, illegitimate or unbelievable.

When Western scholars like Miles (1999: 233) critique the South Asians for not making any significant study of their ancestors' histories regarding disability (although it is not clear whether he is pointing towards non-disabled professionals or people with disabilities), I sense an inability to imagine the loss of agency which comes about when one is 'other' in one's own country. Though he discusses some of the practicalities, the emotional strain of exclusion in its very raw form perhaps goes unnoticed.

Agency is possible only when voices can be raised and heard. Postmodern theory, which measures its competence in terms of justice to heterogeneity, locality and complexity, can provide space that allows for multiple discourses. What is needed in India is an abandonment of the assumptions of essentialism, and concomitantly universalism, and the development of a vision of plurality that focuses on the wholeness of our own bodies. It is here that I feel post-structuralist theory can be of significance, for it is here that a disruption of a unified and individualistic subject is replaced with the indeterminate subject constituted and reconstituted in multiple ways. As Rich (1986: 213) points out, it is important to understand that 'the discourse is about *our* bodies and not "*the* body", which must become the site and the grounds from which to speak' as impaired/disabled. Only then will it be possible to offer a resistance that can challenge the assumptions underlying the cultural constructions of destiny and medicalization. The freedom to understand the plurality and instability of experiential realities could offer creative possibilities for growth.

In the Western world, disability activism has led to an emergent field of disability studies, which is venturing to create theories that conceptualize disabled and non-disabled people as central, harmonizing parts of the whole universe. Scholars such as Thomson (1997: 6) look at 'disability as a social construction – a representation and cultural interpretation of physical transformation or configuration, and a comparison of bodies that structure unequal social relations and institution'. While gender has been viewed as a social construction in the Indian scenario, disability has not been understood in terms of social factors. In the UK, on the other hand, as activists have shifted their focus from service delivery problems to look at some of the oppressive environmental factors, a comprehensive understanding of disability as a social construction is put in the background. Their 'social model' asserts that disability arises from the socially constructed attitudinal, physical and structural barriers created by the dominant ideology of disablist society, rather than an individual's impairments.

Both of these models – constructionist and creationist – are critical of historical treatments of disability as a minoritizing discourse, and promote a universal discourse of disability, which is rationalized by demonstrating its relevance not only for the disabled people in America or the UK, but also for the lives of people across the world. However, this universal discourse ignores the harsh realities of disabled people's lives in countries such as India, which are caught in social and economic marginalization. A postmodern turn in India can clarify that, instead of reinventing the wheel, it will be worthwhile to accept the Western notions as *strands* in a disability discourse that can also look for theoretical positions that would respond to the concerns of the Indian experience of disability.

The contextualization of discourse is imperative. Just as Eurocentric models pose problems in their application to India, we need to recognize that the discourses, cultural responses and subjective perceptions of Indian 'realities' are significantly different. The attraction of post-colonialism, once again, lies in its ability to privilege such diversity. As Corker puts it, '[t]o suggest that particular arguments and particular experiences are wrong is to create a position where theory rules disabled people's experience, rather than one where theory grows from and is therefore *flexible enough to respond to our experience*' (Corker, 1999: 640, italics mine). Post-colonialism can destabilize the totalizing tendencies of imported Western discourse. It brings the possibility of problematizing the norms of given cultural practices and a commitment to take responsibility for modifications that result from the situatedness of knowledge.

When experiences are so vastly different, an examination of specific locales becomes mandatory. The possibility of post-colonialism serving as a vehicle for emancipation also arises from its ability to question the universalistic claims of a disabled identity and a universal disability culture. Erevelles (2000: 27) is critical of locating emancipation solely in the transformation of discursive systems, when the living realities are harsh. However, to me, since disability is not a central feature constituting the lives of people in India, even raising the voices of dissent might be fruitful. The meaning attributed to disability is different for those who speak the language of rights when compared to the language of those who look at disability as a curse. The need is to evaluate the location from which we can challenge the perception of categories of disabled and the able-bodied as fixed, permanent, internally homogeneous and as oppositional. At the same time, a simple celebration of difference or particularity for its own sake should be avoided, when we apply post-colonialism theory to the Indian context, as Probyn (1990: 10) reminds us:

> Knowledges are ordered into sequences which are congruent with previously established categories of knowledge. Location, then, delineates what we may hold as knowledge and, following Foucault, renders certain experiences true and scientific while excluding others.

At this juncture within the Indian milieu, I would not want to argue that 'a particular' theory of disability would comprehensively explain disability. I am aware of the danger in a post-structuralist perspective as it can have the impact of denying the realness or materiality of the impaired body. As Hughes and Paterson (1997: 333–4) put it,

> Poststructuralism replaces biological essentialism with discursive essentialism. The body becomes nothing more than the multiple significations that give it meaning . . . The body and the sensate – in effect – disappear into language and discourse, and lose their organic constitution in the pervasive sovereignty of the symbol. Foucault's concept of bio-politics robs the body of agency and renders it biologically barren. The body becomes a surface to be written on, to be fabricated by the regimes of truth.

However, discourse, according to some authors (White, 1978: 4), is a contemplative enterprise. As such, it is concerned as much with the kind of interpretation as it is with the subject matter with which it is being associated. In addition to visualizing a theory and practice that will problematize the notion of disability as determined by destiny and medical foundations, post-colonialism can be instrumental in setting the tone for engaging in the idea of disability as 'difference' rather than as an oppositional lack or inability. Despite the impressions created, especially in the aftermath of colonial rule, about the multicultural nature of Indian society, in reality there are hegemony and hierarchy that prevail in the construction of social reality. In effect, legitimization of certain differences such as those based on caste have been instrumental in increasing the marginalization of this difference. This is where we need to do what Susan Suleiman (1986) recommends for contemporary feminism, which is to attempt 'to get beyond, not only the number one – the number that determines unity of body or of self – but also to get beyond the number two, which determines difference, antagonism, and exchange . . .' (p. 24). 'The number one' clearly represents for Suleiman the fictions of unity, stability and identity characteristic of the phallocentric world-view. 'The number two' represents the grid of gender, which exposes the hierarchical, oppositional structure of the world-view. Beyond the number two is nothing but endless complication and a dizzying accumulation of narratives. Suleiman here refers to Derrida, in an interview with MacDonald (1982), in which he speaks of a 'dream of the innumerable . . . a desire to escape the combinatory . . . to invent incaluculable choreographies' (p. 76). Suleiman presents Derrida's idea as offering an epistemological or narrative ideal. The implications for India to engage with its multiple realities seem attractive.

Corker's (1999: 635) unease with the argument that 'real differences are based on the socially constructed categories of disability, gender, race, sexuality and class which precisely because they are constructed, embrace a fluidity that cannot mark a collective identity' resonates with me. The boundaries between deaf people, visually impaired people and people with physical impairments remain unchallenged, because the experiential differences and similarities that such people describe are not supposed to be 'real'. This, in my view, is an oversimplification of the issue. The assumption that people with impairments would view the experience of impairment and oppression as identical and subscribe to a general category of disability does not hold water. In India, cross-impairment distinctions are still commonplace. Whereas physically impaired people might see impairment and disability in terms of accessibility issues, rather than the factual information of mobility loss, visually impaired people in India are much more likely to talk about the unavailability of readers and literature in Braille rather than the lack of beeper crossings. Likewise, deaf people in India are at a crossroads with the description of their impairment as hearing loss as there is no space to talk about issues of language and communication. In fact, it is not uncommon to find the labels 'deaf and dumb' in use in many parts of the Indian subcontinent. Developmental disabilities and cerebral palsy have their own specific anomalies. India has certain welfare schemes, such as a discounted airfare, which is given to all visually impaired and those physically impaired who have a disability of 80 per cent and above.

I would thus agree with Corker's view that 'a presupposed internal coherence or unity of impairment requires a stable oppositional category of normality. This institutionalised "normality" both requires and produces the communality of each "voice" of impairment that constitutes the limits of possibilities within an oppositional binary disabled/nondisabled system' (1999: 635). In Indian contexts, such regularity will be difficult to trace. Since individual aspects of disability matter, their clubbing together as one creates tensions. These homogenizing experiences prevent the recognition of cross-disability distinctions, and their specific realities and necessary responses to them. To seek rationality and symmetry within them would be to replicate the fallacy of modernist premises.

Scholars like Bordo (1990: 9) have argued that postmodernism may effect the same kind of erasure of body; and thus erasure of any positioning within space and time that was present in modernism. She reminds us of the metaphors of continuous movement and dance present in postmodern writers and their description of the body as fragmented, changing and inviting a confusion of boundaries. But disabled people possess bodies that are limited and to portray them as otherwise is to negate them. So Bordo asks,

> What sort of body is it that is free to change its shape and location at will that can become anyone and travel everywhere? If the body is a metaphor for our locatedness in space and time and thus for finitude of human perception and knowledge, then the postmodern body is no body at all. The deconstructionist erasure of body is not effected, as in a Cartesian version through a trip to 'nowhere' but in resistance to the recognition that one is always somewhere and limited. (p. 9)

Nonetheless, I believe that a cautiously constructed post-colonialism can deal with this problem. The assertion that theoretical distinctions, criteria of legitimation, cognitive routines and rules are all political, and therefore represent moves of power, is widely accepted. If postmodernism can reject a definition of itself as exemplifying a set of enduring ideals, and acknowledge the political and cultural grounding, it can emerge as a viable option. The focus should be on its being recognized as a set of viewpoints of a time, justifiable as only for a certain time. Being disabled in India does have a context and a certain meaning. In our attempts to change the meaning, we must recognize the multiple political, social, economic and cultural realities. Postmodern discourse, by weaving a tapestry composed of threads of many different hues rather than one that is woven in a single colour, can help in understanding the multiple nuances of 'disabled identity' in India.

References

Appiah, K. A. (1992) *In My Father's House: Africa in the Philosophy of Culture.* Oxford: Oxford University Press.

Bordo, S. (1990) 'Feminism, postmodernism, and gender-scepticism', in Linda Nicholson (ed.), *Feminism/Postmodernism.* New York: Routledge.

Chauhan, R. S. (1998) 'Legislative support for education and economic rehabilitation of persons with disabilities in India', *Asia Pacific Disability Rehabilitation Journal,* 1(2): 46–52.

Corker, M. (1998) 'Disability discourse in a postmodern world', in Tom Shakespeare (ed.), *The Disability Reader.* London: Cassell.

Corker, M. (1999) 'Differences, conflations and foundations: the limits to the "accurate" theoretical representation of disabled people's experience?', *Disability and Society,* 14(5): 627–42.

David, R. D. and Fontana, A. (1994) *Postmodernism and Social Inquiry*. London: Guilford Press.

Derrida, J. and Mcdonald, V. C. (1982) 'Choreographies', *Diacritics*, 12(2): 66–7.

Ellison, R. (1952) *Invisible Man*. New York: Modern Library.

Erevelles, N. (2000) 'Educating unruly bodies: critical pedagogy, disability studies, and the politics of schooling', *Educational Theory*, 50(1): 25–47.

Ghai, A. (1999) 'Education of children with disabilities: an excluded agenda'. Paper presented at *Education in the South Asian Context: Issues and Challenges*, Department of Education, New Delhi, 14–18 November.

Ghai, A. (2001, in press) 'Marginalisation and disability: experiences from the third world', in M. Priestley (ed.), *Disability and the Life Course: Global Perspectives*. Cambridge: Cambridge University Press.

Ghai, A. and Sen, A. (1996) *The Mentally Handicapped*. New Delhi: Phoenix Publishers.

Hughes, B. and Paterson, K. (1997) 'The social model of disability and the disappearing body: towards a sociology of impairment', *Disability and Society*, 12(3): 325–40.

Lyotard, J.-F. (1984) *The Postmodern Condition: A Report on Knowledge*, trans. Geoff Bennington and Brian Massumi. Minneapolis: University of Minnesota Press.

Miles, M. (1999) 'Can formal disability services be developed with South Asian historical and conceptual foundations?', in Emma Stone (ed.), *Disability and Development*. Leeds: Disability Press, pp. 228–56.

Probyn, E. (1990) 'Travels in the postmodern: making sense of the local', in E. K. Sedgwick (ed.), *Tendencies*. London: Routledge.

Rich, A. (1986) *Blood, Bread and Poetry: Selected Prose 1979–1985*. New York: W. W. Norton & Co.

Rutherford, J. (1990) *Identity: Community, Culture, Difference*. London: Lawrence & Wishart.

Sadgopal, A. (2000) *Shiksha Ka Sawa. GranthShilpi*. New Delhi: India Pvt. Ltd. Publications.

Sen, A. (1988) *Psychosocial Integration of the Handicapped: A Challenge to the Society*. Delhi: Mittal Publications.

Smith, A. M. (1995) 'The regulation of lesbian sexuality through erasure: the case of Jennifer Saunders', in Karla Jay (ed.), *Lesbian Erotics*. New York: New York University Press.

Spivak, G. C. (1990) *The Post-Colonial Critic: Interviews, Strategies, Dialogues*, ed. Sarah Harasym. London: Routledge.

Suleiman, S. (1986) '(Re)Writing the body: the politics and poetics of female eroticism', in Susan Suleiman (ed.), *The Female Body in Western Culture*. Cambridge: Harvard University Press, pp. 7–29.

Thomas, M. and Thomas, M. J. (2000) 'Selected readings in CBR', *Asia Pacific Disability Rehabilitation Journal*, Series 1, pp. 84–95.

Thomson, R. G. (1997) *Extraordinary Bodies*. New York: Columbia University Press.

White, H. (1978) *Tropics of Discourse*. Baltimore: Johns Hopkins University Press.

8

Cultural Maps: Which Way to Disability?

Tanya Titchkosky

Introduction

For the past four years, I have lived in a small university town in Nova Scotia and, despite its size, I have seen at least a dozen professionally produced maps of it and many more hand-drawn ones. Some maps are sparse using details only to indicate direction, other maps contain so many details that the path of travel is obscured by the indication of stores and sights along the way. Maps do not simply correspond to the geography of a place. Instead, different maps draw out different meanings that a place can hold. All maps try to impart a sense of the significance of place as this relates to map producers' interpretive relation toward the readers of the map.

Culture, too, gives us many different maps of various things, including disability. Sometimes disability is regarded as a place requiring some delineation of its appearance and its significance. The criteria necessary to qualify for a disability pension, for example, is one such map; government officials use this map to locate disability and to manage disabled people. There are others, such as demographic counts, that map out disability rates in a population. They aim to show what part of a population is made up of disabled persons and to show what part of a person is made up by disability by locating it in the body – 'mobility impairment', 'vision impairment'. These maps point out the severity of the disability landscape by using such terms as 'mild', 'moderate' and 'severe'. These maps are also used as a way to predict one's chances of arriving in the place of disability.

All maps of disability reflect a conception of its place and space within culture. The mapping of disability is an imparting of some version of what disability is and, thus, contains implicit directions for how to move around, through or with it. Disability is mapped differently by various societal institutions and cultural practices and these representations influence one's relation to disability.

In this chapter, I show some of the ways that disability is mapped and how each topography supports a different conception of disability. I try not to follow the paths provided by these maps. Instead, I interrogate the representations of disability found within them. This critical relation to maps and their use serves as an alternative topography that points out the socio-political character of disability. This alternative depicts disability as a social space, constituted from the intersubjective relations to the disabled body, disability identity and interpretive relations that are developed to both. As a way to develop a full sense of the social topography of disability, I make extensive use of my own experience as a dyslexic woman living with a blind person, as well as of the postmodern principle that reality is a discursive accomplishment. My aim is to demonstrate that disability is social and polit-ical, not only with regard to what culture 'makes' out of impaired bodies, but also that the body in all of its vicissitudes already comes to us through cultural maps and is, thus, *always-already* constituted from social and political discursive action.

Mapping blindness: opposition and ambiguity

More than ten years ago I began sharing my life with fellow sociologist, Rod Michalko, who is legally blind. Rod has spent most of his life on the outer-most edge of the legal blindness continuum – '10 per cent of normal acuity'. Measuring a person's percentage of visual acuity is a medico-legal way to map blindness. This map says little about blindness itself, but says much about how far or how close a person is to 'normal' sight.

When I first met Rod I did not experience '10 per cent of normal acuity'. I met Rod as a blind man, but one who could see. He could see . . . but not quite; what I could understand, count on or see as seeing was never all that clear when I was with Rod. It was a confusing state of affairs that threw into question for me what seeing and blindness were suppose to mean. Back in the beginning of our relationship, Rod pointed down and said, 'Your shoelace is undone.' I thanked him, and picked up my pencil . . . and wondered. Per-haps Rod had regained his sight. Yet, if he had, why did he see my pencil as a shoelace? Still, if he is blind, how did he see my pencil? Rod certainly could see but I could not understand what or how.

This confusion flowed from my conception of blindness and sightedness as radically opposite. Either Rod was sighted or he was blind. Fixed opposi-tions, according to Scott (1998: 33), 'conceal the extent to which things presented as oppositional are, in fact, interdependent'. Not only did my conception of blindness as opposite to sightedness conceal their interdepend-ence in Rod, it also concealed from me the need to think about this inter-dependence. I was working with a cultural map that pointed out the land of blindness and that of sightedness with a clearly defined border between the two. What is more, my map did not indicate any border crossings; either you were in the land of the blind or in the land of the sighted. Rod seemed to be on the border. But, instead of thinking about how sight and blindness rely on each other for their meaning, I tried only to decipher whether I was seeing a blind person or not. Such opposition was dependent upon my being secure in the illusion that Rod did not have sight and, thus, was blind, whereas others, including myself, simply had sight. Adhering to these categorical oppositions meant that I possessed sight, really good sight – I saw that my pencil was not a shoelace and in seeing this I also saw Rod as blind. It was not so obvious to me then that blindness – be it 10 per cent, total or what lies between – is not a clear-cut matter. Clearly, my cultural map was oversimplified.

This oppositional understanding conforms to and supports the most common cultural map of blindness – it is *not* seeing. Defining blindness as a kind of negation of sight is regularly expressed in everyday life. During Rod's 10 per cent days, I wondered and others asked me what it was that Rod *could not* see. So common is it to map disability through a series of negations that it might be easy to miss the strangeness of such a process. This strangeness is revealed when we try to map others in a similar fashion, for example, a man is a person lacking a vagina. It would seem ridiculous today to conceive of gender in terms of negation. However, it is still common to regard the disabled body as a life constituted out of the negation of able-bodiedness and, thus, as nothing in and of itself.

If, as Smith (1999: 133) insists, discourse *is* social organization, the every-day ways that the body is spoken of organize being disabled and having able-bodies *as if* they are radically opposed phenomena. Moreover, language recommends that we conceive the able-body as something that just comes along, 'naturally,' as people go about daily existence. People *just* jump into the shower, run to the store, see what others mean while keeping an eye on the kids or skipping from office to office and, having run through the day while managing to keep their noses clean, hop into bed. All of this glosses the body that comes along while, at the same time, brings it along metaphoric-ally. Speaking of 'normal bodies' as movement and metaphor maps them as if they are a natural possession, as if they are not mapped at all. Thus, some people *have* normal visual acuity, normal hearing, normal mobility or normal use of their appendages, whereas others do not. Those who do not *are* dis-abled. A person can *be* blind or a person can *have* sight and it sounds as if these are two very separate things. Clearly, language allows us to speak of our bodies while, at the same time, giving us ways of conceiving of them.

Before I met Rod, I had moved through the world with the implicit assumption that my sight would see whatever needed to be seen – 'naturally'. On our many walks together, I began to question this assumption. Initially, no hand holding, cane nor elbow guidance accompanied us on these walks. I began to pay attention as to how I watched out for bumps and obstacles and to how Rod must be doing the same. Walking with Rod, I paid attention to how my sight worked and I assumed that Rod's partial sight would work the same way, albeit with more effort and overtime. More of 'less of the same' did not, however, capture my experience of Rod's way of seeing. What Rod did was observe me as a sighted person and it was his stance (Harding, 1996: 146) between blindness and sightedness that provoked him to do so. My belief in the illusion that sight is *the* means to observe the world but is not itself observable began to disintegrate and my certainty that blindness is simply the negation of sight became unfixed.

Experiencing and attending to the outer edges of legal blindness can bring to consciousness the ambiguity that lies between sight and blindness and can show that some of the security that sighted people possess is indeed illusory. Wittgenstein (1980, 14e–15e: 75) puts the matter this way:

> I can observe . . . I can also say, 'You see, this child is not blind. It can see. Notice how it follows the flame of the candle.' But can I satisfy myself, so to speak, *that men see?*
>
> 'Men see.' – As opposed to *what?* Maybe that they are all blind?

Of all the things that sight can see, it often does not observe the intimate relation between sightedness and blindness as ways of being in the world. As Wittgenstein indicates, attending to sight usually only occurs in relation to blindness and what we have to say about blindness. Between all the different ways that sight and blindness appear lies something much more meaningful and much more complex: the sheer opposition. Ten per cent of normal vision is not simply the outer limit of blindness, it is also the outer limit of sightedness and it is both at the same time. However, I was soon to discover that culture gives us other maps that almost annihilate the ambiguity that exists between blindness and sightedness.

Fixing ambiguity: medical maps

One day, in yet another of my attempts to see his blindness, Rod and I mapped out what ophthalmologists would refer to as his visual field. Rod focused on the centre of a table top and I moved objects from his point of focus toward the edge of the table, until Rod indicated that the object had appeared in his peripheral vision. I left the objects in the places where Rod began to see them. Soon, using fork, spoon, knife, salt and pepper shakers, the table top displayed a circle of sorts – his field of vision.

There it was – Rod's visual field and his blind spot, concretely represented for me to see. Rod too took a look. He took many looks, moving his gaze around his visual field and blind spot, both the one on the table and the one of his vision. This reminded him of some of his ophthalmological examinations – the same sort of mapping of his vision occurred when he was asked to look at eye charts, or when photographs of his retinas were taken. Despite this somewhat painful reminder of past mapping, Rod worked to give me a representation of his vision and he worked to see this representation for himself.

Mapping, measuring or providing a kind of topography of blind spots and fields of vision is one way to conceive of blindness as well as sight. It is, literally, a static way – Rod could not move if his vision was to be charted and once charted the representation itself was immobile, objectified. As static, such an image is already distanced dramatically from the lived experience of blindness and sight. No matter how precisely produced and minute in its detail, such a map could not tell me how Rod, nor I, nor others, moved, used and lived with this blind spot and this peripheral vision. Although forks and knives are not ophthalmologic tools of examination, the procedure of objectively mapping is tied to the common-sense desire to come to know disability. But such a map told me little. It could not tell me much about how I could or should travel or move with a blind person. This mapping procedure did serve to announce that Rod was different which, of course, we already knew, for why else would we be involved in such an activity?

Measures, such as inability to see the big 'E' on the eye chart, ability to see hand movements at three feet, field of vision charts, photographs of bodily damage, including retinas, or surveys of activity limitations due to bodily differences, help to make blindness, and other disabilities, into a concrete *individual* issue, abstracted from *interpersonal* interaction and interpretation. The social practice of measurement always needs to measure some *thing*, in this case we were making and measuring what Taussig (1980: 3) refers to as 'biological and physical thinghood'. Through such measurement, disability can be made into a thing, a reality in and of a person's body. These measures objectify blindness, making it concrete and easier to deal with, and 'to see', than do the complex self-reflective practices of noticing and reading the work of blind persons as they interact with sighted others in situations, environments and histories not of their own making. 'The thingification of the world, persons and experience . . .' says Taussig (1980: 3) produces a 'phantom objectivity', and 'denies' and 'mystifies' the *body's fundamental nature as a relation between people* (see also Shildrick and Price, 1996).

Among all the different ways to measure blindness there lies in common the fact that these procedures conceive of blindness as essentially a measurable thing of lack and, thus, they map *it* as readily observable, easily quantifiable, impervious to interpretation, set in stone. Arguments regarding appropriate measurements of disability usually only question the contours and shape of *it* as an object and do not question the process of this objectification. Beginning with the unquestioned map of disability as a thing leads to the unexamined presupposition that programmes oriented to ameliorating disability or managing disabled people are just as objectively given as are impaired bodies themselves.

The problem is not simply that such measurement and control practices must take for granted the current social milieu that says that it is right and good to measure, count, track and manage disabled persons. The problem is that this thing-like conception of disability requires, as did Rod and my measurement of it on the table top, a bracketing off of the Really real work involved in being disabled. Disability as objective lack and inability understood as located within a person's body means ignoring disability in relation to the social character of our bodies. It is like giving someone a map of a big city which only indicates its hills, rivers and valleys and telling them to find *Paupers*, a neighbourhood pub. Adhering to the belief that disability is concretely given in some people's bodies requires that we do not get close to the lived actuality of disability.

Interactional maps

There is, nonetheless, a more life-filled reality to disability to which we can attend even within the objectifying practices of measuring and managing disabled people. Consider, for example, what might be learned if we shift our attention away from the objective representation of Rod's vision that was laid out on the table top and 'focus' instead on all that went on *around* the table top. Let us shift our attention away from the map and toward the making of the map.

Around the table top, Rod produced a different image of blindness, one that was more difficult to attend to, but more dynamic, filled with effort, interest and work. Rod had to work to see. He had to take an interest in seeing forks and knives. He had to use his knowledge of a context to figure out what there was to see – what should be seen and what not. The image of blindness produced *around* the table top that day told me that whatever Rod experienced in blindness could only be deciphered by reading the relation between him and the people and the environment around him. Moreover, big blind spot or not, charting its existence could not answer routine questions such as whether I should tell Rod that something was in his way or leave well enough alone.

To gain even a slight understanding of the production of Rod's vision would require that I attend to something much more dynamic than the facticity of his blind spot. In Rod's terms, seeing is a project in so far as we always see through a life (Michalko, 1999: 15–17; 1998: 39–40). The project of seeing for a legally blind person, on the outer edges of both blindness and sightedness, is one filled with conscious effort, will and desire. For sighted people, the project of vision is usually something to which no attention is paid.

But Rod paid attention. His focus was not only on the table top. He focused on that which surrounded the table top and on that which brought it into view. He saw that he was in a bar and that he was surrounded by other table tops around which people sat. Music, sounds of drinking and eating, laughter – all of these sounds Rod 'saw' as his 'being in a bar'. The forks and salt and pepper shakers I used to map his visual field were seen by Rod not only by his peripheral vision but through the lens of being-in-a-bar and being with me and with what I wanted to see. The map we drew was drawn with the material of his life. And as objective as this map was, it was constructed from Rod's 'subjective seeing' of his world. We were transforming Rod's 'seeing' into the objective fact of vision. However, the interactional project of producing a representation of vision is not 'seeable' through an ophthalmological lens.

Any project of vision is accomplished not only in relation to the things and events of the physical world, but also in relation to the habits and customs of a culture – Rod expected to see forks and knives on a table top in a bar . . . and so did I. Vision is accomplished in relation to other people, with conflicting interpretations of what there is to see and with shifting meanings of blindness in different and changing circumstances. What did people see as Rod and I walked into the bar, his hand on my elbow? Did they see blind person and sighted guide? Did they see a couple entering a bar affectionately caressing one another as they did so? Did they see both or neither? Did they see a sighted person mapping out the visual field of a blind person on a table? Did they see two people engaged in animated conversation, perhaps about staging a play or the moves of football players? Perhaps they did not 'see' any of this at all.

Like the people in the bar, Rod's seeing is embedded in the particularity of his body, his interests, his attention, his energy and his effort. Around the table top, Rod worked to give me a representation of his vision. Moreover, he worked to see this representation for himself. In both the making and the observation of his representation of blindness, Rod showed me that being partially sighted meant living with a conscious awareness of vision as an accomplishment. To help or hinder, to experience or ignore Rod in this accomplishment would depend upon the kind of attention that I paid to him. Blindness began to teach me that seeing is culturally organized. Blindness and sight conceived of as a cultural accomplishment, as *work*, more clearly represents that which I actually was experiencing with Rod.

In so far as seeing is cultural, sight is a social accomplishment and blindness is a kind of forced consciousness of the work necessary to achieve it. This is a key lesson that accompanies my shift away from attempts to reduce disability to a concrete reality and towards mapping disability as a complex set of social interactions. This lesson did not simplify my understandings of 'being blind' and 'having sight'. It showed me that there is no way to concretize what will be seen and what will not. There is no definition, rule book or chart which will tell me what being blind or sighted means.

Going blind, needing a better map

My sense of dissatisfaction with cultural maps increased in relation to the fact that Rod's vision began to change. Rod's orientation to his position between sightedness and blindness was more and more being experienced from the side of blindness. The necessary adjustment time between bright light to dim or dim light to bright began to take longer for Rod. The noticing of shoelaces or pencils or anything else on the ground began to disappear. At some point, I too became invisible. I now needed to make my exit or entry into a room aural. As visual cues and markers began to disappear, my dyslexia became more obvious to both Rod and me. Saying 'Turn left', when I meant 'Turn right', could now lead to a collision with unseen objects. I became more anxious about giving correct directions and this seemed to lead to more misdirections. For me, word order within a direction-sentence is often askew, especially if I am rushed: 'There is a chair, at our table, facing the same direction as we did as we walked through the door that we just did.' Or, 'There is a post, past the fence, near the gate, which has been removed.' Rod was losing those visual aids (a missing post, fence or gate?) which had in the past helped him to put straight what I was saying.

Almost every time Rod arrived home he had a story regarding the disappearing visual world he was now living in (Michalko, 1999: 11–15). Almost weekly, one landmark after another would disappear and his vision began to move toward seeing shadows and light. But shadow vision is confusing – is the shadow a post or is the post a mere shadow? Learning to translate the appropriate shadows into solids became an abiding feature of the type of work involved in this form of vision – this included the arduousness of deciphering, memorizing, listening, not only to the ways of sighted people but to the physicality of culture. In this world of multiplying shadows and disappearing people, I said to Rod, 'It is like you are going blind, over and over again.'

Blind people who are going blind are in an awkward state of affairs. All the shifts in Rod's blindness meant a shift in his way of orienting to the world. Every change in vision requires a reorganization of the type of work that is necessary to move through everyday life. Yet, the everyday world remains that place which usually expects nothing other than sighted persons or their opposite. The blind person who is going blind is living testimony to the radical inadequacy of simple dichotomies or simple maps. The richness of the flesh of disability includes 'illegitimate fusions' (Thomson, 1997: 114) between what is assumed to be binary opposites. Given the culture's dominant inclination to frame sight and blindness as opposites, there is no readily available language to express the phenomenon of going blind when one already is.

Between partial sight and total blindness, between dyslexia and going blind, between my vision and Rod's, between all the ways of speaking of blindness and its lived actuality, between all this, and surely more, an ambiguous plurality of perspectives is released into the world. In this diversity, it is possible to map disability as opposition, as a medical thing or as an interactional accomplishment. Yet, it is also possible, indeed probable, that these different maps show us very little about the meaning of disability beyond some observable details. These maps identify some aspect of disability, make it manageable and give the map user a fleeting sense of certainty. Even interactional maps of disability, most often produced by sociologists, do little more than pin down 'attitude and responses' between disabled and non-disabled people (see Titchkosky, 2000). Charting disabled people's interaction with non-disabled others can reveal the routine order of everyday life, for example, that sight is an expected feature of interactional normalcy. However, this knowledge can perpetuate injustice if we do not consider the kinds of relations (orientations) that people develop in regard to such knowledge. After all, there are many ways to make disability thing-like and obliterate any intersubjective discursive consciousness of bodily experience.

There is little new about mapping disability. Western culture has a long history, especially with the Enlightenment, of being very curious about human difference as abnormalcy and pathology, often treating bodily differences as an object of curiosity, conversation and examination (Canguilhem, 1991[1966]; Foucault, 1973). Non-disabled people have spent time and energy mapping human difference through such activities as freak shows, medical rounds, pathology topologies, popular novels, demographics, the generation of statistical probabilities and through surveying and observing disabled persons and non-disabled interactants. Disability has a long history of being mapped as if it is a foreign land, and a distanced curiosity remains one of the most repetitive, debilitating, yet 'normal' ways of regarding the life and work of disabled people.

My account of Rod's changing vision represents the necessity of engaging a plurality of perspectives if disability is to be conceived as a fully social and political phenomenon. Attention needs to be paid to the ways in which people relate to and make use of culturally specific maps of disability and to the ways in which they inscribe meaning onto the lives of disabled people. The power of culture to make up the meaning of blindness, or any other disability, is diverse. There are ways to map how far or how close our bodies come to able-bodied standards, there are statistical maps to indicate the probability of acquiring a disability and there are sociological maps which depict the socially constructed character of 'normal' life. What all these maps share in common is that they reflect, enter and influence culture without necessarily requiring anyone to pay attention to their production and their use. Moreover, these maps influence the destiny of disabled and non-disabled people. These maps delineate 'normal' paths upon which we are to move and live with our bodies and their interpretations. Maps are not just tools, they are cultural products, and thus they are the stuff of culture requiring critical reflection.

There is, however, no way to escape from using some kind of conceptual map as people move and live with disabled persons. *What is unjust about this situation is that these maps are made and remade, used and reused and, yet, there is no cultural imperative to pay attention to such making and such use.* Maps of social space are often oriented to reducing the complexity of a situation and simplifying one's movement through the environment. But there are few people who, when looking at a map of Canada, claim that they are at the same time visiting it. While it is impossible to escape from the power of cultural maps to make up the meaning of its people, it is not impossible to begin to consider what these maps are constructing and how.

Whatever the meaning of the lived actuality of disability may be, it is constructed in relation to the maps of disability that culture provides. Some people may take only short and sporadic trips with disabled people or with the experience of disability, yet all of us, in some way or other, travel with disability. And all of us do so under the guidance of one cultural map or another. None the less, there are few cultural maps that show us how to pay attention to the phenomenon of mapping itself. This chapter has sought to give a topography of some of the common maps of disability. This mapping of maps serves as an alternative topography – this is essential if we are to develop a self-reflective relation to culture and our bodies. Mapping culture's representations of disability holds out the promise of doing and learning something more than merely how to move through a culture in the ways that it has predetermined for us. Mapping culture gives rise to the experience that disability can be interpreted in a multiplicity of ways, each of which holds symbolic social significance, the very sort of significance which makes up the meaning of the bodies and lives of disabled people and the meaning of the relations between disabled and non-disabled identities. The postmodern turn, with its focus on the uncertain and ambiguous character of social life and identity, allows for uncovering interpretive relations that lie at the heart of making up the meaning of disabled people.

References

Canguilhem, Georges (1991 [1966]) *The Normal and the Pathological*, trans. Carolyn Fawcett and Robert Cohen. New York: Zone Books.

Foucault, Michel (1973) *The Birth of the Clinic: An Archaeology of Medical Perception.* New York: Vintage Books.

Harding, Sandra (1996) 'Standpoint epistemology (a feminist version): how social disadvantage creates epistemic advantage', in Stephen P. Turner (ed.), *Social Theory and Sociology: The Classics and Beyond.* Cambridge, MA: Blackwell Publishers Ltd, pp. 146–60.

Michalko, Rod (1998) *The Mystery of the Eye and the Shadow of Blindness.* Toronto: University of Toronto Press.

Michalko, Rod (1999) *The Two in One: Walking with Smokie, Walking with Blindness.* Philadelphia: Temple University Press.

Michalko, Rod and Titchkosky, Tanya (2001, in press) 'Putting disability in its place: it's not a joking matter', in James C. Wilson and Cynthia Lewiecki-Wilson (eds), *Embodied Rhetorics: Disability in Language and Culture.* Carbondale: Southern Illinois University Press.

Scott, Joan (1998) 'Deconstructing equality-versus-difference: or the uses of post-colonial structuralist theory for feminism', *Feminist Studies*, 14(1): 32–50.

Shildrick, Margrit and Price, Janet (1996) 'Breaking the boundaries of the broken body', *Body and Society*, 2(4): 93–113.

Smith, Dorothy (1999) *Writing the Social: Critique, Theory and Investigations.* Toronto: University of Toronto Press.

Taussig, Michael (1980) 'Reification and the consciousness of the patient', *Social Science and Medicine*, 4(1B): 3–13.

Thomson, Rosemarie Garland (1997) *Extraordinary Bodies: Figuring Physical Disability in American Culture and Literature.* New York: Columbia University Press.

Titchkosky, Tanya (2000) 'Disability studies: the old and the new', *Canadian Journal of Sociology*, 25(2): 197–224.

Wittgenstein, Ludwig (1980) *Remarks on the Philosophy of Psychology: Volume II.* Chicago: University of Chicago Press.

9

Defusing the Adverse Context of Disability and Desirability as a Practice of the Self for Men with Cerebral Palsy

Russell P. Shuttleworth

Introduction

The critical analysis of a disabling society has been the bread and butter of disability studies. While a critique of social and cultural barriers is imperative in the struggle for disabled people's emancipation (Shuttleworth, 2000a, 2000b), this primary focus has meant a relative neglect of the creative response to adversity that disabled people can often exhibit. Yet, as Linton (1998) observes, 'The cultural stuff of the [disabled] community is the creative response to atypical experience, the adaptive maneuvers through a world configured for non-disabled people' (p. 5). Nevertheless, any sustained research on creative responses risks being perceived by disability studies as reinforcing the individual model of disability, its valorization of overcoming disability, supercrips and psychological coping and diametrically opposed to social model thinking, and thus it risks being rejected out of hand. While certainly right to be cautious of the heroic inversion of tragedy that often underlies these kinds of discussions, perhaps we need to change some of the terms of our thinking.

From a study I conducted on the search for sexual intimacy for fourteen men with cerebral palsy, I identify several aspects of self and society that helped facilitate their establishment of sexual relationships with others, including cultivating supportive and communal contexts, expanding the masculine repertoire and defusing the adverse structural and symbolic context of disability and desirability. I suggest that the cultivation of especially the latter, borne out of contention and resistance, can result in the affirmation of sexual subjectivity (that is, sexual self-integration) and sometimes also aspires to what Foucault (1986, 1988, 1997) in his later work calls a 'technology' or 'practice of the self', that is, a technique of ethical self-formation in relation to others. While Foucault's post-structural perspective is becoming increasingly influential in disability studies (see, for example, Corker, 1998; Thomson, 1997; Allan, 1996), not surprisingly it is his earlier and middle period work, in which the constructed subject is fully at the mercy of power/knowledge and normalizing practices, that is getting the theoretical mileage. Despite the critical importance of these ideas for our analyses of disability, Foucault's notion of 'practices of the self' is more relevant for the purpose of this chapter.

'The ADA is not gonna get me laid'

One of the major tasks set by the Disability Rights Movement is to work for increased access to social contexts from which disabled persons have previously been denied. Here the social model of disability, in which sociocultural environments are seen as disabling, is the theoretical linchpin in a powerful social movement. However, there is a phenomenological insight inherent in the notion of access that a strict social model approach cannot acknowledge but which nevertheless resonates existentially with our experience: access-obstruction is lived experientially as a continuum of intention and felt sense. Buytendijk (1950) has proposed that our different modes of feeling pleasant or unpleasant signify access or obstruction to the intentional objects of our consciousness. From this perspective, feeling sad, depressed, happy, joyful, hopeful, hopeless, angry, etc., can be directly related to how close our expectations, hopes and desires come to being met. Working for social change within the Disability Rights Movement is one way through an organized effort that the unpleasantness of exclusion from various desired social contexts is being dealt with by many disabled people.

This is all well and good for more publicly defined contexts such as employment, for example. Yet, if we take the above insight seriously, we must acknowledge that access to interpersonal contexts such as dating, romance and sexual intimacy can also be obstructed. The difference between public and private here is that, in the former, if personal preference does not mesh with the ideal of equal access, it is negatively sanctioned (at least at the level of public discourse), yet personal choice is considered mandatory for the latter. In love, personal prejudices reflecting social attitudes towards disabled people, cultural meanings of disability and hierarchies of desirability are thus given free rein. Access to this interpersonal context for disabled people thus cannot rely on the rule of law or public policy. As one man with cerebral palsy so eloquently put it, 'I don't give a flying fuck about the ADA because that's not gonna get me laid!' In addressing the claim of some disability theorists that disability would disappear if all structural barriers were removed, Corker (1999) has observed:

> in the light of our knowledge about the continued oppression of people from black and ethnic minorities and women – both highly 'visible' populations that have had legal protection against discrimination for over

twenty years – it could equally well be argued that the removal of structural barriers would leave the attitudinal and discursive dimensions of
social relations intact, together with their implications for social agency.
(p. 636)

Informed by a broadly critical constructionist and existential-
phenomenological framework, I conducted a series of in-depth interviews
(148 in all) with fourteen men with cerebral palsy (ages 18–51 when I began
interviewing them) who live in the East San Francisco Bay Area, focusing on
their efforts to negotiate sexual intimacy with others. I kept an ethnographic
journal while living with and working as a personal assistant for one of the men,
a long-time friend and employer. I also interviewed seventeen relevant others,
such as wives, girlfriends, ex-girlfriends, family members, personal assistants,
etc., for their perspectives on these men's sexual situation. None of the men is
cognitively impaired. They all have some degree of mobility impairment and
eleven use wheelchairs. Eleven have speech impairments, and four of these
use augmentative communicative devices such as an alphabet board or computer with speech output. Eleven men are white, and three are black. Twelve
men are attracted to women, one man is attracted to men and one man is
primarily attracted to women but has had several brief affairs with men.

Barriers and contention

I learned from pilot interviews with my friend and several other research
participants that my first task should be to explore what all fourteen men felt
were the range of issues in trying to negotiate sexual intimacy with others. All
fourteen men confront an adverse structural and symbolic context of disability and desirability. By this, I mean the entire spectrum of potential
negative influences on these men's sexual situation, but most notably their
own and others' incorporation of cultural images of disability and desirability
that play out in particular interpersonal relations and encounters between
people. This having been said, numerous social and cultural impediments to
establishing sexual intimacy were mentioned, including sociosexual isolation
during their adolescent years, negative or protective parental attitudes, cultural ideals of attractiveness, social expectations of normative functioning
and control, expectations of masculinity, poor body image and lack of sexual
negotiation models (including disability and sexuality education). These and
other contextual aspects effectively operate as power-relational impediments
to sexual inclusion, acting to protect the social (and personal) *normal body*
(read non-disabled) from the symbolic threat of difference in its most intimate relations with the modern sexualized self (Shuttleworth, 2000a, 2000b,
2001, in press).

The next question was how these men contended with those barriers that influenced their efforts to negotiate sexual intimacy. For this task, I relied on several notions culled from recent anthropological and disability studies work. In their narrative accounts, I noted sequences of intentions, felt sense (their immediate feelings when relations either went as they hoped or did not) and their psychic and emotional stance toward others upon emerging from these interpersonal encounters (Shuttleworth, 2000a, 2000b, 2001; Fell, 1977; Buytendijk, 1950). For example, the hope of consent of a desirable woman is one moment of an intentional-felt sense sequence that could end in the pleasure of her embrace or displeasure in her refusal (Fell, 1977: 264–5). I always viewed these sequences of intentions and feelings as only sensible within a culture's system of meanings and structuring of social relations. I also explored the use of metaphors in these men's accounts. In an important statement for the inclusion of phenomenological approaches in anthropology, Jackson (1996) refers to what he calls 'lived metaphors', which disclose 'the interdependency [and unity] of body and mind, self and world' (p. 9). Thus, in research participants' narrative accounts, I searched for metaphors that referred to an integration of their embodied experience, some combination of their bodily, existential, psychic and social sense of their sexual situation within the adverse cultural context briefly sketched above. For example, when one of the men kept telling me 'I feel blocked' from even attempting to negotiate a date with a woman, he was at the same time expressing his implicit comparison to hegemonic ideals of attractiveness, an embodied (felt) sense of others' negative resistance to seeing him in a sexual light and the grip that both of these had psychically on his self-agency (Shuttleworth, 2000b, 2001, in press). For any change of perspective, I searched their stories for epiphanies or turning points (Shuttleworth, 2000a, 2000b, in press; Denzin, 1989), that is, those times when they had a profound insight into their lived situations in the world, what Kasnitz (2001) in a study of leaders in the Disability Rights Movement calls an 'ah-ha!' experience. I also identified research participants' personal themes and contextualized them in relation to the above notions.

Working with this analytical mix revealed three interpersonal modes of experience these men assume in the face of social processes and cultural meanings that attempt to construct them as undesirable in their attempts to find lovers: (1) A mode in which they feel interpersonally immobilized. Here, participants' incorporation of the adverse context and their felt sense of others' negative resistance to sexual negotiations combine to block their sexual agency. (2) A mode in which they risk rejection and attempt to find a lover. Here, participants become active agents in trying to negotiate sexual intimacy with others. (3) A mode in which they interpersonally disengage. Here, participants socially withdraw due to repeated rejection and the futility of trying. This schema should be viewed as a dynamic process. All but a couple of the younger men had moved through these modes and sometimes back and forth especially between engagement and disengagement in the course of their lives.[1]

Facilitatory aspects of self and society

Despite their difficulties, most of the disabled men in this study have experienced sexually intimate relationships at one time or another in their lives; and there are several who managed consistently to do this. While part of these men's success can be attributed to meeting lovers whose criteria are less in line with hegemonic norms and ideals, within the space of interpersonal engagement, establishing intimate relationships could also depend on their cultivation of certain facilitatory aspects of self and society including cultivating supportive and communal contexts, expanding the masculine repertoire and defusing the adverse context of disability and desirability.

An important facilitatory aspect is the cultivation of a supportive context in which one's sexuality is acknowledged and encouraged. Several supportive contexts that provided these men with a space to work on their sexual integration were the Disability Rights Movement, disability-related work environments and peer support from other disabled people in general, communes, avant-garde artistic communities and Internet communities, such as chat rooms. Disability-related work and disability community activities were also contexts in which some of the men actually established relationships with both disabled and non-disabled people. Communal living situations, such as communes, dorms, hospitals or summer camps, are also places where several men found lovers.

Several researchers have noted the dilemmas that disabled men confront in the face of our society's hegemonic ideals of masculinity, such as competitiveness, self-control, independence and individual initiative (Hahn, 1989; Gerschik and Miller, 1996; Shakespeare, 1999; Tepper, 1999; Shuttleworth, 2000a, 2000b, 2001). For the men in this study, confronting the dilemma of how to be masculine when one is disabled cannot be divorced from their interpersonal attempts to establish sexual intimacy with others. That is, the dilemma of disabled masculinity is felt most acutely in interpersonal relations with those to whom they are sexually attracted. Those men who attempted to conduct themselves in rigid accordance with hegemonic masculine ideals and who measured themselves against these ideals were more apt to remain immobilized or socially to withdraw when they fell short; and, indeed, much of the blame for their failure in love was shouldered by their inability to measure up. Those men, however, who perceived hegemonic masculinity as less a total index of their desirability and who could sometimes draw on alternative ideals such as interdependence, prioritizing emotional intimacy, becoming friends first, allowing the other sometimes to make the first move when necessary without feeling less of a man, could better weather rejection and remain open to the possibility of interpersonal connection and sexual intimacy. In this expanded masculinity, ideals often associated with femininity take their place in the masculine repertoire alongside more hegemonic ideals in subjects' psyches and interpersonal practices.

Modes of defusing the context

The possibility of establishing intimacy with others exists only if one remains open toward them. Those men who in some way could consistently defuse the negative potential of the context were better able to sustain or return to interpersonal engagement with others. While participants were all able to render the adverse context impotent on occasion, there were three men who were especially adept at this, each employing a different mode of defusing.

One way to defuse the adverse context was to concede it minimal power. While the desexualization of disabled people is acknowledged to exist in the abstract, its significance and effect in Lenny's own interpersonal relations are seen as negligible.[2] Lenny, who uses a communicative device with speech output and was 45 years old at the time of our interviews, took full responsibility for establishing or not establishing intimate relationships. Feelings of frustration, anger and emotional pain are acknowledged but not indulged in for long. To get a sense of Lenny's minimizing approach, listen to this interchange between us:

(R) Some of the men cite their communication difference . . . as problems in trying to develop relationships. But it sounds like you don't buy into that?

(L) No way, because we communicate 98 per cent of the time non-verbally. Your eyes, body language, gestures, smile and charm. To me that's not a good excuse. . . .

Lenny used few metaphors but a consistent theme in his account was the necessity of risk-taking. Being a long-time motivator in the self-advocacy movement, he also stresses the positive side of disability. For example, during one of the few times he talked about disabled people facing prejudices, he added: 'I feel having CP makes a person more understanding of others because of the prejudices.' Turning points for him occur in terms of specific relationships and also in long-term goal setting. For example, an epiphany occurring as a young teenager is vividly remembered, which brought into focus the need to acquire basic independent living skills for a chance to get a girlfriend:

It wasn't until I saw the girl I had a crush on kissing and making out with another boy in her own backyard when I decided I wanted to prove to her that I was just as good as anyone, and the only way to do that was to get out of Carson. I went to the Rehab Center . . .

Another way of defusing the desexualizing context's power is born out of the perception that it is in fact a sociocultural construction. Here, its influence is acknowledged to a much greater degree. David, who is in his mid-40s and has a speech impairment, recognizes both his own and others' incorporation of some of its images and structures. But he understands that culture is the culprit, transforming his physical difference into a negative value. This understanding sustains him in his search for a lover. His own feelings of frustration, anger and emotional pain are fully recognized and contended with. Integrative or lived metaphors here often focus on risk-taking, but also on subversion of the adverse context. Major epiphanies are felt to occur which provide insight into the constructedness of his interpersonal and sexual situation and thus a poor self-image is confronted and subverted; existential confrontation and subversion in fact become a daily ritual, as he 'walks through the fear' engendered by his image in the cultural imaginary. David dates his turnaround to reading humanistic psychology in a graduate school counselling programme, starting to live in the dorms and garnering an important teaching assistantship:

it became increasingly like I was reaching into society's sleeve and turning it completely inside out. And from the moment of very, very deep despair, I was able to completely turn the situation around. And I chose the most comfortable situation, which was, I would say, I was sane living in an insane world . . . [and] what connects to the sexuality is you have to be a fucking cliff-walker. You need to walk always on the edge of a cliff to see all the beauty instead of the safety and security of the main road. Meaning people on the fringe – and we are – need to position themselves not in the secure mainstream but they need to be on the edge and they need to take risks and gamble. Yeah, it is very painful but walking down that main road is so monotonous and it will never get you laid because you are safe.

The influence of negative constructions of impairment and disability on one's body image and sexual self-esteem is resisted by Lenny through minimizing their significance, and by David through existential confrontation and subversion. Fred, however, moved between minimizing and subversion but would skip any anguish about his situation. Fred was 51 years of age when I began interviewing him and uses a head pointer and alphabet board for communication. Similar to David, he is good at cultivating supportive contexts. Yet, while David simply subverts his own self-image in the cultural imaginary, Fred also subverts the dominant cultural meanings of disability, desirability and masculinity in his everyday relations with others. He tells of being 28 and still a virgin due to his incorporation of the cultural images of himself as ugly and a burden. He began living in communes in the early 1970s, something he had aspired to for several years, and eventually experienced a series of major epiphanies whereby he was able effectively to shed those negative images. An incident that helped crystallize Fred's turning point was when a woman with whom he was becoming physically and emotionally close (albeit they had not had sex yet) rejected him:

(F) But after days of crying I began talking to the second in command who said he didn't understand why I want her . . . but if I did, I should go after her one hundred per cent . . . That was when I dropped my thinking that I was ugly.

(R) What in that situation made you drop that? What aspects of the situation turned that around, the body image?

(F) I could just give up and go back to Louise [a mother figure in Fred's life] and not try again.

(R) In terms of trying again to get a girlfriend?

(F) Yes.

(R) So, did you perceive that the way that you looked at yourself as ugly was a barrier to get a girlfriend? You felt that it was necessary to drop that?

(F) Yes.

(R) You were able to do that at the drop of the hat or did that take some time?

(F) Both.

(R) You had gone through this transformation?

(F) Yes, but not totally.

Shortly after experiencing a number of these kinds of do-or-die epiphanies, Fred had several sexual encounters with women in the commune; and using a variety of ingenious strategies, he managed to convince the woman who had rejected him to change her mind (see Shuttleworth, 2000b). The cumulative effect of these epiphanies eventually enabled him to project more fully his disabled body-self as the source of his power/meaning in the world and as perfect for his calling as a performance artist and to pursue his vision of intimate community. Today, he still uses the notion of interdependency promoted in the commune to his advantage and has been at the forefront of creating a nurturing artistic community, an alternative to mainstream culture in which desirability is not so tied to hegemonic ideals.

Fred especially constructs his sexuality in opposition to the narrow genital and orgasm focus of hegemonic masculinity and to a culturally sanctioned monogamy. He talks a lot about emotional intimacy and erotic playfulness without orgasm, and he focuses on these themes among others in his performances, which are often conducted in the nude, and where audience participation is encouraged. He has been in what he calls group marriages ever since the early 1970s and is currently in a long-term, three-person marriage. As you would expect, Fred's metaphors focus on risk-taking but even more on taboo breaking. The following metaphor, lust as a rogue, comes from one of the many autobiographical essays he gave me to read: 'Lusty is love of living . . . Lusty does what feels good. It breaks taboos, therefore discovers things. It risks being "bad". It is a rogue. It dares to look, to touch, to get turned on.'

Defusing the adverse context as 'a practice of the self'

I want to argue that these men's resistance, in fact refusal, to being seen as undesirable functions as a movement towards sexual self-integration and also aspires to what Foucault (1986, 1988, 1997) calls a 'technology' or 'practice of the self'. In his last works, Foucault shifted his focus from technologies of domination and power to the question of the self's relationship to itself through 'practices of the self'. Foucault maintains that 'technologies of the self . . . permit individuals to effect by their own means or with the help of others a certain number of operations on their own bodies and souls, thoughts, conduct and way of being, so as to transform themselves in order to attain a certain state of happiness, purity, wisdom, perfection, or immortality' (1988: 18). Foucault concerns himself with the history of the care and techniques of the self, especially in relation to sex, employed in pre-modern Greek, Roman and Christian cultures. Not surprisingly, some social commentators have criticized Foucault for abandoning his critical assault on modernity. Best and Kellner (1991), for example, note, 'His later positions seek a cultivation of the subject in an individualistic mode that stands in tension with emphasis on political struggle by oppressed groups' (p. 73). They continue, 'he might have theorized political resistance as a form of technologies of the self, as a creative response to coercive practices . . . but Foucault's later work lacks substantive political dimensions' (p. 70).[3]

Although less overtly political, Foucault's change of focus is, I believe, politically suggestive. Foucault's latter subject is still shaped by the historical context of social and discursive practices. Nevertheless, there is space for some degree of self-transfiguration. While never explicitly elucidating the move from resistance to a technology of the self founded at least partially in resistance to a particular oppression, Foucault does recognize the need for new forms of subjectivity that promote non-normalizing relations with others. Thus, forms of ethical self-constitution in resistance to normative grids of evaluation hold possible political potential.

Other social commentators also draw political implications from Foucault's later work. Rabinow (1997), for example, points to Foucault's advice that gays do not restrict themselves to demanding individual rights but 'give new forms to relational activities' (p. xxxviii). Rabinow emphasizes that, 'This work is not only ethical, it is also political; but it is politics without a program' (p. xxxviii). A key to political change then becomes the self's practices in relations with others. Indeed, for Foucault, care of the self is 'the government of the self by one's self in its articulations with relations with others' (1997: 88). Rabinow further sees Foucault's project as engendering the desire 'to invent a mode of subjectivation in which the ethos would be a practice of thought formed in direct contact with social and political realities' (p. xxxii).

In terms of disability, working within the Disability Rights Movement to acquire basic rights and legal protection for disabled people is the overt, collective goal, but according to Foucault an ethical relation to self and others in one's daily affairs constitutes another avenue by which socio-political change may be effected. I would argue that resistance to the normative gaze, coercive social practices and negative cultural images, while it has importantly led to collective political action, sometimes also manifests as everyday practices of the self in relations with others. An example where both come into play would be the Disability Rights activist who strives in her/his self-social practices in daily life not to reproduce oppressive social relations against people along other identity axes (for instance, gender, ethnicity and sexual orientation).

There are disabled people, however, such as Fred who are in basic agreement with the Movement's civil rights agenda but, because of their radical subversion of other unquestioned social norms and cultural values (in Fred's case, monogamy, wearing clothes in communal and performance contexts, etc.), become alienated from the Movement. Yet, Fred's practices of the self move beyond subversion and are in fact transfiguring: he has been the major initiator in creating an intimate and non-hierarchized community for himself and others, all this without, as Rabinow says, 'a program'.

One of Foucault's goals in changing his focus was to show 'how that long history began, which in our societies, binds together sex and the subject' (1997: 89), that is, sex as constitutive of the self. Thus, one reason for Foucault's new emphasis was simply to extend his history of the objectivization and normalization of the sexualized subject into a more intimate domain: that of the self objectifying itself through practices of self-formation. Foucault, of course, never historically ventured beyond the confines of the West and some anthropologists would certainly argue with his implying an exclusivity for our sexualized selves (see Herdt and Stoller, 1990; Freidl,

1994). Yet, within Western history one does notice an increasingly constitutive role for sex in terms of identity and selfhood. In such a context, securing some kind of sexual intimacy, however defined by the individual, becomes a paramount project of self-constitution. Considered in this light, efforts to negotiate sexual intimacy by the men in this study take on a particular constructive urgency and meaning. From this perspective, the claiming of sexuality by disabled people (Guldin, 2000), against the cultural assumption of their asexuality, is also a bid for full subjectivity. This is one reason why the issue of disabled people's sexuality has assumed such political importance today (Waxman and Finger, 1989; Shakespeare et al., 1996).

The significance of sex for the constitution of the subject and the evaluative gaze that rejects impaired body-selves as undesirable is fertile ground for further resistance. Emerging from resistance to this evaluative gaze, defusing the adverse context is similar in some dimensions to a practice of the self performed by Epictetus and later in Christianity, 'what one might call the "control of representations"' (Foucault, 1997: 103). Epictetus maintains 'that one must be in an attitude of constant supervision over the representations that may enter the mind' (p. 103). What is at issue is to 'determine whether or not one is affected or moved by the thing that is represented, and what reason one has for being or not being affected in that way' (p. 104). For Epictetus the control of representations is aimed at recalling a number of true principles for living concerning death, illness, political life, etc., and is not constituted through resistance. For the men in this study, defusing as a practice of the self is founded in resistance to evaluations of their undesirability whereby they attempt increasingly to control the representational and also situational flux in order to live as sexual subjects. Cultivating supportive contexts and an expanded masculine repertoire were important facilitatory aspects for these men precisely because they promote emotional strength and a flexible gender identity that can assist in achieving this goal.

De Lauretis (1994) views Foucault's focus on self-analysis and other self-transformative techniques as commensurate with Pierce's notion of a deliberately formed, self-analysing habit, the final interpretant. As she argues, 'The new experience of self Foucault describes is, in effect, a habit-change' (p. 312). Colapietro (in de Lauretis, 1999) further distinguishes between self-analysing habits and habits that are not deliberately formed. Earlier, I referred to the account of one research participant who felt blocked from negotiating intimacy with the women to whom he was attracted. Almost all of the men in this study felt this way at one time or another in their lives and were in effect under the spell of a habit that they did not deliberately form. This habitual feeling or pre-reflective (prior to reflection) habit did not emerge from self-analysis but was evoked by the multiple constraints on self-agency within the adverse context of disability and desirability, which these men inhabit.

If de Lauretis is right, and I think she is, the engendering of a practice of the self occurs through an explicit habit change – for the men in this study, in terms of their sexuality, a transformation of the pre-reflective habit that grips their self-agency. Thus, David's and Fred's remembered (or reconstructed) epiphanies mark the breaking of a habit that had kept them immobilized. Accomplishing this habit change as a consistent self-practice, not an occasional breakthrough, affirmed their sexual subjectivity, that is, facilitated their sexual self-integration. Combined with other self-practices borne out of their resistance, the care of their now sexualized selves holds the potential for a transfiguration of self-other sociosexual relations that have yet to be realized as such. While the possibility of refusing to reproduce oppressive social relations is not necessarily tied to the claiming of sexual subjectivity, other subversive and transfiguring moves require the establishment of a sexualized self.

Two examples of the latter are several men's claims of a more creative sex life with their significant others because of their disability and a sexual politics of disability that is not wholly constituted by the logic of our traditional cultural avenues for securing sexual intimacy with others. In response to our many discussions on disability and sexuality, Fred has recently proposed a bold plan. He asked me: 'If I get a group of people who are willing to go into institutions to have sex with crips who cannot get out, would you think about how to do it?' I asked him if he had heard of the book *Crip Zen*, in which the author fantasizes about getting a bunch of sex workers to do just this. He said that he had. I then went through all the likely barriers that would be put in his way: moral outcry by the public, liability of the institution, concerns about the potential for sex abuse, etc. 'There would be no money involved,' he added. 'I want civil rights workers. Not mercy fucking, not paid, not helpers.'

As we talked further, I began to realize the radical intent of his proposal. On one level, it would be an effort to provide some sexual experiences for disabled people who were severely restricted in the institutional settings (or quasi-institutional settings such as group homes) in which they lived; on another level, it held the potential for subverting and perhaps transfiguring our traditional avenues in which sexual relations are validated or stigmatized. These traditional sexual avenues tell the story of securing a dating or love relationship, the stigmatization of having to pay for illegal sex because of some self-deficiency or the use of a sexual surrogate because of a purported lack of sociosexual development. The fact that today sex has taken on such key constitutive meaning for the expression of identity, as the truest expression of self to other relations and as essential to a high quality of life, makes it a marker of distinction. There are the haves, the haves with varying degrees of stigmatization and the have-nots, and the have-nots are often pitied for being unfulfilled selves. In order for sex really to become a human rights issue for all disabled people, not just those who live independently in the community (and whose chances are therefore to relative degrees enhanced), these traditional avenues and their role in maintaining the exclusion especially of more significantly impaired people from sexual activities would have to be undermined. Fred should certainly expect a host of barriers to his project – barriers that on an unacknowledged level will be erected in order to maintain the significance and distinctions that achieving sexual subjectivity represents for us.

Acknowledgements

The research in this chapter was assisted by a fellowship from the Sexuality Research Fellowship Program of the Social Science Research Council with funds provided by the Ford Foundation.

Notes

1. Elsewhere I have referred to this process as a dynamic intersubjective process (Shuttleworth, 2000a, 2000b, 2001, in press). This idea highlights the fact that human subjects act upon and affect each other's thoughts and feelings during interpersonal encounters and thus draws attention away from the objective features of interactions. My understanding of intersubjectivity does not strictly adhere to its phenomenological usage. I refrain from using this notion in the present chapter for accessibility's sake.
2. All names used in this chapter are pseudonyms.
3. Darke (1996), however, has attempted to show how women's resistance to the disease construction of menopause could also be seen as a 'practice of the self'. In the long run, she does not see this notion as being of much use because it lacks an interactive dimension. Although it is true Foucault provides us with no explicit interactive analytical key, he does maintain that ethical self-practices are performed in the context of articulation with others and offers some suggestive implications.

References

Allan, J. (1996) 'Foucault and special educational needs: a box of tools for analyzing children's experiences of mainstreaming', *Disability and Society*, 11(2): 219–33.
Best, S. and Kellner, D. (1991) *Postmodern Theory: Critical Interrogations*. New York: Guilford Press.
Buytendijk, F. (1950) 'The phenomenological approach to the problem of feelings and emotions', in M. Reymert (ed.), *Feelings and Emotions: The Moosehead Symposium in Cooperation with the University of Chicago*. New York: McGraw-Hill.
Corker, M. (1998) *Deaf and Disabled, or Deafness Disabled? Towards a Human Rights Perspective*. Buckingham: Open University Press.

Corker, M. (1999) 'Differences, conflations and foundations: the limits to "accurate" theoretical representation of disabled people's experience?', *Disability and Society*, 14(5): 627–42.

Darke, G. (1996) 'Discourses on the menopause and female sexual identity', in J. Holland and L. Adksins (eds), *Sex, Sensibility and the Gendered Body*. New York: St Martin's Press.

de Lauretis, T. (1994) *The Practice of Love: Lesbian Sexuality and Perverse Desire*. Bloomington: Indiana University Press.

de Lauretis, T. (1999) 'Gender symptoms, or, peeing like a man', *Social Semiotics*, 9(2): 257–70.

Denzin, N. (1989) *Interpretive Interactionism*. Newbury Park: Sage Publications, Inc.

Fell, Joseph P. (1977) 'The phenomenological approach to emotion', in D. K. Candland, J. P. Fell, E. Keen, A. I. Leshner, R. M. Tarpy and R. Plutchik (contribs), *Emotion*. Monterey: Brooks/Cole Publishing Company, pp. 252–85.

Foucault, M. (1986) *The Care of the Self (The History of Sexuality, Volume 3)*. New York: Vintage.

Foucault, M. (1988) *Technologies of the Self: A Seminar with Michel Foucault*. Amherst: University of Massachusetts Press.

Foucault, M. (1997) *Ethics: Subjectivity and Truth*, ed. P. Rabinow. New York: New Press.

Freidl, E. (1994) 'Sex: the invisible', *American Anthropologist*, 96: 833–44.

Gerschick, T. and Miller, A. (1996) 'Gender identities at the crossroads of masculinity and physical disability', in M. Gergen and S. Davis (eds), *Toward a New Psychology of Gender*. New York: Routledge, pp. 455–75.

Guldin, A. (2000) 'Self-claiming sexuality: mobility impaired people in American culture', *Sexuality and Disability*, 18(4).

Hahn, H. (1989) 'Masculinity and disability', *Disability Studies Quarterly*, 9(3): 1–3.

Herdt, G. and Stoller, R. J. (1990) *Intimate Communications: Erotics and the Study of Culture*. New York: Columbia University Press.

Jackson, M. (1996) 'Introduction: phenomenology, radical empiricism, and anthropological critique', in M. Jackson (ed.), *Things as They Are: New Directions in Phenomenological Anthropology*. Bloomington: Indiana University Press, pp. 1–50.

Kasnitz, D. (2001) 'Life event histories and the US Independent Living Movement', in M. Priestley (ed.), *Disability and the Life-Course*. Cambridge: Cambridge University Press.

Linton, S. (1998) *Claiming Disability: Knowledge and Identity*. New York: New York University Press.

Rabinow, P. (ed.) (1997) 'Introduction', in M. Foucault, *Ethics: Subjectivity and Truth*. New York: New Press.

Shakespeare, T. (1999) 'The sexual politics of disabled masculinity', *Sexuality and Disability*, 17(1): 53–64.

Shakespeare, T., Gillespie-Sells, K. and Davies, D. (1996) *The Sexual Politics of Disability: Untold Desires*. London: Cassell.

Shuttleworth, R. (2000a) 'The search for sexual intimacy for men with cerebral palsy', *Sexuality and Disability*, 18(4): 263–82.

Shuttleworth, R. (2000b) *The Pursuit of Sexual Intimacy for Men with Cerebral Palsy*. Doctoral dissertation, University of California, San Francisco-Berkeley.

Shuttleworth, R. (2001) 'Symbolic contexts, embodied sensitivities and the lived experience of sexually relevant, interpersonal encounters for a man with severe cerebral palsy', in B. Swadener and L. Rogers (eds), *The Semiotics of Dis/ability: Interrogating the Categories of Difference.* New York: SUNY Press.

Shuttleworth, R. (in press) 'Experience and meaning in the pursuit of sexual relationships for men with cerebral palsy', in E. Makas and D. Kasnitz (eds), *Proceedings of the 1998 Society for Disability Studies Conference.* Lewiston, MI: Society for Disability Studies.

Tepper, M. (1999) 'Letting go of restrictive notions of manhood: male sexuality, disability and chronic illness', *Sexuality and Disability*, 17(1): 37–52.

Thomson, R. G. (1997) *Extraordinary Bodies: Figuring Physical Disability in American Culture and Literature.* New York: Columbia University Press.

Waxman, B. F. and Finger, A. (1989) 'The politics of sex and disability', *Disability Studies Quarterly*, 9(3): 1–5.

10

Changing the Subject: Postmodernity and People with 'Learning Difficulties'

Dan Goodley and Mark Rapley

Introduction

This chapter examines the contributions of post-structuralist theory, and a postmodern stance, to understandings of 'learning difficulties/intellectual disability'[1] in contemporary disability theory. We outline two areas of work that illustrate the power of the postmodern concepts of deconstruction and the reconceptualization of language use as social practice offered by conversation analysis and discursive psychology. We *challenge* both the modernist construction of 'learning difficulties' as naturalized impairment, and also demonstrate that phenomena frequently understood as being an essential feature of 'intellectual disability' are better understood as *aspects of social interaction.* What we seek to do then is to show how two – apparently theoretically divergent – approaches can offer convergent *alternative* conceptions of the notion of 'learning difficulty' that acknowledge the socially and linguistically constructed nature of the social world. The approaches we adopt differ in their research practices and their breadth of focus, but both point to the same conclusion – that the current, modernist, notion of intellectual disability as a given form of being in the world is unsustainable. In both our conversation analytic examination of how the 'acquiescence' of people with 'intellectual disability' is actively constructed in psychological assessments, and in our deconstruction of (British) disability studies texts, we see that it is *assumptions and ways of talking* about disability that are crucial to the production of persons as incompetent. Both approaches point to the political consequences of these ways of talking: to the silencing of people with intellectual disabilities. Both approaches thus draw our attention to disability as a *socially produced* phenomenon in a *social* world, and social worlds, we argue, are worlds that can be changed.

Firstly, we outline a discursive psychological approach that provides a resource for unpacking the situated social construction of 'acquiescence bias' and interactional 'incompetence', which are usually seen as being inevitable *dispositional attributes* of people described as 'intellectually disabled'. In contrast, we suggest that – by making their linguistic construction explicit – these notions can be critically re-examined.

Secondly, we draw upon post-structuralist methods of enquiry – specifically deconstruction – to examine the taken-for-granted construction of 'learning difficulties' as naturalized impairment. The notions of 'inscribing impairment' and 'promoting independence' are examined, alongside a critical inspection of the theoretical dominance of materialism in British disability studies literature. We suggest that post-structuralism adds to – rather than detracts from – the need for politicized social theory by providing a political and social vision of impairment in relation to 'learning difficulties'.

We conclude that analytic methods drawn from theoretically divergent areas of postmodern social theory demand a critical revision of the modernist subject, bringing together interaction, impairment and disability as co-existing *social* and *political* artefacts of disablement.

'Acquiescence bias' – dispositional attribute or situational artefact?

Discursive psychology[2] offers a reconceptualization of the theoretical and methodological practices of the psy-complex (Rose, 1985, 1999). Starting from the premiss that, in the most profound sense, language talks the world into being, discursive psychology insists that (research) 'methods' are always and already 'theory' in disguise (Edwards *et al.*, 1995). The approach is explicitly social constructionist and treats language not as *a medium* for 'telementation' (Taylor and Cameron, 1987) – the transmission of thoughts between minds – but rather as *the site* where social objects such as 'thoughts', 'minds' and 'intellectual (dis)abilities' are produced in talk in the conduct of social action. As we see later in this chapter, in a deconstruction of 'helping' professionals' talk of ways of being in the world in terms of 'syndromes' and 'symptoms', discursive psychology similarly grants prior status to language: without the *prior* existence of language, such 'psychological' things as 'intellectual (dis)abilities', 'syndromes' or acquiescence 'biases' can, quite literally, not sensibly be talked of. Discursive analyses thus draw on work in conversation analysis and ethnomethodology (Sacks, 1972, 1995; Garfinkel, 1967; Schütz, 1962) to examine *naturally occurring interaction* in order to understand the ways versions of the world and our cultures' common knowledge of (the nature of) disability are produced in and through interactional practices.

'Acquiescence bias' – the official version

In 'standard' accounts of the interactional competence of 'intellectually disabled' people, the notion that people are unreliable reporters of their own subjectivity is firmly entrenched. The utterances of people with 'intellectual disabilities' are not to be trusted as veridical reports of their actions, beliefs or feeling states. This version of what 'being intellectually disabled' means is routinely reproduced across the academic literatures and is perhaps (still) best summarized by the first substantive paper on the phenomenon: 'When in doubt, say yes: acquiescence in interviews with mentally retarded persons' (Sigelman *et al.*, 1981a). Since then the literature has reified 'acquiescence bias', and translated what was always potentially readable as a sensible interactional strategy for powerless people confronted with authority, into an essential(ized), and implicitly also discreditable, component of the 'intellectually disabled' identity.

This literature claims that one can 'validly' gain access to the views of people with 'intellectual disabilities' only with extreme difficulty (Heal and Sigelman, 1990). If there is a dispute between a person so-labelled and a carer or professional, the suspect voice is that of the person with an 'intellectual disability', whose in-built 'acquiescence bias' precludes accurate reporting. But what is the foundation of the concept? The Sigelman *et al.* studies (1981a, 1981b, 1982, 1986) involved people with 'mental retardation' in long-stay institutions. They noticed that some people would answer 'yes' to mutually contradictory questions about their happiness in a formal interview schedule. In follow-up interviews, incorporating paired 'factual' questions about the person's residence (one accurate, the other not) and other questions to which 'no' was the correct answer, people were asked, for example: 'Are you Chinese?' (none of the sample was) and 'Do you know how to fly an aeroplane?' (a little unlikely, perhaps, if one has lived all one's life in an institution).

Based on this rather bizarre methodology, it was concluded that 'the rate of acquiescence is staggering' (1981a: 56) and that 'because mentally retarded persons asked yes or no questions tend to acquiesce, their answers are likely to be invalid'. Having thus reified 'acquiescence' as a naturalized aspect of 'mentally retarded persons', while simultaneously obliterating the capacity of such persons to say anything 'valid' in response to questioning, Sigelman *et al.* offer neither a clear specification, nor an analysis, of when 'acquiescence' may occur (it might, sometimes, be an appropriate interactional strategy). It is simply something that 'mentally retarded persons' do. For instance: 'acquiescence is the tendency to say yes regardless of question content' and 'acquiescence is one particular type of response bias' (1981b); it is 'contradicting oneself on oppositely worded questions' or offering 'conflicting answers to . . . parents or carers' (1982). What may, for another group, be glossed as 'disagreement' is constructed as an essentialized incompetence (see also Booth and Booth, 1994).

However, we do not know *how* people *actually* responded to inane questioning about their aviation skills or ethnicity; rather we have to take on trust that their answers (and *ipso facto* the answers of all 'mentally retarded persons') not just to peculiar questions but, by implication, to *all* questions are 'invalid'. The active production of acquiescence in and through psy-complex practices is, however, visible if the tools of discursive psychology are brought into play. If the fine details of actual interactions between psychologists and people described as 'intellectually disabled' are examined, both the artefactual nature of 'acquiescence' and the interactional resilience of people with 'intellectual disabilities' come into focus. In the remainder of this section, a brief examination of some of the ways that incompetence is produced *by virtue of* standard psy-complex procedures is provided.[3]

Producing acquiescence

If we look at actual interviews, using 'real' questions, 'acquiescence bias' assumes a rather different cast. It is, of course, a definitional feature of interviews that the normal, egalitarian distribution of question and answer turns at talk is suspended. This imbalance can *produce* what some might call 'acquiescence', particularly in situations where interviewers have a schedule which specifies exactly the range of possible 'right' answers. In Extract 1, the interviewer can only accept 'never', 'sometimes' or 'always' as 'valid' answers, and s/he is obliged (by standard psy-complex research procedures) to offer the interviewee all three possible answers prior to accepting one as 'belonging' to the respondent.

Extract 1:

```
01  I    d'you feel out of place (. .) >out an'
02       about in< social (.) situations
03  AN   n    ⌈o:
04  I         ⌊Anne? (.) never?
05  AN   no
06  I    sometimes?
07  AN   °no°
08  I    or usually
09  AN   sometimes I do:
10  I    yeah? (. .) ok we'll put a two down for
11       that one then (sniff)
```

Anne's reply at line 3 ('no') would seem to be clear and unambiguous. But, by line 9, her answer has changed from a claim 'never' to feel 'out of place in social situations' (line 5) to yes, sometimes she does. What better example of the 'if in doubt, say yes' phenomenon? Anne has offered clearly contradictory responses. But if this interaction is examined more closely, we can see that the production of contradiction is, entirely, the work of the interviewer. The interviewer refuses to accept a perfectly acceptably designed, thrice-repeated, answer that, 'no', Anne does not feel out of place in social situations. It is a combination of the *requirements of the interview schedule*, and the *assiduous-*

ness of the interviewer's pursuit of them, that *produces* the change in Anne's response, not some hazily defined defect in Anne which renders her incapable of 'validly' responding. Interviewees, if they are competent conversationalists, will, in the face of the demands of the interviewer, change their position (and thereby seem to be 'acquiescing') until the trouble brought about by these demands has been resolved (Antaki and Rapley, 1996). What we see in Extract 1 is not a natural defect essential to 'mental retardation', but rather a demonstration that 'mentally retarded persons' may have as sophisticated a grasp of the preference organization of interaction as their supposedly non-impaired interlocutors.

'Acquiescence' and resistance

The consequence of the widespread and uncritical acceptance of the notion that people with 'intellectual disabilities' are, essentially, incapable of 'validly' reporting on their own subjectivity is that they are thereby silenced. This silencing is not necessarily something to which people with 'intellectual disabilities' will willingly acquiesce. The final two extracts demonstrate the breach of two major conventions of conversation management: the production of preferred second pair parts and the provision of an explanation for the implied inadequacy of a response. That such acts of resistance are offered to people who the interviewees know are in a position of power over them is testament more to the resilience than the 'retardation' of these people (see also Marková and Foppa, 1991; Rapley and Antaki, 1996).

In Extracts 2 and 3 the interviewer uses the conversational device known as a 'pass' (Schenkein, 1978) to solicit an explanation of the previous speaker's last utterance. Although apparently an innocent echo, the 'pass' very specifically locates some part of what was said as requiring accounting, whilst at the same time declining explicitly to name it. Bluntly, interviewees are under pressure to acquiesce to the interviewer's (implicit) demand for an alternative answer to the one offered.

Extract 2:

```
01  I     ri:ght (. .) oh that's good (1 sec) em: (1
02        sec) do >you<
03  Bob   ((hhhhh))
04  I     ever feel lonely (.) Bob
05  Bob   eh?
06  I     do you ever feel lonely
07  Bob   no:
08  I     no (. .) not ever
09  Bob   no:
10  I     no:
```

The 'pass' comes at line 8. By repeating 'no', Bob's candidate answer (line 7) is produced as requiring justification. When Bob does not take up the subsequent pause which the interviewer offers with a revised opinion, the interviewer explicitly marks Bob's answer as problematic: 'not ever?'. Refusing to acquiesce to the by now explicit demand for an alternative answer, Bob restates his view and rejects the interviewer's proposed reformulation. Extract 3 again illustrates resistance to interviewer demands. In this extract, rather than deploying a simple pass (which occurs in line 7), the interviewer also reformulates the questionnaire item (line 10), reversing the polarity of the question, to be told – for the third time – that the answer to the question is, in fact, 'no'.

Extract 3:

```
01   I     yeah?
02         (3 sec) .hh are there people living with you who (.) who bother
           you (.) sometimes (..) or hurt you or: (.)  ⌈m-
06   Bob                                              ⌊no
07   I     make you angry or  ⌈(pester you) (.) no?
08   Bob                      ⌊n:o
09         (1 sec)
10   I     so y y' like the people you live with
11   Bob   yes:
12   I     yeah?
```

This is, in any context, extraordinary pressure. In a professional examination of a person described as 'intellectually disabled', the resolution displayed by Bob in the face of explicit (and possibly highly consequential) pressure for a reconsideration of his answer is remarkable. Taken together, the instances of coercion and of resistance in the conversational data reproduced above suggest that the existing 'acquiescence' literature cannot offer an adequate description of the competence of people described as 'intellectually disabled'. These data, we argue, are sufficient to call into question the very notion that people with an 'intellectual disability' are inherently unable to report 'validly' on their own feeling states; that they are incapable of resisting the pressure of professionals to acquiesce to their view of things. This is demonstrably not the case.

Deconstructing 'learning difficulties'

From individual to social deficit – modern impairments and materialism
In the second part of this chapter we examine another aspect of postmodern theorizing that is crucial to the development of disability theories that are

fundamentally social and pose a political challenge to the taken-for-granted grand narrative of 'learning difficulties as naturalized'. The starting point for our second postmodern analytical turn is the dominance of materialism in British disability studies literature that aligns itself with a social model of disability. The influential work of Barnes (1998), Finkelstein (1996) and Oliver (1996) offers varying forms of insightful and consistent materialist analyses of the social, economic and cultural conditions of capitalism that create 'disability' – the exclusion of people with impairments from main-stream life (UPIAS, 1976). As the disability movement's big idea (Hasler, 1993), the social model has been concerned with theorizing and changing social exclusion:

> The social model of disability is, first and foremost, a focus on the environmental and social barriers which exclude people with perceived impairments from mainstream society. It makes a clear distinction between impairment and disability: the former refers to *biological characteristics of the body and mind*, and the latter to society's failure to address the needs of disabled people. This is not a denial of the importance of impairment. It is, however, a concerted attempt to provide a clear and unambiguous framework within which policies can be developed which focus on those aspects of disabled people's lives *which can and should be changed*. (Barnes, 1998: 78, our italics)

We align ourselves without hesitation with this call. Social theorists and researchers must face the real oppressive conditions of disablement if they are to be suitable allies of disability activists. It is clear to us how such political and social aims may be seen to lie uneasily with postmodern social theory. Those concerned with praxis – bringing together politicized theory and action in a dialectic manner – may view postmodernism's emphasis on the 'wordy' nature of the world as ignoring the real material conditions of oppression. Yet, while this may be advanced by some as a problem with postmodernism, there are *also* problems with the ways materialism has been used in relation to disability. Corker (1999) argues that the dominance of materialist thinking in literature aligned with a social model of disability encourages dichotomous thinking, privileging the social and public world over personal and private experiences. As Barnes puts it, the social model of disability is, first and foremost, a focus on environmental and social barriers. Consequently, as Thomas (1999) has observed, materialists often view any discussion of impairment as watering down the social model of disability, as analysis inevitably collapses to resemble mere 'sentimental autobiography' (Barnes, 1998). *Impairment in the modern, materialist world remains charac-teristically biological and not an aspect of disabled people's lives that can or should be changed.*

Postmodern impairments and post-structuralism

A critical engagement with postmodern thinking can provide the necessary materials for politicized and social theories of impairment. While materialist critiques provide firm and powerful visions of exclusionary society, post-modernism *also* provides opportunities for developing a 'theory of disability as oppression [that] recognises and, *in the present context, emphasises the social origins of impairment'* (Abberley, 1987, in Barton and Oliver, 1997: 176, our italics). If we take Marx's (1845) thesis that human essence is 'the ensemble of social relations' belonging to a particular form of society, then we need also to interrogate theoretical critiques to see how they capture the social relations of the society that they claim to examine. Whereas discursive psychological analyses can show us the moment-by-moment playing out of 'the ensemble of social relations' in talk-in-interaction, there is also a requirement for sus-tained critical examination of the ways in which grand theories of disability themselves talk their object of knowledge into being.

Disabled people are more than aware that they occupy a particular place in a service industry and that many modes of (psychological) research – as we have shown above – while rhetorically geared towards positively affirming their position in society, actually recreate their very conditions of disable-ment. The disability industry aims to restore normality, organizing intrusions into disabled people's lives on the basis of claims to discrete and *limited knowledge* and skills (Oliver, 1996: 37, our italics). A particular postmodern view – post-structuralism – acknowledges the cultural, discursive and insti-tutional basis of these human interventions and intrusion (Foucault, 1970, 1975, 1983). Here, knowledge claims about disabled people are located in modernity's general obsession with the confessing and knowing human sub-ject. In practice, 'knowing' is far removed from its seemingly humanitarian ends. As Foucault puts it: there is a price to be paid in human subjects speaking 'the truth' about themselves. Truths do not emerge out of thin air. They are tied to particular institutions (and related research practices) such as medicine, psychology and social work – the 'psy-complex' – which enjoys dominance in the network society (Corker, 1999). Psy-complex practitioners create discursive truths that serve to inform and to govern human subjects' relation to impairment as a naturalized and *pathological phenomenon*. A theory of disability that maintains a *biological* vision of impairment threatens to leave these truths in the realms of the essentialist rather than the socio-logical – in the hands of the very institution that such a theory purports to challenge. In contrast, impairment in a postmodern world need no longer be understood as inevitably biological or the stuff of sentimental biography. Instead, it becomes an aspect of disabled people's lives that can be theorized as part of a politicized vision of disablement.

Deconstructing impairment

While some materialists have argued that we need to engage with medical sociology in order to *flesh out* social understandings of impairment (Barnes, 1998; Thomas, 1999), much (more) can be gained from a post-structuralist social theory of disability. In particular, our experiences with people with the label of 'learning difficulties' suggest that this labelled, objectified and 'othered' group is subjected to peculiar varieties of interventions symptomatic of late capitalism, which are the very stuff of postmodern analyses. Building on our earlier examination of research interactions, we now turn to two other types of oppressive intervention and offer alternatives, via *deconstruction*, as storied through our involvement with people with 'learning difficulties'.

Inscribing and challenging impairment

Fairclough (1992) suggests that deconstruction involves untangling the discourses utilized in the technologies of governance employed by the psy-complex. For people with 'learning difficulties', identity is governed in a number of professionalized contexts. Accordingly, a variety of discourses are brought together in this process, such as psychologized notions of 'mind', which, when applied to people with 'learning difficulties', emerge as 'syndromes' and 'mental impairments'. These objects contribute to the seduction of psychological discourse and, when adopted, lead to particular assumptions about people who are so-labelled:

> The special school's Christmas performance. I take my seat at the back, amongst an audience of family members, teachers, support staff and local dignitaries, to whom students sang, danced and acted. Enter stage left, Hugh. A slight teenage lad, Hugh performed to piano accompaniment the classic Tom Jones number 'It's not unusual'. As his performance was greeted by enthusiastic applause, a teacher turned to me and shouted above the noise, 'It's his syndrome you know – it makes him so extroverted.' (taken from Goodley, forthcoming)

In this ethnographic moment, Hugh's actions are *discursively framed* in terms of the available object of 'syndrome'. Following Butler (1993: 129), Hugh's 'personhood' is understood as a set of naturalized violations of, or injuries to, his very 'personhood'. All that may be spoken of meaningfully in relation to Hugh is a 'syndrome'. Deconstruction goes further to unearth the 'historical *a priori*' (epistemes or discourses) that not only delimit the totality of experience in a field of knowledge, but also, in defining the permissible mode of being of objects in that field of knowledge, *produce* the things that are (to be) 'known'. In this sense, then, learning-difficulty-as-impairment must be understood relationally, historically, practically and critically. As Fairclough

(1992) and Wetherell and Potter (1992) have pointed out, not only is the deployment of one *particular* discourse rather than another always a political act, but also power struggles occur in, through and over discourse(s), as elements of social and personal change. This view resonates with our own experiences: in addition to the analysis of the inscription of psychologized understandings of (in)competence upon persons in discourse – be it 'acqui-escence bias' or syndrome-driven 'extroversion' – we have been drawn to the ways in which people with 'learning difficulties' discursively *resist* categories of object and forms of subject that are thrown at them in a disabling 'network society'. What critics of postmodernism such as Thomas (1999) ignore is that close and detailed attention to the qualitative nature of social life (as we have already seen in this chapter) opens up possibilities for challenging taken-for-granted narratives such as impairment-as-essentialized-biological-insult:

> Karen had recently had a meeting with an educational psychologist because, she joked, 'I'm dumb in the head'. A supporter who works at the college suggested that this meeting be arranged because Karen 'was not joining in in class'. Karen disagreed – 'No, I was bored'. (from Goodley, 2000)

According to Fairclough (1989: 28), the social nature of discourse and practice always implies social conventions: assumptions of and about the 'retarded' become second nature in professional interventions and, as Danforth and Navarro (1998) have shown, such professionalized knowledges readily come to permeate lay discourse. However, human subjects may also be *enabled* through being constrained: being socially constrained does not preclude being creative. Where there is power there is also, inevitably, resistance (Foucault 1975) – as evidenced both by Karen's reaction and Bob's refusal to allow a psychologist to tell him what the 'quality' of his life 'really' was.

Impairment and interdependence
Booth and Booth's (1994, 1998) research on parents with 'learning difficulties' clearly shows how assumptions commonly held by professionals tend to frame parenting skills in terms of the 'impairments' owned by each parent. The dominance of the positivist paradigm and the influence of psychological research on professional practice, which we critiqued above, is not coincidental. Booth and Booth's work draws attention to the ways in which professionals approach the task of support with epistemological assumptions that promote deficit thinking: problems will arise in parenting because of the psychological deficits of the parents. In contrast, and in line with the social model's turn to the disabled person as *social being*, Booth and Booth unravel the (lack of) social networks surrounding the parents that contribute to what we might term 'fitness to parent'. They argue that parenting competence may

more properly be seen as a distributed feature of parents' social network rather than as an individual attribute:

> The notion of what might be termed 'distributed competence' attests to the fact that parenting is mostly a shared activity and acknowledges the interdependencies that comprise the parenting task. (Booth and Booth, 1998: 206)

Such a social conceptualization of the notion of competence allows for a relational and *interdependent* stance in relation to assumptions about parenting (in)competence and hence impairment. Like the 'quality' of any particular life (Rapley, 2001), 'fitness for parenting' is not, of necessity, an individualized quality, but rather a product of social and relational networks. The rise of the self-advocacy movement, both nationally and internationally, constitutes another sociocultural context inhabited by people with 'learning difficulties' (Williams and Shoultz, 1982). Recent research suggests that such contexts exhibit a variety of relational qualities in which notions of 'learning difficulties-as-lacking' can be revisited (Goodley, 2000). Specifically, the workings of self-advocacy groups question the idea that people with 'severe learning difficulties' causally disable social relationships:

> Rachel arrives at the meeting of her self-advocacy group by minibus from the local 'Autistic Community'. She does not speak often. She spends her time quietly and apparently contentedly smelling her fingers and looking around the room. She doesn't appear to interact with any of her friends. At break-time Bill asked her if she would like a cup of coffee or tea. Erica, who lives with Rachel, replied, 'She likes coffee don't you Rachel?' Bill looked at Rachel, 'Coffee then?' (taken from Goodley, 2000)

The above vignette could be read in terms of personal tragedy: with Rachel being unable to contribute actively to the group as a consequence of her impairment (in this case, autism). However, we can see how Rachel's solitary actions provide a catalyst for other self-advocates to act. Indeed, without Rachel's apparent 'inactivity', a chance for interdependence would have been lost. If we choose to understand self-advocacy groups as contributing to the development of collective self-empowerment then Rachel becomes *essential* to this development. Such events invite us to reconsider how we conceptualize (in)dependence. Reindal (1999) argues that the social model of disability tends to emphasize the dichotomy of independence–dependence. This modernist view of the human subject emphasizes voluntary and rational components of the human condition. Yet, as Rachel reminds us, there is a need to situate the self in relational understandings. If we maintain the independence–dependence dichotomy, independence remains an individualized quality with related essentialist views of the subject kept in place. Post-structuralist critiques of modernity's emphasis on the individual suggest a need to turn to the public, signifying activities of collectivities of subjects. Here the subject is no longer the 'solipsistic subject that constitutes through its faculty of reason, transcendental apprehension, self-consciousness and so forth' (*ibid.*, p. 361). Instead the possibility of self-hood is reinterpreted in light of this *expanded identity* (*ibid.*, our italics) a situated, enlarged subject – the subject as a social movement – where *inter*dependence is crucial to the formation of notions of autonomy evident in parenting and self-advocacy, to name but two areas of disabling and enabling social life.

Towards a social theory of impairment
Some disability theorists see a turn to impairment as an unnecessary diversion from the 'real material stuff' of disabling society. A post-structuralist stance suggests that this way of thinking, based as it is on a Cartesian either/ or distinction (disability or impairment), needs to be deconstructed in ways that bring impairment and disability together as co-existing *social* and *political* facets of disablement. Viewing impairment as the stuff of tragedy and medicalization implies that we are not yet ready to 'do social theory' with impairment. Fortunately, the resistance of people with 'learning difficulties' and their experiences of disablement (where naturalized views of impairment are at the core of oppression) offer us lived examples that enable the re-socializing of impairment (Goodley and Moore, 2000) as part of, and in addition to, materialist understandings of disabling society. A critical post-modern stance encourages us to work with these incidents of resistance as part of the political struggle against disablement.

Conclusion

This chapter has drawn attention to the damage done by assumptions of 'learning difficulties'/intellectual disabilities as a naturalized, individualized, embodied pathology. In the first part of the chapter we examined accounts of acquiescence as a dispositional characteristic of persons. We demonstrated how, through the talk of psy-complex practitioners, incompetence can be inscribed onto interviewees, who themselves were seen to mobilize everyday practices of conversational interaction to resist such inscriptions. In the second part of the chapter, we suggested that materialist interpretations within disability studies ignore the socially contested nature of impairment. We drew attention to professional interventions that imported discourses of impairment into social settings and so (re)produced conventional social forms for governing the 'deficient' individual. We also noted how asocial visions of people with 'learning difficulties' fail to recognize social and cultural contexts in which 'capacity' is the mark of interdependence. Both parts of the chapter make clear two things. First, that impairment is up for grabs in the discursive world. Second, that we need to be attentive to the challenges posed by people with the label of 'learning difficulties'/intellectual disabilities. Such a sensitivity is enabled by a view of the world which does not separate impairment and disability as binary oppositions but throws both into the dynamic world of discourse and practice.

Notes

1. Our choice of terminology reflects those labels that prevail in our respective locations. For example, the term 'learning difficulties' is chosen because it is the term preferred by many in the British self-advocacy movement. As one self-advocate puts it, 'If you put "people with learning difficulties" then they know that people want to learn and to be taught how to do things' (quoted in Sutcliffe and Simons, 1993: 23).
2. See Edwards and Potter, 1992; Potter, 1996; Edwards, 1995, 1997; Wetherell and Potter, 1992, for extended treatments of the approach.
3. Transcripts have been simplified and line numbering amended (see Rapley and Antaki, 1996). Transcript conventions are in Appendix 1.

Appendix 1

Transcription notation
The transcription conventions used here were derived from those developed by Gail Jefferson (see Atkinson and Heritage, 1984: ix–xvi).

(.) (. .) (. . .)	Pauses of approximately a fifth of a second, half a second and one second
(2 secs)	A roughly timed period of no speech
hh	An 'h' denotes an out-breath. The more hs, the longer the out-breath
(slurps)	A description enclosed in double brackets indicates a non-speech sound
cu-	A dash denotes a sharp cut-off of a prior word or sound
°soft°	Degree signs indicate that speech is noticeably quieter than the surrounding talk
>fast<	'Greater than' and 'less than' signs indicate that the talk
<slow>	they encompass was produced noticeably quicker than the surrounding talk; the reverse for 'slow' talk
he ⌈llo ⌊hello	Square brackets between adjacent lines of concurrent speech show overlapping talk.

References

Abberley, P. (1987) 'The concept of oppression and the development of a social theory of disability', *Disability, Handicap and Society*, 2(1): 5–21.

Antaki, C. and Rapley, M. (1996) 'Questions and answers to psychological assessment schedules: hidden troubles in "Quality of Life" interviews', *Journal of Intellectual Disability Research*, 40(5): 421–37.

Atkinson, J. M. and Heritage, J. (eds) (1984) *Structures of Social Action: Studies in Conversation Analysis*. Cambridge: Cambridge University Press.

Barnes, C. (1998) 'The social model of disability: a sociological phenomenon ignored by sociologists?', in T. Shakespeare (ed.), *The Disability Reader: Social Sciences Perspectives*. London: Cassell.

Barton, L. and Oliver, M. (1997) *Disability Studies: Past, Present and Future*. Leeds: Disability Press.

Booth, T. and Booth, W. (1994) *Parenting under Pressure: Mothers and Fathers with Learning Difficulties*. Buckingham: Open University Press.

Booth, T. and Booth, W. (1998) *Growing up with Parents Who Have Learning Difficulties*. London: Routledge.

Butler, J. (1990) *Gender Trouble*. New York: Routledge.

Butler, J. (1993) *Bodies That Matter: On the Discursive Limits of Sex*. New York: Routledge.

Corker, M. (1999) 'Differences, conflations and foundations: the limits to "accurate" theoretical representation of disabled people's experiences', *Disability and Society*, 14(5): 627–42.

Danforth, S. and Navarro, V. (1998) 'Speech acts: sampling the social construction of mental retardation in everyday life', *Mental Retardation*, 36(1): 31–43.

Edwards, D. (1995) 'Sacks and psychology', *Theory and Psychology*, 5(3): 579–96.

Edwards, D. (1997) *Discourse and Cognition*. London: Sage.

Edwards, D., Ashmore, M. and Potter, J. (1995) 'Death and furniture: the rhetoric, politics, and theology of bottom line arguments against relativism', *History of the Human Sciences*, 8(2): 25–49

Edwards, D. and Potter, J. (1992) *Discursive Psychology*. London: Sage.

Fairclough, N. (1989) *Language & Power*. London: Longman.

Fairclough, N. (1992) *Discourse and Social Change*. Cambridge: Polity Press.

Finkelstein, V. (1996) 'Outside, "Inside Out"', *Coalition*, April: 30–6.

Foucault, M. (1970) *The Order of Things*. London: Tavistock Publications.

Foucault, M. (1975) *Discipline and Punish*. London: Allen Lane.

Foucault, M. (1983) 'The subject and power', in H. L. Dreyfus and P. Rabinow (eds), *Michel Foucault: Beyond Structuralism and Hermeneutics*. Chicago: University of Chicago Press.

Garfinkel, H. (1967) *Studies in Ethnomethodology*. Englewood Cliffs, NJ: Prentice-Hall.

Goodley, D. (1998) 'Stories about writing stories', in L. Barton and P. Clough (eds), *Articulating with Difficulty: Research Voices in Special Education*. London: Paul Chapman.

Goodley, D. (2000) *Self-advocacy in the Lives of People with Learning Difficulties: The Politics of Resilience*. Buckingham: Open University Press.

Goodley, D. (forthcoming) 'Challenging epistemologies of "Learning Difficulties"', *Disability and Society.*

Goodley, D. and Moore, M. (2000) 'Doing disability research: activist lives and the academy', *Disability and Society*, 15(6): 861–82.

Hasler, F. (1993) 'Developments in the Disabled People's Movement', in J. Swain, V. Finkelstein, S. French and M. Oliver (eds), *Disabling Barriers – Enabling Environments.* London: Sage.

Heal, L. W. and Sigelman, C. K. (1990) 'Methodological issues in measuring the quality of life of individuals with mental retardation', in R. L. Schalock (ed.), *Quality of Life: Perspectives and Issues.* Washington: American Association on Mental Retardation.

Marková, I. and Foppa, M. (eds) (1991) *Aysmmetries in Dialogue.* Hemel Hemptsead: Harvester Wheatsheaf.

Oliver, M. (1996) *Understanding Disability: From Theory to Practice.* London: Macmillan.

Potter, J. (1996) *Representing Reality: Discourse, Rhetoric and Social Construction.* London: Sage.

Rapley, M. (2001) 'The social construction of quality of life: the interpersonal production of well-being revisited', in K. D. Keith and R. L. Schalock (eds), *Cross-Cultural Perspectives on Quality of Life.* Washington: American Association on Mental Retardation, pp. 155–72.

Rapley, M. and Antaki, C. (1996) 'A conversation analysis of the "acquiescence" of people with learning disabilities', *Journal of Community and Applied Social Psychology*, 6: 207–27.

Rapley, M. and Ridgway, J. (1998) 'Quality of life talk and the corporatisation of intellectual disability', *Disability and Society*, 13(3): 451–71.

Reindal, S. M. (1999) 'Independence, dependence, interdependence: some reflections on the subject and personal autonomy', *Disability and Society*, 14(3): 353–67.

Rose, N. (1985) *The Psychological Complex.* London: Routledge and Kegan Paul.

Rose, N. (1999) *Governing the Soul: The Shaping of the Private Self.* London: Free Association Books.

Sacks, H. (1972) 'An initial investigation of the usability of conversation for doing sociology', in D. Sudnow (ed.), *Studies in Social Interaction.* New York: Free Press, pp. 31–74.

Sacks, H. (1995) *Lectures on Conversation, Vols. 1 and 2*, ed. G. Jefferson; Introduction by E. A. Schegloff. Oxford: Blackwell.

Schenkein, J. N. (1978) 'Identity negotiation in conversation', in J. N. Schenkein (ed.), *Studies in the Organisation of Conversational Interation.* New York: Academic Press.

Schütz, A. (1962) *Collected Papers Vol. 1: The Problem of Social Reality*, ed. and intro. M. Natanson. The Hague: Martinus Nijhoff.

Shaw, J. A. and Budd, E. C. (1982) 'Determinants of acquiescence and nay-saying of mentally retarded persons', *American Journal of Mental Deficiency*, 87: 108–10.

Sigelman, C. K. and Budd, E. C. (1986) 'Pictures as an aid in questioning mentally retarded persons', *Rehabilitation Counselling Bulletin*, 29: 173–81.

Sigelman, C. K., Budd, E. C., Spanhel, C. L. and Schoenrock, C. J. (1981a) 'When in doubt, say yes: acquiescence in interviews with mentally retarded persons', *Mental Retardation*, 19: 53–8.

Sigelman, C. K., Budd, E. C., Spanhel, C. L. and Schoenrock, C. J. (1981b) 'Asking questions of retarded persons: a comparison of Yes–No and Either–Or formats', *Applied Research in Mental Retardation*, 2: 347–57.

Sigelman, C. K., Budd, E. C., Winer, J. L., Schoenrock, C. J. and Martin, R. W. (1982) 'Evaluating alternative techniques of questioning mentally retarded persons', *American Journal of Mental Deficiency*, 86: 511–58.

Sigelman, C. K., Schoenrock, C. J., Spanhel, C. L., Hromas, S. G., Winer, J. L., Budd, E. C. and Martin, P. W. (1980) 'Surveying mentally retarded persons: responsiveness and response validity in three samples', *American Journal of Mental Deficiency*, 84(5): 479–86.

Sutcliffe, J. and Simons, K. (1993) *Self-advocacy and Adults with Learning Difficulties: Contexts and Debates*. Leicester: National Institute of Adult Continuing Education in association with the Open University Press.

Taylor, T. J. and Cameron, D. (1987) *Analysing Conversation: Rules and Units in the Structure of Talk*. Oxford: Pergamon Press.

Thomas, C. (1999) *Female Forms: Experiencing and Understanding Disability*. Buckingham: Open University Press.

UPIAS (1976) *Fundamental Principles of Disability*. London: Union of the Physically Impaired Against Segregation.

Wetherell, M. and Potter, J. (1992) *Mapping the Language of Racism: Discourse and the Legitimation of Exploitation*. Hemel Hempstead: Harvester Wheatsheaf.

Williams, P. and Shoultz, B. (1982) *We Can Speak for Ourselves*. London: Souvenir Press.

11

Madness, Distress and Postmodernity: Putting the Record Straight

Anne Wilson and Peter Beresford

Introduction

Postmodernist discussions highlight difference, diverse subjective realities and the reappraisal of rationalist assumptions about knowledge and understanding. Interestingly, however, such debates do not yet seem to have had a significant impact or influence on psychiatric and 'mental health' policy or analysis, where medicalized interpretations continue to predominate. Indeed, it could be argued that such interpretations are actually increasing in force as an emphasis on the 'dangerousness' of mental health service users, and the search for objective organic origins for their 'condition' and status, dominate political and media agendas in the wake of decarceration policies (Beresford, 2000).

The failure of psychiatric discourse to pay serious attention to alternative understandings and interpretations of madness and distress also seems particularly significant, given the emergence of the major new understandings and interpretations associated with the growth of the mental health service user/psychiatric system survivor movement since the 1980s. There are now clear and well-argued challenges to psychiatric orthodoxies from users' perspectives (for example, Barker *et al.*, 1999). There also seems to be a popular preparedness to acknowledge distress as something that is part of *all* of us. Yet psychiatry's structures seem to be impervious to these developments and its diagnostic empire is apparently expanding, like some unstoppable juggernaut, to include new groups and new 'disorders' (Kutchins and Kirk, 1999). Psychiatry's resistance to the insights offered by broader critiques of the Enlightenment and of modernism is both the context and the starting point of our discussion. We ask from where does psychiatry gain its continuing authority? What forces are helping it to persist in the face of the very contrary concerns of postmodernity? These are key questions which concern us as psychiatric system survivors.

While their administrative categories overlap, the relation of madness and distress to disability is complex and contested (Plumb, 1994; Beresford *et al.*, 1996). It also highlights the issue of competing constructions of madness and distress and provides a framework for considering these in the context of

UNIVERSITY OF WINCHESTER
LIBRARY

postmodernist ideas and developments. In this chapter, we explore the socially constructed nature of 'mental illness' from our perspectives as psychiatric system survivors. We pay particular attention to three current interpretations of madness and distress: dominant psychiatric interpretations, popular media interpretations and psychiatric system survivors' own conceptualizations. In doing this, we are conscious of the fragmentation of such conceptualizations and that each has implications for the other. As a result, it is not always easy or necessarily appropriate to separate them and, in this discussion, the reader will therefore find they are interleaved.

In pointing to the socially constructed nature of 'mental illness', we do not wish to deny or play down the very real mental and emotional distress that we and other psychiatric system survivors experience. We nevertheless view this as part of a broader continuum of distress and well-being; a continuum upon which *all* people would place themselves, in different positions and at different times in their lives. We need to be explicit: the world does not consist of 'normals' and 'the mentally ill'; it consists of *people*, all of whom may experience mental and emotional distress at some time(s) in their lives. Our task here is to examine the role of dominant discourses of 'mental illness' in accentuating and perpetuating that distress and 'difference' through the construction of users of mental health services as Other – a separate and distinct group.

To develop our discussion, we turn to psychiatry's own administrative processes and explore the role of psychiatric record keeping in the professional construction of madness and mad people. We also examine the function of psychosurgery and other destructive so-called 'treatments' in the simulation and public understanding of 'mental illness', madness and distress. We focus in particular upon the documentation of individuals' medical/psychiatric records, as ostensible *evidence* of mental illness. In terms of contact with 'officialdom', an individual's psychiatric record, once written, constitutes the dominant version of that person and serves to place restrictions, which are frequently severe, on future life opportunities, understandings, rights and possibilities. Individuals identified as 'mentally ill' also serve collectively as material for professional and academic theorizing of 'mental illness' – including 'postmodernist theorizing' (for example, Parker *et al.*, 1995; Fee, 2000a) – and the stereotypes and discourses of 'mental illness' thus generated.

Dominant discourses of 'mental illness', madness and distress are framed in terms of 'individual pathology', 'disorder' and *'permanency* of defect'. Even where there is beginning to be a challenge to the latter, it is still framed in medical terms of 'remission' or 'recovery'. The attempt of psychiatric system survivors and our organizations to articulate our own understandings of our experiences come up against the overarching dominance of medicalized definitions and explanations of 'mental illness', or the analyses and interpretations of non-survivor 'experts' and academics. Because of the power and dominance of these approaches, it can be difficult even to begin to make sense of our own experience outside of frameworks provided by 'experts', whose theories and powers may extend to every aspect of our lives, not least our identity as 'mentally ill' (non-)persons. Indeed, the identities of those survivors subjected to the damaging 'treatments' of the psychiatric system may be further eroded, compromised or damaged by 'side effects', iatrogenic (medically generated) 'disorders' or misinformation. Having our brains damaged through tardive dyskinesia (brain damage *caused* by neuroleptic medication prescribed for 'psychotic illness'), lobotomy or electroconvulsive 'therapy' (ECT) must in some sense 'make us different persons'. So must the 'counselling' or 'therapy' aimed at helping us to 'accept' or 'come to terms with' *our* 'mental illness' and consequent impaired status as persons.

Both of us have been subjected to the psychiatric system's definition, scrutiny, interpretation, 'diagnosis' and 'treatment' of our mental and emotional distress. Though we have, so far, survived our contact with the system, our transgressions from the 'psychonorm' have been documented and preserved in perpetuity in medical/psychiatric records which continue to impact upon our lives long after they were written. In recent years, we have attempted to make sense of our experiences in terms other than the dominant discourses supplied by the psychiatric system.

There is a growing interest in social approaches to madness and distress in the psychiatric system survivors' movement. However, as yet no equivalent of the social model of disability, developed by the disabled people's movement, has been developed by mental health service users/survivors, which could offer a philosophical basis and/or focus for action. At the same time, the social model of disability is likely to need further development if it is to provide a suitable framework for such social approaches to madness and distress. Individual/medical model approaches to mental and emotional distress and ideas of personal tragedy accord with our experiences of contact with the psychiatric system. Psychiatric system survivors are also frequently assigned to the same administrative categories as disabled people. For example, we are included in community care services, disability benefits and the Disability Discrimination Act. However, as we have already said, the relation of madness and distress to disability is complex and contested. It is likely that any reworking of the social model, as it relates to psychiatric system survivors, which takes account of issues of mind as well as body, will also be complex.

Dominant psychiatric interpretations of madness and distress

Psychiatry is predicated upon putative 'mental illnesses' and their valid and reliable diagnosis and treatment. Its textbooks unquestioningly promote the existence of psychopathology in the form of 'psychoses' and 'neuroses' (see, for example, Hughes, 1991). Psychiatrists further classify 'psychoses' and 'neuroses' into numerous subgroupings or diagnostic categories. Jennifer Hughes (1991: 3) suggests that this classification has three purposes: aiding clinical management, by providing a rational guide to treatment and prognosis; facilitating communication between professionals; and facilitating research into causes, prevention and treatment.

From our perspectives, having been on the receiving end of this diagnostic process, the categorization and classification of our mental and emotional distress has served no useful purpose. Both of us have experienced psychiatrists' enhanced interest in some aspects of our distress and the 'playing down' of other aspects in order that it, or we, conform to a specific diagnostic category and prescribed 'treatment'. Our experience of mental and emotional distress does not fit neatly with psychiatry's classificatory system. This is echoed by Louise Pembroke (1994a), who explains how her distress was categorized into separate pigeon-holes:

> That behaviour was *eating disorder*.
> This behaviour was *schizophrenic*.
> That behaviour was *personality disorder*. (Pembroke, 1994a: 19)

She goes on to argue that she does not experience the categorized distress in isolation:

> I don't have a *Bulimic* or a *Schizophrenic* day. This definition and separation of the facets of my distress is not helpful. The rigid frameworks psychiatry, psychology **and** therapy employ serve only to fragment and objectify people . . . It was hardly surprising then that some workers found my behaviour difficult to relate to . . . Only certain combinations of behaviour were *understandable*, if they slotted neatly into symptoms 1–6, paragraph 8. (*ibid.*)

The psychiatric diagnostic process is dependent upon, and derives its legitimacy from, its alleged links with modernist medicine and science (Boyle, 1999). The conventional view in psychiatry is that 'mental disorders' parallel our understanding of physical disorders. They occur in the individual and are 'discovered' by rigorous scientific research (Kutchins and Kirk, 1999). 'Scientific' approaches underpin both the process of validating particular constructions of 'mental disorder' (defining the diagnostic categories) and the diagnostic process itself, where psychiatrists assess individual patients' indicative symptoms or signs in order to establish whether or not they are 'suffering from' particular forms of 'mental illness' or 'disorder'. To aid the diagnostic process, the American Psychiatric Association has devised the *Diagnostic and Statistical Manual of Mental Disorders* (DSM), which lists diagnostic criteria for a plethora of psychiatric disorders.

Herb Kutchins and Stuart Kirk (1999) argue that the DSM, which is increasingly also being used in the UK, is based on an illusion of science and is fundamentally flawed. The committees of psychiatrists who make decisions about including new diagnostic categories in the DSM do not always agree among themselves and sometimes resort to voting on crucial decisions. In some instances, even the pharmaceutical companies who produce psychiatric medications have contributed directly to the development of these diagnostic categories (*ibid.*, p. 13). In addition, Kutchins and Kirk cite a number of research studies which report psychiatrists, trained in using the DSM, failing to agree whether or not a specific disorder is present in an individual patient. There are problems therefore with both the validity of the DSM's diagnostic categories and with their reliability. These problems are not unique to the DSM and extend to other psychiatric diagnostic systems (Thomas, 1997; Boyle, 1999).

Though the psychiatric profession has continued its search for biological causes or 'genetic markers' for 'mental illnesses' such as 'schizophrenia', there is still no definitive 'laboratory test' for any specific 'mental illness' (Kutchins and Kirk, 1999; Thomas, 1997; Boyle, 1999). Psychiatrists are therefore dependent upon diagnostic tools when diagnosing someone as 'suffering from schizophrenia'. Despite the fact that these tools lack validity, and psychiatrists may differ as to whether or not we are 'suffering from' a specific 'mental disorder', *once we have been diagnosed, 'our diagnosis' is recorded (in perpetuity) in our medical and psychiatric records.*

Medical/psychiatric records

A patient's psychiatric record documents information about that individual relevant to their diagnosis and 'treatment'. This information is collected and recorded by mental health professionals. Each professional operates within her/his own particular theoretical perspective(s). According to their views on the epidemiology of 'mental illness', they will have different ideas about what counts as an indicator of specific 'mental illnesses' and which aspects of a patient's behaviour or history they should write into the record (Herpin, 1981).

Because, as we have said, there is no 'laboratory test' for specific 'mental illnesses', psychiatrists resort to recording subjective judgements about patients' behaviours and symptoms, citing these as indicators of presumed psychopathology. As a psychiatric patient, it can feel as if everything you say or do is being taken down and recorded to be used in evidence against you. At the time of our original contact with the psychiatric system, both of us intuitively felt reluctant to reveal everything about our distress to the mental health professionals we consulted. Years later, when one of us (A.W.) saw her psychiatric records, she felt vindicated in her reluctance to reveal her inner-most secrets to the psychiatrists, as she found herself described in 'her' records in the most negative and damning of terms. One psychiatrist even intimated it would be a good thing if she moved out of the area.

Psychiatric records tend to document problematic or difficult features of the patient's 'illness' and do not usually record the unproblematic or positive aspects of his/her daily life. A record therefore creates a partial and negative picture of its subject. Despite its prejudicial content, the record may be 'used as a guide' by the professionals who write in and consult it, to the extent that the subject her/himself may eventually become convinced of the profes-sionals' negative conceptions (Herpin, 1981). Both of us have experience of being influenced by professionals' overly negative perceptions of our distress and 'prognosis'. These perceptions have been based purely on their interpre-tations and our medical records, rather than on any contemporary problems or distress.

Since 1991, patients have been permitted access to their personal medical records (this does not normally apply to records written before that date). However, some patients may be denied access to their records if, 'in the opinion of the practitioner, such information would be likely to cause ser-ious harm to the physical or mental health of the individual' (Access to Medical Reports Act 1988, s. 7(1); Access to Health Records Act 1990, s. 5(1)(a)(i)). The courts may also support GPs' decisions to withhold infor-mation from psychiatric system survivors. For example, Peter Jenkins (1997) cites the case of R. v. Mid-Glamorgan FSHA (1993), where the court refused permission for a patient with 'a history of depression and psychological problems' to access her medical records. It can be very difficult, if not impossible, for patients to request correction of misleading or inaccurate records or argue their own defence if they do not even know what is written about them.

It is also difficult for patients to contribute to the writing of 'their own' record. One of us (A.W.) wrote her own account of the events leading to her diagnosis (many years before) as having 'schizophrenia' and asked for this to be placed on the medical records held by her GP, alongside the letters and reports written by psychiatrists. When a third party subsequently requested further information on and copies of all records relating to her 'psychiatric history', her GP omitted Anne's account from the information forwarded. He argued that, despite the fact that Anne's account had clearly been written by Anne and was signed by her, to have made reference to it or included it 'would have sanctioned its content'.

Since there is no objective verification for specific 'mental illnesses', the medical/psychiatric record assumes inflated importance in the evidencing of presumed psychopathology. As medical records are ineradicable, they also serve to make permanent and immutable the ostensible psychopathological difference or 'disorder' of those diagnosed 'mentally ill'. They become the 'proof' of our 'pathology'. The records themselves are deemed indubitable evidence of our transgression from the 'psychonorm'.

Liz Davies has written of when she was diagnosed as having 'schizo-phrenia' as an eighteen-year-old. She describes a visit to her GP *thirty-two years later* for treatment for migraine.

> As I took my prescription from her outstretched hands, and smiled my thanks, she looked down at my medical card and said in a rather interested voice, 'I see it says here that you had schizophrenia when you were eighteen.'
>
> My vulnerable heart constricted with the shock. I thought my whole connective tissue had collapsed inside, the structural edifice on which I built my social life just melted away. In a thin voice I heard myself say, 'That was a mistaken diagnosis. I'm absolutely horrified to find it's still on my medical record. You just can't imagine how awful that seems to me!'
>
> As I started to explain to her what had happened, the tears welled up in my eyes and heart. . . . Thirty-two years had passed, yet I still bore the scar, with a wound as raw and fresh under the surface of its thin skin as on the day it was first inflicted. It had taken many years to plaster over this crack, and the knowledge that it had remained all this time in black and white on my medical record had stripped the plaster off in one fell swoop. Ouch!
> (Davies, 1999)

A specialist palliative care social worker has also written of how, working with people who are dying, the existence of any formal psychiatric record, however tenuous or long ago, was likely to affect the way in which professionals interpreted patients' responses to their situation, symptoms and treatment. To this degree, the authority of psychiatric diagnosis can haunt the individual to the grave (Croft, 1996).

Both of us have had similar experiences to Liz Davies when visiting our GP for physical ailments. Having a 'psychiatric record' can also prove prob-lematic in other areas of our lives. Psychiatric system survivors may face discrimination when applying for life insurance, mortgages, visas to travel or work abroad, when making applications to become registered childminders, foster or adoptive parents (McNamara, 1996: 199), or when seeking fertility treatment (Steinberg, 1997: 86–7). This discrimination appears to be based on a belief that people who – *according to their medical/psychiatric records* – have 'a history' of mental or emotional distress can never fully recover.

It may be that the Disability Discrimination Act will afford some protection in some of these areas, though we are aware so far of only one successful case (MIND, 1999). The Human Rights Act may also work to the benefit of mental health service users, although there remains the possibility that our rights may be seen to be subordinated appropriately in the interests of our 'treatment' (Hirst, 1999).

Academic and professional discourses

Sociologists have used societal reaction or labelling theory (Lemert, 1951; Scheff, 1966) to provide explanations of the 'secondary deviance' (internalizing the identity imposed upon us) of people identified as 'mentally ill'. These explanations do have a certain resonance with our own experience. However, they perhaps fail to acknowledge the complexities of the interaction between public and professional perceptions of 'mental illness' and 'the mentally ill'; academic theories about the aetiology of 'mental illness' (including biogenetic explanations); the role of the pharmaceutical companies; the iatrogenic effects (physical and psychological) of 'psychiatric treatment' and *our* understandings of our original madness and distress. All of these impact upon our perception of our*selves* and our place in the social world.

As suggested above, individual medical/psychiatric records play a key part in the reification of 'mental illness'. In addition, descriptions of mad people and 'their' 'mental illnesses' are included in textbooks resulting in (stereo)-typical views of particular 'syndromes' and 'conditions'. Many of these are extremely negative. For example, according to the *Oxford Textbook of Psychiatry*, 'the main features of chronic schizophrenia are apathy, lack of drive, slowness, and social withdrawal . . . Once the chronic syndrome is established, few patients recover completely' (Gelder *et al.*, 1993: 268). Similarly, Allan Young (1996: 5) describes schizophrenia as 'a common disorder, causing a huge burden of morbidity and cost to the general population, as well as an unmeasurable burden to the patients and their families'. These descriptions are clearly fully underpinned (and reinforced) by personal tragedy theory (Oliver, 1996). For mental health service users who, on learning of 'their' diagnosis, choose to read about 'their' 'condition' and prognosis, such descriptions can be devastating and leave the holder of the diagnosis feeling utterly hopeless. But texts that focus upon social perspectives on 'mental illness' may be no less negative. For example, Len Bowers (1998) notes that 'the mentally ill person is often bad-mannered, poorly socially skilled, or given to committing minor infractions of the law, but it is the way in which they do so that is irrational and unreasonable' (Bowers, 1998: 17). He further claims, without supporting evidence, that 'the mentally ill' cannot explain or justify their own (irrational) behaviour in rational terms (*ibid.*, p. 18).

Mad people are also documented and portrayed in other ways within academic and professional discourse – for example as 'case studies' discussed at conferences or published within academic or professional journals. We find this aspect of academic/professional discourse particularly disturbing. Firstly, it is rare, in our experience, for psychiatric system survivors' consent to be sought before their 'case' is used. Though names and identifying features may be changed, the description of the service user's life and 'illness' may still be recognizable to the individual and others who know her/him. Such behaviour is based upon the assumption that service users and academics/professionals are members of two discrete groups that do not, and perhaps cannot, overlap.

These 'case studies' also occasionally include photographs or 'video evidence' of 'mentally ill' people. For example, an article in the *Journal of the American Medical Association* (Freeman *et al.*, 1954) contains 'before' and 'after' photographs of patients subjected to lobotomy 'treatment'. In displaying these pairs of, what appear to us to be, staged photographs, the authors contribute (graphically) to stereotypes of the 'deranged mental patient' (and thus of 'mental illness') *and* demonstrate the efficacy of their brain-damaging 'treatment'. Publication in a scientific/medical journal lends spurious validity to the lobotomy procedure and epitomizes psychiatry's dual illusions of biologically based 'mental illnesses' and physical/scientific 'cures' for mental and emotional distress.

Though neither of us was photographed when we were in hospital, we were both included in videos that were used for training. These, too, will have contributed to constructions of 'mental illness' and its 'treatment'. Our consent was sought before these videos were made but we have no idea who they were shown to, if we were identified by people who watched them or whether they are still in use.

'Case studies', like the information included in an individual's medical record, also present a partial and incomplete picture of the individuals concerned. Collectively, they serve to construct stereotypes of people 'suffering from' particular 'mental disorders'. Since tests for specific 'mental illnesses' cannot be objectively verified, without these *descriptions* of individual patients and their distress, it would not be possible to identify and classify, or even discuss, 'mental illnesses'. Where psychiatric system survivors have succeeded in publishing their own accounts or records of their experience, these too are being used as material for academic theorizing (see, for example, the postmodernist analysis of Elizabeth Wurtzel's (1995) autobiography, *Prozac Nation* (Fee, 2000a)).

Iatrogenic 'treatments'

We, along with many other psychiatric system survivors (see, for example, Chamberlin, 1988; Campbell, 1989; O'Hagan, 1993; Pembroke, 1994a, b), believe that any original distress we experienced has been compounded and perpetuated by the psychiatric system. Some psychiatric 'treatments' can have damaging physical effects (often euphemistically referred to as 'side effects'). For example, ECT can cause actual brain damage (Arscott, 1999) and neuroleptic medication can cause tardive dyskinesia: uncontrollable movements of the jaw, tongue and lips (Thomas, 1997). There may also be psychological 'side effects' of these treatments. Research by Lucy Johnstone (1999, cited by Arscott, 1999: 103) found that people who had received ECT experienced 'feelings of humiliation, increased compliance, failure, worthlessness, betrayal, lack of confidence and degradation and a sense of having been abused and assaulted'. It is not unusual for people experiencing tardive dyskinesia to be unaware that this is a 'side effect' of the medication they are taking (for example, Clay, 1999). They may instead be told that they are causing these uncontrollable movements themselves because of some deep-seated psychological problem, as was the experience of one of us (A.W.).

Perhaps the most extreme example of damaging psychiatric treatments is the lobotomy, already discussed above in a different context. 'Between 1948 and 1952 tens of thousands of mutilating brain operations were performed on mentally ill men and women in countries around the world' (Valenstein, 1986: 3). In the course of these operations, 'a surgeon inserted [into a patient's brain] any of various instruments – some resembling an apple corer, a butter spreader, or an ice pick – and often without being able to see what he was cutting, destroyed parts of the brain' (*ibid.*). By 1960, the practice of lobotomy had been drastically curtailed, though psychosurgery is still occasionally employed. In October 1999, the former pop star, Lena Zavaroni, was reported as having died 'following radical brain surgery for serious eating disorder' (Thorpe and McVeigh, 1999), which she had specifically requested.

The effect of lobotomy (and modern forms of psychosurgery such as cingulotomy, amygdalotomy and thalamotomy) is to produce 'deactivation' – diminished initiative and emotionality. Though psychosurgery is only rarely performed today, deactivation in the form of neuroleptic-induced 'chemical lobotomy' is extremely widespread, with comparable destructive effects. Deactivation is a primary effect of all neuroleptics, including the newer 'atypical' neuroleptics such as clozapine and risperidone:

> The neuroleptic deactivation effect so closely resembles psychosurgery in its clinical impact because it disrupts the same regions of the brain. Classical lobotomy, for example, cuts the descending fibers from the frontal

lobes to deeper brain structures, while the neuroleptics tend to impair the ascending dopaminergic fibers. (Breggin, 1997: 16)

Another damaging effect of psychiatric treatment and an additional layer in the construction of 'mental illness' and 'mentally ill' people is the convincing of patients themselves that they are truly 'mentally ill'. When one of us (A.W.) was first admitted to hospital, she did not consider that she was 'suffering from a mental illness' and was reluctant to take medication. In an attempt to 'persuade' her to take neuroleptics, the psychiatrists first listed all the things that were 'wrong with her'. These would apparently be rectified by adjusting the dopamine levels in her brain. It can be very difficult, especially if you are young and relatively inexperienced, to counter psychiatrists' pronouncements that you are 'mentally ill'.

Psychiatric patients are encouraged to 'come to terms' with their mental illness and advised that they may be unable to cope with stressful occupations, if they can work at all. Both of us received such unhelpful advice. It was suggested to Peter that he might be able to get a job as a clerk and Anne was advised to become a shop assistant. Fortunately, somehow or other, we found it possible to disregard these negative predictions and have both worked successfully for many years in demanding and sometimes stressful jobs. With the benefit of hindsight, it seems to us now that the psychiatrists' 'prognoses' were concerned with devaluing and subverting our understanding of ourselves. While the expression may seem extreme and also dated, there are parallels with both the logic and intention of wartime brainwashing techniques (Hickey, 1999; Hastings, 2000), where the aim was to change the beliefs of prisoners of war to make them consistent with the political ideology of their captors.

Popular and media interpretations of 'mental illness'

The public and political expression of psychiatry's medical and administrative categorizations seems to be the increasing polarization of madness and distress into two categories – of the 'threateningly mad' and the 'worried well'. This development might be seen as a move to more postmodernist understandings that appreciate difference and diversity. In practice, however, it seems to serve both to dismiss and to devalue the experience and distress of those of us not seen as 'ill' enough to require public resources for support, and to reinforce assumptions about a discrete and separate group of mad people that constitutes a threat to the rest of society.

The media and public treatment of both the life and death of Princess Diana highlights this issue. She became a focus for competing views about madness, distress and femininity. These were frequently polarized on the basis of gender, as well as according to whether they were offered before or after her death. Critics condemned her as feckless, disordered, psychopathic and destructive. Supporters viewed her as a marker to highlight the 'normality' and tragedy of distress, particularly eating distress, and the possibility of challenging and triumphing over it (Engel, 1997; *Sun*, 1998). Supporters praised her for her charitable good works – although significantly she never associated herself with any 'mental health' charities (*Disability Now*, 1997). Her iconic status also ensured that the subtext of her status as a mental health service user (or at least as a subject of private therapy) could be that it was all right to be distressed, so long as you were rich, beautiful and powerful.

The subtleties and complexities of public categorizations of madness and distress are highlighted by the survey by MIND (the mental health charity) of mental health service users'/survivors' views of the media. The *Daily Mail*, which has been at the forefront of a media frenzy about the threat and danger from mental health service users linked with the 'care in the community' policy, was rated fourth in order of unpopularity for 'handling mental health issues very badly', beaten only by the *Sun*, 'all tabloids' and the *Daily Mirror*. However, when asked which newspaper, programme or magazine 'handled mental health issues very well', the *Daily Mail* came *eighth* overall in order of popularity (MIND's own bi-monthly journal, *Openmind*, came first) (MIND, 2000: 12). David Crepaz-Keay, of Mental Health Media, sees this discrepancy as a product of *news* stories which are frequently negative and stigmatizing (telling 'us' about a threatening 'them') and of *health* features which are often supportive and informative (telling 'us', including the 'worried well', what 'we' can do when 'we' experience distress) (Crepaz-Keay, 2000, personal communication).

This distinction between the 'dangerous mad' and the 'worried well' mirrors psychiatry's separating out of people's madness and distress into broad categories of 'psychoses' and 'neuroses' which are, we believe, unhelpful, as they suggest that those who are diagnosed 'neurotic' are perhaps *less Other* than people diagnosed 'psychotic'. This reinforces the *Otherness* of those of us identified as 'psychotic'. It also serves, by association, ironically to reinforce the *Otherness* of people labelled 'neurotic'. The two of us experience mental and emotional distress. Sometimes our distress is more extreme than at other times, but we place ourselves alongside everyone else on a continuum of mental and emotional distress and well-being: a continuum that does not show binary opposition between 'the mad' and 'the not-mad'. Psychiatry's purpose, however, is to identify and diagnose 'mental illness' and, in so doing, to mark out and police the conceptual divide between those who 'suffer mental illness' and those who do not.

Conclusion

We have outlined above some aspects of dominant expert discourse on madness and distress and their impact upon mental health service users and psychiatric system survivors. Though the movement of psychiatric system survivors does not share one agreed view of the psychiatric system and its failings, psychiatric system survivors, as documented above, have for several years written critically about their own experiences of the system. It appears to us that little attention is being paid to survivors' critiques in 'postmodernist' texts on madness and distress, which, like the modernist accounts before them, continue to be authored by 'experts' and academics who do not have experience as users or recipients of the psychiatric system. This failure to include the local, situated analyses and knowledges of people on the receiving end of public policy, particularly welfare policy, reflects a broader failing of some aspects of postmodernism (Croft and Beresford, 1998). Whereas Dwight Fee's (2000b) edited collection admits the role of 'mental health patients' in the production of knowledge, it does not have a place for them. This failure on the part of conventional postmodernist discussion represents a lost opportunity, by omitting the diverse subjectivities which it highlights. Hopefully, books like the present volume will begin to compensate for this.

Other issues are also raised for mental health service users/survivors by conventional discussions of the social model of disability. The distinction these draw between impairment and disability, where impairment is taken to refer to assumed biological characteristics of the body and mind, is likely to be problematic. Some disabled authors, however, have written of the socially constructed nature of impairment (for example, Abberley, 1987). It is these discussions which may make more sense for psychiatric system survivors, for our starting point cannot be the unquestioning acceptance of the reification of 'mental illness'. In a social model analogy, we cannot take 'mental illness' as the 'given' often accepted of physical/sensory impairment.

Ideas of perceived biological impairment of the mind clearly do underpin (or indeed *are*) medicalized modernist approaches to madness and distress. However, a social model of madness and distress which focused on society's failure to accommodate people with such 'perceived impairments of the mind' could, we believe, further contribute to the reification of 'impairment of the mind' and run the risk of reinforcing ideas of psychiatric system survivors as Other.

If we are to develop a social theory of madness and distress, we need to be clear about our common difference as psychiatric system survivors. In our view, any understanding of that difference should *vigorously contest* the role of the psychiatric system and, in particular, of medical/psychiatric records and discourses, in the reification of 'mental illness'. This is closely consistent with postmodernist commitments to the 'deconstruction of grand narratives' on the basis of difference and may be one of the ways in which postmodernist critiques can be helpful here. We do not consider that our 'minds', or those of other psychiatric system survivors, are impaired, damaged or 'sick' in any way. Yet it is precisely because the psychiatric system has *perceived us* in this way that we have, at times in our lives, been indoctrinated into believing that we really are 'mentally ill'. The challenge we now face as mental health service users/survivors is to make it possible for our own critiques and discussions to develop and counter the dominance of existing medicalized and ritualized individual discourses. Until we achieve this, the likelihood is that, ironically, modernist explanations of madness and distress will continue to flourish in an age of postmodernity. For psychiatric system survivors, a key route to making this challenge is likely to be strengthening the links of our discourses with those of disabled people.

References

Abberley, P. (1987) 'The concept of oppression and the development of a social theory of disability', *Disability, Handicap and Society*, 2(1): 5–19.

Arscott, K. (1999) 'ECT: the facts psychiatry declines to mention', in C. Newnes, G. Holmes and C. Dunn (eds), *This Is Madness: A Critical Look at Psychiatry and the Future of Mental Health Services*. Ross-on-Wye: PCCS Books, pp. 97–118.

Barker, P., Campbell, P. and Davidson, B. (eds) (1999) *From the Ashes of Experience: Reflections on Madness, Survival and Growth*. London: Whurr Publications.

Beresford, P. (2000) *Mental Health Issues: Our Voice in Our Future*. London: Shaping Our Lives/National Institute for Social Work.

Beresford, P., Gifford, G. and Harrison, C. (1996) 'What has disability got to do with psychiatric survivors?', in J. Read and J. Reynolds (eds), *Speaking Our Minds: An Anthology*. Basingstoke: Macmillan, pp. 209–14.

Bowers, L. (1998) *The Social Nature of Mental Illness*. London: Routledge.

Boyle, M. (1999) 'Diagnosis', in C. Newnes, G. Holmes and C. Dunn (eds), *This Is Madness: A Critical Look at Psychiatry and the Future of Mental Health Services*. Ross-on-Wye: PCCS Books, pp. 75–90.

Breggin, P. (1997) *Brain Disabling Treatments in Psychiatry: Drugs, Electroshock, and the Role of the FDA*. New York: Springer.

Campbell, J. and Oliver, M. (1996) *Disability Politics: Understanding Our Past, Changing Our Future*. London: Routledge.

Campbell, P. (1989) 'Peter Campbell's story', in A. Brackx (ed.), *Mental Health Care in Crisis*. London: Pluto Press, pp. 11–20.

Chamberlin, J. (1988) *On Our Own*. London: MIND Publications.

Clay, S. (1999) 'Madness and reality', in P. Barker, P. Campbell and B. Davidson (eds), *From the Ashes of Experience: Reflections on Madness, Survival and Growth*. London: Whurr Publications, pp. 16–36.

Croft, S. (1996) 'How can I leave them? Towards an empowering social work practice with women who are dying', in B. Fawcett, M. Galloway and J. Perrins (eds), *Feminism and Social Work in the Year 2000: Conflicts and Controversies.* Bradford: University of Bradford.

Croft, S. and Beresford, P. (1998) 'Postmodernity and the future of welfare: whose critiques, whose social policy?', in J. Carter (ed.), *Postmodernity and the Fragmentation of Welfare.* London: Routledge.

Davies, L. (1999) 'Avalon', in P. Barker, P. Campbell and B. Davidson (eds), *From the Ashes of Experience: Reflections on Madness, Survival and Growth.* London: Whurr Publications, pp. 80–112.

Disability Now (1997) 'Disability world mourns Diana', *Disability Now*, October: 1.

Engel, M. (1997) 'Today Diana is laid to rest and will enter our legends', *Guardian*, 6 September: 1 and 3.

Fee, D. (2000a) 'The project of pathology: reflexivity and depression in Elizabeth Wurtzel's *Prozac Nation*', in D. Fee (ed.), *Pathology and the Postmodern: Mental Illness as Discourse and Experience.* London: Sage.

Fee, D. (ed.) (2000b) *Pathology and the Postmodern: Mental Illness as Discourse and Experience.* London: Sage.

Freeman, W., Davis, H., East, I., Sinclair Tait, H., Johnson, S. and Rogers, W. (1954) 'West Virginia lobotomy project', *Journal of the American Medical Association*, 156: 939–43.

Gelder, M., Gath, D. and Mayou, R. (1993) *Oxford Textbook of Psychiatry*, 2nd edn. Oxford: Oxford University Press.

Hastings, M. (2000) *The Korean War.* London: Pan Books, pp. 339–51.

Herpin, N. (1981) 'Off the record: the consequences of constructing dossiers on clients', in G. Albrecht (ed.), *Cross National Rehabilitation Policies: A Sociological Perspective.* London: Sage.

Hickey, M. (1999) *The Korean War: The West Confronts Communism 1950–1953.* London: John Murray, pp. 337–46.

Hirst, J. (1999) 'Reading the Rights Act', *Community Care*, 2–8 December: pp. 20–2.

Hughes, J. (1991) *An Outline of Modern Psychiatry*, 3rd edn. Chichester: Wiley.

Jenkins, P. (1997) *Counselling, Psychotherapy and the Law.* London: Sage.

Johnstone, L. (1999) 'Adverse psychological effects of ECT', *Journal of Mental Health*, 8(1): 69–85.

Kutchins, H. and Kirk, S. (1999) *Making Us Crazy: DSM – The Psychiatric Bible and the Creation of Mental Disorders.* London: Constable.

Lemert, E. (1951) *Social Psychology.* New York: McGraw-Hill.

McNamara, J. (1996) 'Out of order: madness is a feminist and a disability issue', in J. Morris (ed.), *Encounters with Strangers: Feminism and Disability.* London: Women's Press.

MIND (1999) *Landmark Discrimination Case.* London: MIND, Press Release, 24 December.

MIND (2000) *The Daily Stigma: Counting the Cost, Mental Health in the Media.* London: MIND, 9 February.

O'Hagan, M. (1993) *Stopovers on My Way Home from Mars: A Journey into the Psychiatric Survivor Movement in the USA, Britain and the Netherlands.* London: Survivors Speak Out.

Oliver, M. (1996) *Understanding Disability: From Theory to Practice.* Basingstoke: Macmillan.

Parker, I., Georgaca, E., Harper, D., McLaughlin, T. and Stowell-Smith, M. (1995) *Deconstructing Psychopathology*. London: Sage.

Pembroke, L. (ed.) (1994a) *Eating Distress: Perspectives from Personal Experience*. London: Survivors Speak Out.

Pembroke, L. (ed.) (1994b) *Self-Harm: Perspectives from Personal Experience*. London: Survivors Speak Out.

Plumb, A. (1994) *Distress or Disability: A Discussion Document*. Manchester: Greater Manchester Coalition of Disabled People.

Scheff, T. (1966) *Being Mentally Ill: A Sociological Theory*. London: Weidenfield & Nicolson.

Steinberg, D. (1997) *Bodies in Glass: Genetics, Eugenics, Embryo Ethics*. Manchester: Manchester University Press.

Sun (1998) 'Diana: the people's pictures, Part 2': 24-page tribute free with the *Sun*. London: *Sun* (undated).

Thomas, P. (1997) *The Dialectics of Schizophrenia*. London: Free Association Books.

Thorpe, V. and McVeigh, T. (1999) 'Anorexia claims life of child pop star who never grew up', *The Observer*, 3 October: 3.

Valenstein, E. (1986) *Great and Desperate Cures: The Rise and Decline of Psychosurgery and Other Radical Treatments for Mental Illness*. New York: Basic Books.

Young, A. (1996) 'Introduction', in H. Freeman (ed.), *Options for Improving Patient Care in Schizophrenia*. London: Royal Society of Medicine.

12

Countering Stereotypes of Disability: Disabled Children and Resistance

John Davis and Nick Watson

Introduction

Disabled children are presented in much of the research literature as passive, vulnerable and dependent. Research that originates from within social policy, for example, documents how disabled children experience a range of social and economic difficulties (Shakespeare and Watson, 1998). There is also an emphasis on care, on the services they receive, and this characterizes disabled children as a drain on society; they are presented as a burden. Educational research on disabled children focuses on how recent changes to the education system (for example, national testing, league tables, devolved management and the National Curriculum) act to reduce opportunities for disabled children (Davis and Watson, 2001). Social psychology and developmental psychology, by proposing a universal model of 'normal' child development, pathologizes those children who fail to achieve certain developmental criteria (Woodhead, 1999). Medical and paramedical research prioritizes research into cure and much medical sociology and nursing research concentrates on how the disabled child and his or her carers 'cope' with the consequences of impairment (Priestley, 1998).

This discourse is reinforced in both the popular media and in literature and images used by charities. Disabled children are often presented as sad and despairing. In promotional literature produced by, for example, Children in Need, Telethon and Action Research for the Crippled Child, the message is very much that, without the help of donors, these children's lives will not be worth living. Also, cure is often offered as the only possible way to improve the life chances of disabled children. It is all about changing the individual, tackling impairment; there is little recognition of the role of society in creating the problems faced by the child. Indeed, many of these organizations, it could be argued, often promote the very social practices that many within the disabled people's movement suggest encourage their exclusion from the mainstream of society, in, for example, their support of segregated schools. Implicit in these images is the idea of a 'normal' child/childhood. The presence of an impairment excludes a child from taking part in that normal childhood; their childhood is invalidated by the impairment.

However, this characterization has not gone unchallenged. The disabled people's movement and its allies have, through the social model, repositioned the disabled child from the object to the subject (Shakespeare, 1994). Disability, it argues, is not to be seen as a problem of the individual, or arising as a consequence of impairment, but is the product of a society that is organized so as to exclude disabled people. For example, self-organized groups of disabled people, supported by professional bodies such as the Centre for Studies on Integration and Education, have campaigned against current educational policy, demanding that disabled children must be included in mainstream schools. However, there is a danger in this approach. It presents disabled people as a homogeneous grouping, as if there is an essential element to the disability experience.

This homogenization of disabled children is reinforced by the UN convention on the rights of the child and the Children's Act (1990) and the Children (Scotland) Act (1995) (James et al., 1998). Whilst these acts have led to the recognition that disabled children can form opinions and that these opinions should be taken into account by service providers and policy-makers, they mask differences both between and within groups. They overlook the fluid and diverse nature of children's lives.

Writers from the new social studies of childhood have provided a method through which this diversity can be uncovered (James and Prout, 1990; Christiensen and James, 2000). This theoretical approach has provided the tools and the ethics for a new approach to childhood, one that collects and interprets the views of children and, importantly, works so as to include children in processes of change (Alderson, 1995). Building on this, we have shown how a reflexive method can enable the development of a more nuanced understanding of disabled children (Davis, 1998; Davis et al., 2000). We argue that much research on disabled children rests on a fairly unreflexive acceptance of the distinction disabled/non-disabled and child/non-child. There is an essentialist and totalizing understanding of both disability and children as categories. We start from an awareness that the current understandings of disability and disabled children are historically contingent and are not stable descriptive classifiers. This rejection of meta-narratives and general theories in favour of an emphasis on local narratives and piecemeal and contingent understandings is, many would argue, an endorsement of postmodernism (Seidman, 1994). The recognition of fluidity and multiplicity and the rejection of a central organizing principle is pivotal to much that is described as postmodern. We do not intend here to enter into a debate about the meaning of postmodernism or post-structuralism, but use the terms as convenient descriptors of a trope. Suffice it to say, we argue that our work falls broadly within what is described as postmodernism/post-structuralism in that our work considers 'social, moral and political consequences, the practical purposes of knowledge and their situational impact' (Seidman, 1994: 17).

Our reflexive, ethnographic approach has enabled us to illustrate how adults and children construct notions of disability and utilize these constructions during social interaction. We have demonstrated that, very often, disabled children's opportunities are restricted because other people's perceptions lead to oppressive practices (see Corker and Davis, 2000; Davis and Watson, 2000; Davis and Watson, 2001). Disabled children encounter adults and children and organizational structures that contribute to the conditions in which self-empowerment flourishes. As such, we have demonstrated the fluid and contingent nature of disabled children's everyday lives.

In this chapter, we build on this body of work by discussing disabled children's diverse patterns of resistance. In contrast to medicalized constructions of resistance (e.g., concepts like oppositional defiance disorder in psychology/psychiatry), we establish that disabled children's resistance is understandable and is a response to oppressive cultures, structures and individuals. In essence, we see this text as an opportunity to construct a competing discourse which presents disabled children as agents and not passive, dependent victims. In so doing, we attempt to represent the diversity of disabled children's lives at the same time as exploring how the processes of mobilizing discourses concerning disabled children, by specific adults and children, is embedded within the structural organization of specific locations.

Resisting structural oppression

Disabled children encounter a variety of structures in their day-to-day-lives. These structures are both material, such as schools and educational policy, and cultural, deriving from belief and attitude systems. In the example below, Mark's comments clearly show how the attitudes of other, non-disabled children, mitigate against his, and other disabled children's, inclusion during football.

JOHN [Mark asks if we can chat about the recent football match against the mainstream school.]

MARK: I hardly got a touch. And one of our pupils, Egan, hogged the ball all the time. And it was only the partially sighted people who got a chance. And they wouldnae pass ti us, the blind people.

JOHN: And did you do anything about that?

MARK: Well, when he first did it I had a mind to chuck him oot, but it's no up ti me, it's up to the coach. So ah thought, get on wi' the game.

> Egan just does it to show off. I'm tryin' ti get the ball but he's always on the ball.
>
> JOHN: Do you think you could change that at all?
>
> MARK: When I shout, Egan! Egan!, he just doesn't listen. It's the same with the resti them. If ah was the manager I'd ban him or I'd put him on the subs' bench and get a good person to take his place. It wasn't just Egan, it was Alan who did it as well. And it also happens to Brian. Ah feel sorry for Brian. He doesnae come ti football much. Like ma best dream would be ti captain. But ah dinnae complain. Ah'll just have ti wait 'til it's ma time. Egan was captain the last time and he just passed it to Andrew. And he was suspended from school one game and when he was suspended ah got more of the ball. He's a right complainer, that lad. Like come on ref, he pulled ma shirt. He's always saying that. See if he was, see if he was called off-side, he'd argue wi' the ref, so ah think I'd be glad if he got sent off. And it's just a wastei the time ti argue wi' the ref, 'cause the ref gives it the other way. And I think, ha ha Egan you're no gettin' your own way this time. He thinks we're crap. He probably thinks blind people can't, can't play.

In this example, Mark is unhappy with the way the football is organized, with the coach and with Egan. However, he internalizes his resistance and he does not suggest that he could make any immediate attempt to change Egan's mind. Mark does not see his problem as being blind, it is about the organization of the football, clearly a social model analysis. Yet, he wants people, such as the coach, to act on his behalf. His solution (if he were the coach) would be to exclude Egan from taking part, thus reproducing the very situation that he is experiencing.

Mark identifies oppressive practice and locates the source of that practice: discrimination against blind people. However, there is a danger that this example presents him as a passive victim of the society he lives in. This would be unwise, because it is not so much that he does not resist as that he keeps his resistance inside. In contrast to this example, other data collected in mainstream and segregated school settings suggests that disabled children can adopt more overt strategies through which to assert their own agency. Indeed, this can involve children expressing their feelings through immediate physical and verbal resistance.

Physical and verbal resistance

Many children we met resisted an identity imposed by other children in ways that did not lead to dialogue:

ANDREW: I used to get in trouble [when he went to a mainstream school] with other kids 'cause like I was getting made fun of, slagged, and that. I just went up to one of them and I gave the left hook and booted them like anything and that when he was down. Anyway, while he was lying there I says to him, 'Want ti take the piss ooti us again then?' I just go mental like. I just dinnae take it. [At a whisper] See if anyone em called me a blind little cunt then I'd say. Like I might take it once or twice but then I'd just go for them.

JOHN: How would that go down here?

ANDREW: You wouldnae need ti dae it here.

JOHN: What about outside the school?

ANDREW: That doesnae really come inti it. It's like captivity here.

Here Andrew asserts his right to his own identity, and clearly displays his agency. This shows us an example of the heterogeneity of disabled children: some resist internally whilst others overtly resist. However, when comparing Andrew and Mark, it is important to note that Andrew is both somebody who at times has to be resisted (Mark, in earlier conversation, also accuses Andrew of not passing the ball) and has to resist other children. Many other children in the school told us how Andrew was capable of bullying. Andrew can be both bullied and the bully – disabled children can oppress each other and can oppress and be oppressed by non-disabled children. His role changes with the structural location he is in (mainstream or special school, home or school). This suggests that not all disabled children react in the same way to the same situation. Their behaviour changes, depending on where they are and whom they are with. Indeed, even in this case Andrew is willing to put up with a 'slagging' once or twice before he resorts to violence.

We have illustrated that some forms of bullying in 'special schools' involve disabled children utilizing adult ableist discourses against each other (Davis and Watson, 2001) and that very often these discourses relate to ideas concerning hierarchies of impairment. However, it would be unwise to assume that the children who are least overtly resistant are also those who experience the most severe impairments. We soon came to learn that, whatever the physical impairment attributed to a child, they were capable of exhibiting agency and resistance. This is clear from this example involving Guy, a child with severe and multiple impairments who did not employ spoken words to communicate:

JOHN [Rita is working with Guy in her interaction class. She has a stethoscope and is listening to Guy's breathing.]

RITA: [to John] I've just been on a course about breathing and swallowing so I'm just gonny have a listen. Guy, is it OK if I listen?

GUY   [Smiles]

RITA: [after listening for a while] Could you make a noise for me?

GUY: Ahhhhhhhhh.

RITA: That's great thanks, do you want to listen [to Guy]?

GUY   [Moves his hand, he's lying on a mat on the floor, across his body towards Rita and smiles]

RITA: Yes, you would, good here we go.

GUY   [Listens to his breathing; Rita holds his hand with the listening end of the scope and puts the other bits in his ears.]

RITA: Why don't you make a noise again?

GUY: AHHHHHHHHHHHH.

RITA: Ok, now you can stop [taking the scope away].

GUY: Ahhhhhhhhh . . . eh . . . ahhhhhhhhhhhhhhhhh [with eyes completely closed].

JOHN   [At first I think he is in pain or he has drifted off in his mind but Rita starts to walk away and Guy opens his eyes very slightly, watches her, pauses for a second, then continues moaning. Rita moves away a few more times and, each time she moves away, he stops moaning to watch her, then starts to moan again when she stops moving.]

RITA: Guy, what's wrong? Do you want the scope back?

GUY   [Moves hand and stops moaning]

RITA: Oh, so you do, sorry, Guy [Puts the scope back on for him to listen to].

    [after a while] Could I have another go now and get you to swallow for me? [Takes the scope back] OK, swallow again, a missed that one.

LAURA: [Comes in] Hi, John. [to Rita] Oh, what's this then?

RITA: We've just been listening to Guy breathing and swallowing; it's a bit like a short breath and then a big one, like he's getting ready to have a breath with the first one, isn't it Guy? [to Laura] He's had a listen too. I think he quite enjoys it.

LAURA: [to me and Rita, ignoring Guy] Yes, it's fascinating, it's not like us, you know, like normal breathing is in and out and quite regular but Guy, it's like he sucks in to get going and then suddenly it's a big intake. [Demonstrates] Ah. [pause] Ahuuuuup.

RITA: Yeh [to me], all the children have different ways of breathing like.

LAURA: [Interrupts] Helen's incredible, she doesn't breathe for ages.

RITA: Yeh and you wonder, you know, you think that she'd have to breathe.

LAURA: [Interrupts again] It's really frightening. When we were on holiday, I checked on her in the middle of the night and she wasn't breathing for ages. I thought, please Helen, please breathe, and I got her up, rubbing her back and saying to her, come on now, Helen, and she woke up startled and thought what the heck's going on here? I just didn't realize.

Prior to this interaction the research team had assumed that Guy was unable to employ overt resistance. However, here Guy is seen by John and Rita to demonstrate agency by demanding the stethoscope back. In contrast to John and Rita, Laura does not pick up on the significance of Rita's interaction with Guy. Ignoring Guy, she turns the discussion into an opportunity to reinforce the discourse that these children are not 'normal'. She makes no attempt to incorporate Guy into the discussion whilst she talks about him. Guy makes no effort to attract her attention. Rita attributes meaning to Guy's behaviour and she enters into a process of communication and exchange. In opposition to this, Laura creates social space between herself and Guy, stigmatizing him as different and 'not normal'. As part of the process of creating social space, Laura draws on past experiences, where she discovered these children were different from herself. As Merleau-Ponty (1962) would see it, Laura and Rita come to the interpretation of Guy's actions from different pre-objective positions. Rita assumes she can connect with Guy and interpret his agency and does not assume she knows what his bodily movements mean. However, she and Guy try to negotiate meanings and close the gap between their different ways of communicating and their different bodily practice (Bourdieu, 1978). In contrast, Laura predefines Guy's body as different, strange and difficult to read and does not attempt to negotiate meaning with Guy.

Elsewhere, we have argued that, though children like Guy are capable of agency, whether their behaviour is read as such depends on the reflexive capacities of the interpreter (Davis *et al.*, 2000). We also argued that, for resistance to be read as meaningful, cultural exchange has to occur between the participants within a social setting. If this does not occur, for example in a school setting between adult and child, the child's behaviour can be labelled as innate, biologically stimulated, a consequence of impairment and as lacking meaning.

However, in coming to such a conclusion we do not want to downplay the importance of impairment in children's lives. The material consequences, the here and now of having an impairment, were mentioned by some of the children. In the following example Liam talked about blindness:

As he was kicking the ball about, Liam, out of the blue, said: 'Nick, you're luckier than me, you've got sight, you can see when things are coming. I've always wondered what it would be like to be able to see. Do you wish you could walk properly?'

NICK: Why?

LIAM: Cos I wish I could see.

I replied that at times I did, but not all the time. Liam then asked me to come into his room for a chat, saying that there are things that he didn't want people to hear and that there might be something we wanted to discuss. Got into his room and I asked him what it was that he wanted to talk about:

LIAM: I'm happy to talk about anything as long as it's nothing to do with blindness.

NICK: Why?

LIAM: I don't like talking about blindness.

Here, Liam is talking about the impact of impairment on his life and his feelings about his impairment. He is aware of the difference that he, as a blind child, experiences. However, he did not wish to dwell on the issue, resisting further questions. These data are included to show that impairment is always already present as what Thomas (1999) would call 'impairment effects'. We cannot write the body out of disabled children's lives, yet in recognizing the importance of impairment effects we should not assume, as Laura and those who work within the medical model do, that the meaning of impairments are pre-given. Indeed, many children resist identities foisted onto them by others that relate to stereotypical views of impairment.

Resisting impairment as a dominant status

Many of the children we interviewed and worked with described to us how many people only saw them in terms of their impairment. As Sheila commented:

> Yeah. Like the chemistry teacher, I go up and ask him a question, it's like he's always apologizing because he says, 'Oh, I'm sorry the writing is not as big as.' And I'm like, 'I just came to ask you a question about chemistry.' And he's like, he just thinks I'm disabled.

This approach is patronizing and reductive. The teacher reads all Sheila's actions through her impairment. This is a mistake made by many adults, even us as researchers:

> JOHN   [The teacher asks me to help Candis go up in the lift on the way to the next class. The teacher tells me that one of her impairments means she has to use the lift and that the school policy is that she should have an adult with her. As we get into the lift,

Candis gets in first. I reach across and press the button for the floor we're going to. Candis flinches; I realize I shouldn't have done that.]

JOHN: I'm sorry. I suppose you know how to press the button yourself?
CANDIS: Yes.
JOHN: I'm sorry, I shouldn't have done that. Do adults very often do that to you?
CANDIS: They're always doing it. It's really annoying. But I try to get my own back on them by doing something they don't like.

Candis resists being patronized by adults, specifically here through the use of body language. However, she also verbally resists adults, as in this example:

JOHN   [The English teacher makes a huge issue about the way that Candis was spelling the word 'matches'. Takes her about seven attempts to get the spelling right.]
TEACHER: Have you got it now? Can you spell it? Can you say it for me?
CANDIS: Maatches.
TEACHER: Yeah, listen to the sound. It's mat-ches, mat-ches, mat-ches, mat-ches [emphasizing the syllables in a really patronizing way].
JOHN   [Candis gets really annoyed.]
CANDIS: I did hear you, you know.
TEACHER: What?
CANDIS: I did hear you the first time, you know. This is what these things are for [pulling out her ears]. I've got ears you know [in a way which suggests the teacher is mixing this up with her other impairments].
JOHN   [The teacher isn't very impressed by this. However, Candis is saved from a telling off by another teacher interrupting the class.]

Sheila and Candis perceive their teachers' approaches to be unnecessary. Candis challenges the teacher angrily. In contrast, John gets off lightly, probably because his reflexive apology opens up the possibility for dialogue. However, as the next section shows, it should not be assumed that disabled children are only capable of resisting perceptions of their impairment.

Day-to-day resistance

Whilst the examples above show children resisting around their impairment, resistance was also commonplace around issues that affect all children, for example, the wearing of school uniforms:

JOHN   [George was really annoyed that the head teacher had put a suggestion to people that people who travelled away at the weekend and were boarders would have to wear the school uniform at all times. He had an argument with Fergy about this during their residential section weekly meeting.]

GEORGE: What happened at the meeting is [the head teacher] has asked parents and staff to write in what they think of the uniform and when they should wear it and that some teachers are complaining about people coming in with casual clothes.

FERGY: [The head] is wanting uniforms to be worn Monday to Friday.

LINA: No way.

FERGY: He's gonni send out a sheet to pupils, staff and everyone connected with the school, and he thinks it will happen. [The head] thinks there's too many pupils wearing no uniforms, and it's not good for people coming in. I think that's fair enough.

GEORGE: [Interrupts] But the pupils at the mainstream secondary school don't have to wear uniform. They can just put on their home clothes.

FERGY: [Interrupts again] There'll be no training shoes in school as well . . . [The head] said it was OK for boys and girls to wear shirts and ties and that the education committee are all for it.

GEORGE: I'm completely against it, because it's easier for my mum on a Monday if I don't come in with a school uniform.

LINA: But if day pupils can wear it on a Monday, so can you. So can the residential.

GEORGE: Well, I wouldn't go as far as breaking the rules.

FERGY: You're gonni have to lump it.

GEORGE   [Goes off to get a cup of tea]

JOHN: What do you think he'll do?

FERGY: He'll have to wear it.

This shows how children are often pressured to conform as a group. However, it also demonstrates that they respond to this structural requirement in different ways. These children all share a similar impairment and have all been to the same secondary school. Yet, contrary to much writing on disabled children that seeks to present them as the product of their impairment, this has not served to create a homogeneous group. Fergy and George have different views concerning the imposition of school uniforms: Fergy appears to place a value on conformity, George on rights. Fergy uses the power of the school structure as an explanation for why George should change. George privileges the needs of his mother over those of the school. They both draw on notions of autonomy, equity, structure, individuality, collectivization and much more when asserting their different perspectives. They have different value systems, which relate to wider life issues. In Bourdieu's (1978) terms, they are competing to impose their own definitions of legitimate practice.

Fergy is a member of the school council, the oldest in the group, expected to go on to university, and comes from an affluent background. George is a working-class boy, from a single-parent family. It is easy to explain this conflict in terms of the children's different structural/cultural backgrounds. However, not all working-class children in the school opposed the school uniform and not all middle-class girls supported the way the school was organized. Indeed, Mark and Andrew came from similar backgrounds yet their behaviour when resisting was quite different. We would suggest that different children have different capacities to resist the people and organizations that they encounter and that this capacity is situated in both locality and time. Therefore, as James and Prout (1995) argue, the culture of childhood is fluid and children are flexible social actors. For example, many of the children used resistance in a very strategic way. If they saw benefit to be gained from not challenging, then they allowed perpetrators to get away with patronizing behaviour. For example, when Bobby went to the Boys' Brigade he was often sidelined, ignored or treated in a patronizing manner. At the end of the session, however, he was given a large bag of sweets and, whilst he was aware of the way he was treated, for him the benefits outweighed the costs.

Discussion

The multidimensional nature of resistance documented here contrasts with writers in, for example, the field of education, who only discuss resistance in terms of class conflict. Authors such as Hargreaves (1967), Willis (1977) and Ball (1981) suggest that resistance within schools stems from class conflict underpinned by structural and cultural inequalities. Hargreaves (1967) argues that the streaming structure of schools results in children being treated unequally and consequently their views and aspirations are reduced in scope. Ball (1981, 1987) contends that, even where streaming was removed, the teachers' attitudes meant that they labelled certain children as non-achievers and this had a detrimental effect on their educational attainment. For Willis (1977), working-class children, 'the lads', were responding to their material location within society. He believed that class consciousness led 'the lads' to reject the values of the education system. All these theorists are arguing that resistance emerges through and in opposition to structures. Recent work by Adams et al. (2000) is based very much within this paradigm. In their exploration of 'special' education, whilst they recognize difference between schools, they show little awareness of the fluid process of interaction within, and between, groups of adults and children. Elsewhere, we have argued that much research within 'special' education does little more than reproduce the structural determinism that is found in educational sociology (Davis and Watson, 2001).

As an alternative perspective, we suggest resistance amongst disabled children is not solely the consequence of material differences between themselves and adults or other children. Disabled children also resist during daily interaction. They resist the imposition of identities founded on notions of impairment; the everyday value systems of other children and adults that differ from their own; and the local processes of organization which structure their lives. We argue that, like other social actors, at different times and in different settings disabled children can be both winners and losers, bullies and bullied, humorists and the subject of ridicule. Different people within the same social interaction can read the social practice of resisting in different ways. The process is extremely fluid. Disabled children are, above all, complex social beings. Value systems, as James and Prout (1995) have suggested, are open to challenge. Children who experience the same impairment do not behave in the same way, they are not a homogeneous group (Priestley *et al.*, 1999), and nor for that matter are children of the same gender (Davis, 1996; Thorne, 1993), race/religion (Fleming, 1991) or class (Davis, 1996, 1998, 1999).

We often encountered angry children both in and out of school. There is, as we have shown both here and in other work (Davis and Watson, 2000, 2001), a 'real' basis for this anger. It is a response to a threat to themselves or to their values. In the same way that we need to move away from a model that fixes the identity of disabled children and from pathologizing them on the basis of their impairment, we also need to move away from a model that places all its emphasis on structural disablement. That is, we need to understand the complex web of issues that underpins disabled children's behaviour, and the complex identities that lie within each child. Rather than simply seeing disabled children as only being shaped by deterministic forces such as disabling practices and barriers, social class, gender or ethnicity, we need to recognize that individuals are engaged in a process of reflexive self-constitution (Lash and Urry, 1994). However, this should not be seen as an argument to privilege agency over structure. Both are in play at the same time, each can be given equal weight as an explanation for social practice or there can be oscillation between the two. They cannot be disaggregated from each other or everyday cultural processes.

Disabled children live within a society whose cultural values and socio-cultural relations and physical environment operate so as to create a stereotypical image of what a disabled child should be. At the same time, these structures and values can only be what people hold them to be. Structure, culture and agency are fused in every social setting. This fusion is not fixed in either time, place or person; it is fluid and open to change and, as such, so are disabled children. Therefore, it would be unhelpful to cling to fixed characterization of disabled children as a homogeneous grouping who simply experience the same forms of oppression (e.g., Middleton, 1999). This characterization, in contrast to the data presented above, writes out the diversity within these children's lives.

Conclusion

These data challenge the hegemony that exists around disabled children and disabled childhoods. Disabled children are not passive, vulnerable or incompetent. They are neither solely the victims of impairment, nor are they always silent victims of a society that is structured so as to exclude them. Whilst the social model has obvious political potency, its material basis creates barriers to the investigation of the lives of disabled children (Shakespeare *et al.*, 1996). Our analysis, as we have argued above, could be read as a post-structural account. That is, it could be argued there is no centre, no appeal to a unifying discourse on disability or on disabled childhoods. By drawing on different children's stories in different settings we have attempted, following Marcus (1986), to close the distance between wider systems and local accounts at the same time as accounting for the multifaceted nature of the lives of disabled children. This process has been assisted by our ability to employ data from a number of different localities.

This chapter has presented contrasting versions of disabled childhoods. We have done so by employing verbal and non-verbal voices of adults and children and by illustrating different forms of resistance (silent, body language, oral, violent, overt, internal). Our aim has been to contribute to the circumstances in which dialogue occurs by developing a text which is anti-hegemonic (goes against the norm) and which demonstrates the fluid synthesis of issues of agency, culture and structure. In so doing, we have been able to question commonly held assumptions associated with medical and social models of disability. We have staged the voices in our text and put some signs up as a way of directing the reader but hopefully our voice is not so strong that it prevents others from developing their own readings. The extent to which this is 'co-operative story making' (Tyler, 1986) is up to the reader to decide. However, we would highlight a danger here that, despite our post-structural leanings, our work in itself will act as an instrument of normalization (Corker, 1999a).

As such, the status of this chapter is somewhat ambiguous. It is a text that illustrates the multiple realities of people's lives but, in a sometimes overt or allegorical way, there is a single message. This text challenges other academic and non-academic texts that represent disabled children as passive, vulnerable and incompetent social actors. It does so because our perspective has been influenced both by the opinions of the children we worked with and by writing and research in a number of areas such as the new sociology of childhood, disability studies and post-structural anthropology.

Yet, our hope is that, rather than setting up a new discourse which will become as oppressive as those we have criticized here, we are actually, by illustrating the fluid nature of disability, contributing to the circumstances in which people can stimulate change in their lives. By illustrating the different multiple-perspectives of disabled children and the people they interact with, our hope is that those who read our work might be able to utilize these illustrations as a starting point from which to understand each other's every-day perspectives and practices. Rather than creating a new dogma, we aim to contribute to the conditions in which dialogue, self-confidence, self-emancipation and mutual respect can flourish (Corker, 1999b; Shakespeare, 1997). It is our conclusion that the fulfilment of this aspiration will come about not only when people stop characterizing disabled children as a uniformly vulnerable, passive group but also when they stop homogenizing and pathologizing the people that disabled children interact with on a daily basis. In other words, if we are to demand heterogeneity for disabled children, then adults who work with children must be accorded the same status.

Finally, we would like to suggest that, though there is much to be gained by engaging with so-called post-structural and postmodern approaches, we would warn against assuming that there is anything extraordinary or new in these approaches. Indeed, as Corker (1999b) indicates, notions of dialogics come from Bhaktin, whom Campbell (1996) calls 'old as the hills'. Campbell further argues that there is little new in many so-called postmodern and post-structural approaches ' "Cauld kail het again" in Hugh MacDiarmid's words – (cold cabbage heated up again) . . . It's the same old stuff put in whizz-bang language' (p. 66). 'Cauld kail' or not, post-structural analysis certainly provides much food for thought. It provides a way of moving from an approach based on foundationalist principles to one that, as Lemert (1995) argues, enables an incorporation of difference as a primary feature of modern life.

Acknowledgements

We would like to thank Marcus Redley and the editors for their helpful comments and encouragement regarding this chapter.

References

Adams, J., Swain, J. and Clark, J. (2000) 'What's so special? Teachers' models and their realisation in practice in segregated schools', *Disability and Society*, 15(2): 233–46.

Alderson, P. (1995) *Listening to Children: Children Ethics and Social Research.* London: Barnardo's.

Ball, S. J. (1981) *Beachside Comprehensive.* Cambridge: Cambridge University Press.

Ball, S. J. (1987) *The Micropolitics of the School.* London: Routledge.

Bourdieu, P. (1978) 'Sport and social class', *Social Science Information,* 17: 819–40.

Campbell, A. T. (1996) 'Tricky tropes: styles of the popular and the pompous', in J. MacClancy and C. McDonaugh (eds), *Popularising Anthropology.* London: Routledge.

Christiensen, P. and James, A. (eds) (2000) *Conducting Research with Children.* London: Falmer.

Corker, M. (1999a) 'A view from the bridge: an interdisciplinarian's overview of the social relations of disability studies', *Disability Studies Quarterly,* 19(4): 305–17.

Corker, M. (1999b) 'New disability discourse, the principle of optimization and social change', in M. Corker and S. French (eds), *Disability Discourse.* Buckingham: Open University Press.

Corker, M. and Davis, J. M. (2000) 'Disabled children – invisible under the law', in J. Cooper (ed.), *Law, Rights and Disability.* London: Jessica Kingsley.

Davis J. M. (1996) 'Sport for all? An ethnographer's interpretation of the underlying factors influencing children's participation in PE and sport and their consequences for an efficacious implementation of the guidelines for PE of the 5–14 Curriculum and Assessment in Scotland: national guidelines: Expressive Arts.' PhD thesis, University of Edinburgh.

Davis, J. M. (1998) 'Understanding the meanings of children: a reflexive process', *Children and Society,* 12(5): 325–35.

Davis, J. M. (1999) 'Culture, structure and agency in Lothian PE settings', *1998–99 Scottish Centre Research Papers in Sport, Leisure and Society, Scottish Centre for Physical Education Sport: Edinburgh,* 3: 1–14.

Davis, J. M. and Watson, N. (2000) 'Disabled children's rights in every day life: problematising notions of competency and promoting self-empowerment', *International Journal of Children's Rights,* 8(3): 211–28.

Davis, J. M. and Watson, N. (2001) 'Where are the children's experiences? Analysing social and cultural exclusion in "special" and "mainstream" schools', *Disability and Society,* 16(5): 671–88.

Davis, J. M., Watson, N. and Cunningham-Burley, S. (2000) 'Learning the lives of disabled children: developing a reflexive approach', in P. Christiensen and A. James (eds), *Conducting Research with Children.* London: Falmer.

Davis, J. M., Watson, N. and Priestley, M. (1999) 'Dilemmas of the field: what can the study of disabled childhoods tell us about contemporary sociology?' Paper presented at the 1999 BSA conference *For Sociology.* University of Glasgow, 6–9 April 1999.

Fleming, S. (1991) 'Sport schooling and Asian male youth culture', in G. Jarvie (ed.), *Sport Racism and Ethnicity.* London: Falmer.

Hargreaves, D. H. (1967) *Social Relations in a Secondary School.* London: Routledge and Kegan Paul.

James, A., Jenks, C. and Prout, A. (1998) *Theorising Childhood.* Cambridge: Polity Press.

James, A. and Prout, A. (1990) 'Contemporary issues in the sociological study of childhood', in A. James and A. Prout (eds), *Constructing and Reconstructing Childhood*. London: Falmer.

James, A. and Prout, A. (1995) 'Hierarchy, boundary and agency', *Sociological Studies in Children*, 7: 77–99.

Lash, S. and Urry, J. (1994) *Economies of Sign and Space*. London: Sage.

Lemert, C. (1995) *Sociology after the Crises*. Oxford: Westview Press.

Marcus, G. (1986) 'Contemporary problems of ethnography in a world system', in G. E. Marcus and J. Clifford (eds), *Writing Culture: The Poetics and Politics of Ethnography*. Berkeley: University of California Press.

Merleau-Ponty, M. (1962) *Phenomenology of Perception*. London: Routledge and Kegan Paul.

Middleton, L. (1999) *Disabled Children: Challenging Social Exclusion*. London: Blackwell.

Priestley, M. (1998) 'Childhood disability and disabled childhoods: agendas for research', *Childhood*, 5(2): 207–23.

Priestley, M., Corker, M. and Watson, N. (1999) 'Unfinished business: disabled children and disability identities', *Disability Studies Quarterly*, 19(2): 90–8.

Seidman, S. (1994) 'Introduction', in S. Seidman (ed.), *The Postmodern Turn: New Perspectives on Social Theory*. Cambridge: Cambridge University Press.

Shakespeare, T. (1994) 'Dustbins for disavowal: cultural representation of disabled people', *Disability and Society*, 9(3): 283–301.

Shakespeare, T. (1997) 'Researching disabled sexuality', in C. Barnes and G. Mercer (eds), *Doing Disability Research*. Leeds: Disability Press.

Shakespeare, T., Gillespie-Sells, K. and Davies, D. (1996) *The Sexual Politics of Disability: Untold Desires*. London: Cassell.

Shakespeare, T. and Watson, N. (1998) 'Theoretical perspectives on research with disabled children', in C. Robinson and K. Stalker (eds), *Growing up with Disability*. London: Jessica Kingsley.

Thomas, C. (1999) *Female Forms: Experiencing and Understanding Disability*. Buckingham: Open University Press.

Thorne, B. (1993) *Gender Play: Girls and Boys in Schools*. New Brunswick: Rutgers University Press.

Tyler, S. (1986) 'Postmodern ethnography: from document of the occult to occult document', in J. Clifford and G. Marcus (eds), *Writing Culture: The Poetics and Politics of Ethnography*. Berkeley: University of California Press, pp. 122–40.

Willis, P. (1977) *Learning to Labour*. Aldershot: Gower.

Woodhead, M. (1999) 'Reconstructing developmental psychology: some first steps', *Children and Society*, 13(1): 2–20.

13

Estranged-Familiarity

Rod Michalko

Far from being unambiguous, transparent and static, 'knowledge and know-ing' are wrapped in ambiguity and opaqueness and are steeped in the con-stant flux of cultural movement. The 'knower', too, as postmodern theory has taught us, is cloaked in such ambiguity and movement. The process of know-ledge production is surrounded by issues of authority and legitimacy. What counts as knowledge? Who counts as a knowing subject? These are questions that have been raised by postmodernism, thus problematizing more trad-itional versions of knowledge and knowing. Traditionally, the 'knowing sub-ject' has been understood as one who knows by virtue of her methodological ability to remove her subjectivity. This removal of subjectivity has been con-ceived of as a development of a standpoint (often a scientific one) which permits the knower to 'see objectively'.

In the following pages, I will attempt to problematize this version of knowledge through addressing the roles of 'seeing' and of 'sight' as they play themselves out in the discourse that comes to signify the 'knowing subject'. I will make use of an interaction I was present at between Jenny, an eight-year-old blind girl, and her Orientation and Mobility instructor, Cheryl. Cheryl was teaching Jenny how to use the white cane. What follows is based on some 'observations' Jenny made during one of these lessons. As a way to enter Jenny's observations, her knowledge of the world, I begin with the work of Donna Haraway.

> There is a premium on establishing the capacity to see from the peripheries and the depths. But here lies a serious danger of romanticizing and/or appropriating the vision of the less powerful while claiming to see from their positions. To see from below is neither easily learned nor unproblematic, even if 'we' 'naturally' inhabit the great underground terrain of subjugated knowledges. (Haraway, 1998: 193)

It is often the case that danger accompanies that which comes at a premium. Developing the capacity to see from the periphery or from the depths (from the margins) is undoubtedly a premium, but it too comes with dangers. There are the dangers of romanticization and of appropriation of which

Haraway speaks, but there are others. I will address one of these – one which I consider to be especially cogent for disabled people as well as for the ongoing development of disability studies.

Periphery, depths, below, underground, margins – all of these are apt metaphors for the equally metaphoric imagined geographical location of disabled people. After all, we (disabled people) live somewhere in the midst of the socially organized ideas and practices of society. Where we live, however, is rarely experienced as 'in-the-midst'; indeed, we often experience our geography as bordering the hustle and bustle of this midst. To stay with this spatial and thus visual metaphor, we see this midst from below, we look up at it; we see it from the margins, we look at it from across a border; we experience it from where we live.

Like any location, this one too has its local knowledges, not the least of which is that, while this locale is *in* society, it is not in the *midst* of it. It is within this piece of local knowledge that danger lurks. Unlike some dangers which are relatively clear and even marked with warning signs, this one is not obvious at all and there are no warning signs posted; this is what makes it the most dangerous of all dangers. This is the danger that comes from seeing local knowledge as just that, local. The danger arises when such knowledge is understood as mere experience, and thus relevant *only* in and to a particular locale. Even celebrations of the recognition of knowledge as *located*,[1] celebrations that stretch from Nietzsche to classical anthropology, from Mannheim to postmodernism, contain an element of this danger. What counts as knowledge in one locale does not in another and such local knowledge is often seen as detrimental to moving from one locale to another.

Let me give an example of this danger as it relates to disability, in particular blindness. On one of my research outings a few years ago, I accompanied an Orientation and Mobility (O&M) instructor, Cheryl, on her lesson with an eight-year-old blind girl, Jenny. Jenny is totally blind and has been so since birth. At the time, she was attending 'blind school', as she put it, a school some fifteen hundred miles from her home. Jenny made the two-hour plane ride to her school in the autumn, returning home during school holidays and, of course, for summer vacation. During this particular summer, Jenny was beginning to learn to use the white cane; she was receiving O&M instruction.

I was at Cheryl's side as we walked down the street following Jenny, who was only a few feet in front of us using her new white cane. Suddenly, Jenny's white cane struck something at the edge of the pavement and, just as suddenly, Jenny stopped and exclaimed 'What's this?!' Like a good O&M instructor, Cheryl said, 'What do you think it is?' Jenny said that she didn't know. 'Like a tree, like a dead one or something,' Jenny offered. 'No,' said the good instructor, 'think. Try again. What do you think would be just off the sidewalk there?' Jenny kept touching the object, saying that she did not know what it was. More encouragement from the instructor and more increasingly frustrated I-don't-knows from Jenny.

Finally, and with much frustration, Jenny said, 'What's this, Rod?' Like a not-so-good sociologist, 'A telephone pole,' I said. 'Telephone pole!' Jenny repeated several times. 'Yeah,' I said, 'a telephone pole.' Again, Jenny asked me what it was. Again, I told her it was a telephone pole. Quiet now, Jenny kept touching the pole. Then, she said, 'Rod, is there a phone somewhere on this pole?' I was about to tell her that there wasn't, but suddenly I realized that I didn't know; maybe there was a phone at the top of the pole. Because of my visual impairment, I couldn't see to the top of the pole and even though I never had before, I now wondered whether there was a phone up there, maybe for maintenance purposes; I really didn't know. I immediately turned to sighted Cheryl and asked her if there was a phone at the top of the pole. She laughed and said that there wasn't. Jenny then asked why it was called a telephone pole if there wasn't a phone on it. I explained that there were wires at the top of the pole that went to the tops of the houses, down through the walls and that that's where telephones were plugged in. Jenny seemed to accept this explanation but continued to touch the pole.

After touching the pole a little while longer, her hands moving around and up it, Jenny asked, 'How high is it?' I looked up at the pole and lazily tried to judge its height. 'I don't know,' I said, 'it's pretty high.' 'I think it's as high as the sky,' Jenny said. I told her that I thought she was right. A few more seconds of touching the pole and Jenny changed her mind and did so quite emphatically. 'No, it doesn't go to the sky.' I asked her why she changed her mind. Jenny explained, 'If they went up to the sky, then planes would bump into them.' She said that the plane she took to and from school never bumped into any telephone poles. Although the plane ride was bumpy sometimes, Jenny explained that it wasn't from bumping into telephone poles. I asked her about this too. Jenny said that the flight attendant sometimes takes her into the cockpit of the plane to talk to the pilot. She said that the pilot told her that 'turulance', as she put it, made the plane ride bumpy and, therefore, it could not be telephone poles that did so. I told her that she was probably right and, even though Jenny was reluctant to leave the telephone pole, we moved on and the lesson with Cheryl continued.

Except for telling me that there was no phone on top of the pole, Cheryl remained quiet during this entire exchange. After dropping Jenny at her home following the lesson and returning to her car, however, Cheryl broke her silence and did so dramatically. She chided me for not letting Jenny figure out for herself that what her cane struck was a telephone pole. But she was especially vehement about something else; Cheryl said that I had given Jenny an 'unrealistic picture of telephone poles'. She said, 'You gotta be very careful with congenitally blind kids.' Cheryl elaborated by saying that totally blind kids 'don't have concept development'. I asked Cheryl to elaborate further and I was very surprised by her response. She explained that Jenny had no concept of the sky and what it was. What surprised me was how Cheryl so confidently 'knew' that Jenny was bereft of the concept of the sky when she (Jenny) so confidently spoke of it. Language and concepts did not seem to have any connection at all . . . in Cheryl's eyes. Jenny's explanation of telephone poles, aeroplanes and the sky apparently had no effect on Cheryl. Cheryl concluded by saying that she had a lot of work to do with Jenny on the concept of the sky, now that I had given her (Jenny) an 'unrealistic picture'. Finally, and by way of driving home the point to me, Cheryl gave me one more illustration. She said that Jenny once told her that carrots were little round circles. This was wrong, according to Cheryl, and she took Jenny to a supermarket to 'see real carrots', as she put it. Cheryl was amazed at Jenny's response to 'real carrots'. Jenny told Cheryl that she liked the carrots better when they were little circles. Cheryl used this example to demonstrate just how much work on concept development she had to do with Jenny.

Cheryl is right, in one way. Jenny is blind and when this is 'seen' as 'Jenny can't see', what can she possibly know about the sky? The sky, after all, cannot be touched and even when it is windy or when a smog fills the sky, no one speaks of hearing or smelling the sky. The sky can only be seen. And carrots are not little round circles, after all. Cheryl does have a lot of work to do; it is the work of enlightening the 'ignorance' which comes from Jenny's inability to see. But there is another way to understand this story being told in these Orientation and Mobility lessons – a story which lies buried and thus outside the 'field of vision' of the objective knowledge (sight)/objective knower (seeing subject) narrative.

We can treat this story as narrating two pieces of local knowledge – two knowledges – one of the sky and one of carrots – located in the space of blindness. Jenny depicted knowledges, of the sky and of carrots, to Cheryl and me, and did so from the location (standpoint) of blindness. Cheryl saw a problem with this depiction; the problem was that Jenny's knowledge was local and thus, in the case of the carrots, Jenny's knowledge was wrong and, in the case of the sky, simply non-existent. It was knowledge gleaned from the location of blindness and thus defective. Cheryl learned *nothing* of the sky or of carrots from Jenny. Cheryl learned only what she already knew – that Jenny needed a lot of work on concept development.

Jenny was learning how to use a white cane as a mobility device and she was learning about carrots. But there was a hidden curriculum and Jenny was learning something else – she was learning that she had local knowledge, knowledge that came to her *through her blindness*. Herein lies the danger of local knowledge; Jenny is learning that her knowledge is located *only* in the space of her blindness and that this knowledge does not count and is even defective in the imagined geography of sightedness. Jenny is learning that her space of blindness is a private space and that it is a detriment to her movement and understanding of the public space of seeing and sights. Jenny is learning that the *sensus privatus*, which is her blindness, neither belongs nor counts in the *sensus communus* of the 'sighted world'.

Jenny's depiction of her local knowledge of the sky and of carrots taught Cheryl that there is indeed work to be done; it taught her nothing of seeing and sight. This is not surprising since, for Cheryl, Jenny's knowledge of the world was located 'in her eyes' (Magee and Milligan, 1995: 45) and since her eyes did not work, neither did her knowledge. Jenny's eyes did not see and so her knowledge was local to blindness in so far as it was bereft of visual concepts, concepts which, according to Cheryl (rehabilitation), need to be developed.

But the development of these concepts is not so easy; it is not merely a matter of explaining them to Jenny, as I did in the case of telephone poles, or even of demonstrating them, as Cheryl did in the case of the carrots. There is a much more fundamental starting point to Jenny's development of visual concepts than this. Jenny must first be convinced that what she sees (experiences) is wrong and incorrect; indeed, she must be convinced that her sensory experience of the world is defective and that this *defect* is detrimental both to her coming to know the world and her participation in it. Jenny must cross the border from blindness into sightedness and she *must*, according to rehabilitation, leave blindness behind in order to make this crossing effectively (Michalko, 1999: 96–102). After all, blindness would only mess up the 'sighted world' with 'defect', with telephone poles that reach the sky and with little round circles of carrots.

This understanding of blindness did not allow Cheryl to see anything in Jenny other than the lack of visual concept development. When, for example, Jenny told Cheryl that she liked carrots 'better' when they were little round circles, Cheryl 'heard' the need for 'a lot of work'. She 'heard' Jenny's remarks as a lack of the understanding of what carrots are and not as her preference for eating carrots when they were cooked. Cheryl also told me that it was wrong of me to let Jenny think that the sky 'was only as high as a telephone pole'. This was more puzzling to me than the carrots, since it presupposed some finite point at which the sky began and the earth ended. Jenny's comments on the sky did not generate any wonder or even curiosity in Cheryl regarding the received knowledge of her homeland, the 'sighted world'. And why should it? For Cheryl, knowledge of the world is widespread and not local. Not only is Cheryl's knowledge 'localized in her eyes', everyone's is, and this transforms any sense of local knowledge into the ubiquitous and global knowing and knowledge that comes, and comes so 'naturally', with sight.

But what of Jenny? What will she make of all this Orientation and Mobility, this concept development, this rehabilitation? What will she make of the understanding that what she sees is defective? Like other blind people, Jenny did learn that most people see and that the world is seeable. She did develop an image of what it means to see. Jenny even learned to imitate[2] this knowledge – she learned to use phrases such as 'See you later' and she even learned to look towards the voice of the person with whom she was speaking, she learned to make 'eye contact'. Jenny learned many more things about the sighted world as well. In short, Jenny became very familiar with the sighted world in which she lived.

Well and good – but dangerous. The danger is that Jenny may lose her self in this familiarity. Jenny may become so familiar with the 'sighted world' that she may come to identify closely with it – so close, in fact, that she may come to *see* herself as a sighted person with the sight missing or, in the vernacular of the day, as a person *with* a disability. Jenny may come to 'see' her local knowledge as local and, as such, as irrelevant, defective and even as detrimental to treating her blindness as happenstance and thus as an obstacle that must be overcome in order to know and participate in the 'sighted world'. Like Cheryl, Jenny may learn *nothing* about her self, others and the world *from her blindness*. She may emerge from that 'underground terrain of subjugated knowledge' of which Haraway speaks, from the terrain she so 'naturally' inhabits.

This is the danger of which I wrote earlier. It is the danger of losing focus on the view from below, from the periphery, from the margin – from disability. It is the danger of losing the dialectic of an 'estranged-familiarity' (Michalko, 1999: 106–13) held out to us as a possibility of our disabilities. It is the danger, to borrow from Oliver (1996: 95–109), of being a 'non-walker' who becomes so familiar with walking that her non-walking loses its estrangement and becomes nothing other than 'strange'. The underground terrain which harbours the local knowledge of non-walking is discarded in favour of the more generalized familiar knowledge and the ideological and hegemonic 'goodness' of walking. It is to treat as *real* Oliver's (*ibid.*) desire for leglessness, and thus legs, to be irrelevant. It is for Jenny to treat her knowledge *in blindness* as irrelevant. It is to annihilate any border between knowledge from below and from above and it is to annihilate any estrangement *within* those of us who come above ground and develop a familiarity with those who so 'naturally' move there. If this desire is realized, what would become of disability studies? And, more importantly, would disabled people then move 'in the midst' of society? Even though these questions are not answerable in any direct way, they do deserve some attention.

Cheryl does recognize both estrangement and familiarity in Jenny, but this recognition posits the one *against* the other. Familiarity, for Cheryl, is the goal of Orientation and Mobility while estrangement is the barrier to such an end. That telephone poles reach the sky and that carrots are little round circles are experiences and concepts that represent an estrangement from the 'sighted world'. For Cheryl, these experiences are generated from *inside* the estrangement of blindness and are thus *outside* the familiarity of sightedness. Cheryl's goal for Jenny – the work that needs to be done – is to 'rehabilitate' this estrangement, this inside 'view', by replacing it with the more familiar 'view' *from* the sighted world – a view which is still outside of Jenny's 'point of view'. Cheryl's goal is to transform Jenny's estranged-familiarity into familiarity *only*; Cheryl's work is oriented to transforming Jenny's wonder regarding the sky and telephone poles into no wonder at all.

Such a goal, however, presupposes the binary oppositional and exclusionary character of estranged-familiarity. Nothing can be gained from the 'inside of blindness', especially when the goal is to attain the 'outside of sightedness'. Cheryl (rehabilitation) must dispense with the former in order to attain the latter and must do so by formulating the two as disparate categories which are not amenable to integration. Only Jenny can be integrated, according to rehabilitation. But this integration involves the need for Jenny to dispense with her estrangement (her blindness) and live strictly and only within the familiarity of sightedness. This rehabilitation version of integration *requires* that blindness and sightedness be 'seen' as opposite to one another where the former is conceived of as an 'unrealistic' expression of the 'reality' of the latter. No integration between the two, no conversation, no dialogue is possible. The 'rehabilitation' of estrangement amounts to treating it as the result of a 'defective' physiology – the 'defective' view *from the inside* of blindness – and to remedy this 'defect' through rehabilitation's version of 'work'. Cheryl's first task is to convince Jenny of the defective character of the *view* from *inside* blindness and then to *give* Jenny the 'correct' view. Thus, the only thing to be done with estrangement – the view from the inside – is to dispense with it.

But, as Diana Fuss (1991: 1) says, 'The figure inside/outside cannot be easily or even finally dispensed with; it can only be worked on and worked over – itself turned inside out to expose its critical operations and interior machinery.' Try as she might, Cheryl *cannot* dispense with Jenny's estrangement. No matter how much work Cheryl does with (on-to?) Jenny, she (Jenny) will always have her 'view' from inside blindness.

The difficulty is that Cheryl conceives of estranged-familiarity or, as Fuss puts it, inside/outside, not as a 'figure' representing a standpoint, but instead as two distinct and measurable ways of sensing the world – the one wrong and the other correct. For Cheryl, estrangement is strictly and only the opposite of familiarity, the inside bears the same relation to the outside and, most importantly, blindness is the opposite of sight.

Still, Jenny is like everyone else; everyone has an estrangement, an inside, a subjectivity. But not all subjectivities and their knowledges are interpreted under the rubric of the 'like-everyone-else'. Those of disabled people certainly are not. Jenny's knowledge of telephone poles, the sky and of carrots is not shared by everyone else. What is to be done with Jenny's subjectivity and knowledges? Cheryl's rehabilitation choice? – work on it, work over it, expose its operations and interior machinery – but not in the way Fuss is suggesting. Cheryl's work is composed of *showing* Jenny that her subjective knowledges are not only irrelevant, but are detrimental to the acquisition of objective (real) knowledges, knowledges that come *from within sight.* The interior machinery that Cheryl 'sees' *in* Jenny's blindness is the *faulty* machinery of eyesight *broken* by blindness.

The danger of treating local knowledge and of treating disability as irrelevant is that the 'view from disability' may be dismissed by others and ignored by us (disabled people). But the danger, as Fuss (*ibid.,* p. 2) puts it, is that 'the figure inside/outside [estranged-familiarity], which encapsulates the structure of language, repression, and subjectivity, also designates the structure of exclusion, oppression, and repudiation.' This is the danger that hovers over disabled people when we and others desire to treat our disabilities as irrelevant. If we do so, then we will see nothing wrong with excluding, oppressing and repudiating our 'view' from the inside. After all, who among us would not desire to exclude the 'view of distortion'. Orientation and Mobility is teaching Jenny just that – to dispense with the distortion that comes *from her blindness.* This is the 'real tragedy' of disability – the tragedy of the oppression that seduces disabled people into dispensing with *their* 'view' from disability, a seduction enacted by the imagined figure of the 'like-everyone-else' held out to disabled people as a 'real' possibility. And yet, the reality of such a possibility is always dispensed with by the 'interior machinery' of able-bodiedness, a machinery that continuously works to exclude disability as itself a 'real possibility'.

And what of disability studies? What danger lies in wait for it when the subjective knowledges of disability are conceived of as local and thus as irrelevant? Without a version of local knowledge as estranged-familiarity, and without the inside/outside understood as a *figure* that acts to expose critically the operations and interior machinery of the *background* of 'normalcy' against which this figure stands, subjective knowledges *from disability* 'run' the danger, as Haraway says, of being appropriated, romanticized and melded into the background of the 'like-everyone-else'. This appropriation would lead the figure of disability studies into the background of the 'study of disability', with its programme of prevention and rehabilitation from the biomedical side, together with its programme of documenting 'negative attitudes' toward disability from the social scientific and humanities side. This is dangerous, and this is why we need Jenny's telephone polls that reach the sky and her little round circles of carrots. Disability is *precisely* the turbulence, as Jenny puts it, so necessary to those who understand and experience the world as a taken-for-granted unified reality seeable and knowable *only* from eyes that see.

Notes

1. For an excellent contemporary feminist development of the social location of knowledge, see Smith (1987, 1999).
2. I develop the idea of mimesis in relation to disability in my manuscript 'Politicizing Disability', currently being reviewed at the University of Toronto Press.

References

Fuss, D. (1991) *Inside/Out: Lesbian Theories, Gay Theories*. London: Routledge.

Haraway, D. (1998) 'The persistence of vision', in Nicholas Mizoeff (ed.), *The Visual Culture Reader*. London: Routledge, pp. 191–8.

Magee, B. and Milligan, M. (1995) *On Blindness*. Oxford: Oxford University Press.

Michalko, R. (1999) *The Two in One: Walking with Smokie, Walking with Blindness*. Philadelphia: University of Temple Press.

Oliver, M. (1996) *Understanding Disability: From Theory to Practice*. New York: St Martin's Press.

Smith, D. (1987) *The Everyday World as Problematic: A Feminist Sociology*. Toronto: University of Toronto Press.

Smith, D. (1999) *Writing the Social: Critique, Theory and Investigations*. Toronto: University of Toronto Press.

14

Image Politics without the Real: Simulacra, Dandyism and Disability Fashion

Petra Kuppers

Introduction

These would be the successive phases of the image:

1. It is the reflection of a basic reality.
2. It masks and perverts a basic reality.
3. It masks the absence of a basic reality.
4. It bears no relation to any reality whatever: it is its own pure simulacrum.
(Baudrillard, 1988: 170)

Postmodern ways of thinking of the world, and their icons of the hyperreal and the simulacra, fascinated broad sections of scholars, students and the media from the mid-1980s onwards. For Baudrillard, the postmodern simulacrum emerges out of historical change in the relationship between society and 'the Real'. After previous ages, in which the hierarchical relationship between something 'real' and its representation are undermined, the simulacrum of the postmodern period occurs when 'the Real' has become an obsolescent category. No 'originals' exist, and we live in an endless string of references, discourses, images. For Baudrillard, this state is tinged with melancholy – a dangerous state – for it can give rise to a hunger for overwhelming images to live by, to anchor social reality in one set of images, rather than live with the constant onslaught of diverse images – in a word, 'fascism, that overdose of a powerful referential in a society which cannot terminate its mourning' (Baudrillard, 1988: 181). But, at the same time, the postmodern order of the simulacrum also has other effects on the efficacy of political action, and the sphere of politics:

For example: it would be interesting to see whether the repressive apparatus would not react more violently to a simulated hold up than a real one? For a real hold up only upsets the order of things, the right of property, whereas a simulated hold up interferes with the very principle of reality. Transgression and violence are less serious, for they only contest the *distribution* of the real. Simulation is infinitely more dangerous since it always suggests, over and above its object, that *law and order themselves might really be nothing more than a simulation.* (Baudrillard, 1988: 177)

The explanatory power and seduction of these thought structures are exciting and still retain their glamour. But as the world around us changes, cultural studies moves on from the image-obsessed 1980s and early 1990s. The order of simulacra, where references are free-floating and endlessly manipulated, has given way to a vision of society which acknowledges the power of discourse in interaction with the viewer's agency. Media literacy and a renewed respect for the abilities of viewers mean that few people in the twenty-first century would subscribe to the idea that people really associate shaped turkey chunks with the freedom of open farm country, smoking with cowboys and computer game shoot-ups with the everyday activity of crime prevention.

At the same time, though, all the above examples of connotations have a place in the understanding of the way that cultural meaning shifts and manifests itself. It is just that the 'complete headspace' world does not seem to have arrived yet. Thus, people know about hen batteries and flesh factories, lung cancer and the physical pain of injury. They negotiate a world which is still shaped by media images (how many people have been inside a factory farm?), but where ethical decisions combined with personal, bodily experience steer the path through the plethora of available images.

The early postmodern vision of a helpless viewer bombarded with imagery can be seen to be tempered by those strands of post-structuralist thinking that describe agency and power as a complex network of shifting structures. But the shifted political terrain outlined in Baudrillard's quotation above has made its impact felt on identity politics and their strategies which can be seen to have moved away from 'positive images' to a more complex 'image politics'. Disability studies in the humanities has taken up discourse analysis of cultural representations, the placement of disability as a signifier and cultural marker (see, for example, Hevey, 1992; Thomson, 1996; Mitchell and Snyder, 1997), but so far, very few contemporary image exegeses exist that go far beyond the modernist paradigm asking for either 'truthful depiction' or 'positive images'.

In this article I concern myself with these tenuous relationships between images and society – linkages that can be established between image, 'live person' and viewer in an image-saturated, fast-lived media environment, and the opportunities that the death of the 'natural' can offer to contemporary disability representation. In particular, I focus on representations and the media love affair with (some) stylish disabled people. With this, I circumvent the basic, modernist, feminist, identity politics question – is this image a good thing? – and instead find postmodern, ambivalent answers which see these images as part of a living cultural landscape.

The images under discussion all negate the 'natural' relationship between surface and interior (or representation and the real) – they belong to genres in which the modern coincidence of meaning and shape is overtaken by the baroque, excessive, self-referential, quotational postmodern simulacrum: '[t]he territory no longer precedes the map, nor survives it. Henceforth, it is the map that engenders the territory – PRECESSION OF SIMULACRA' (Baudrillard, 1983: 1). For identity politics, the age of simulacra means that identity is always already map rather than essence. The self is not clothing itself in its 'natural' clothes, but chooses (consciously and unconsciously) its social persona from an array of imagery which makes up the legend of the social map. But the act of choice itself is already part of this world of the simulacrum: this 'choice' is layered into the map of shopping, fashion, representation, convention, genericity, and refers to no single moment of self-directed activity. In the world of simulacra, the self is not originary, but surface effect.

Constellation beauty

To trace discourses of surface and resistance, of quotation and negation of any grounding 'natural', I will investigate the uncanny resemblance between aspects of two cultural moments. First, the 1890s, with its *Yellow Book*, the illustrations of Aubrey Beardsley and the fashionable dandies in their salons, and second, the 1990s, where disabled people feature as fashion highlights, and where contemporary theorists make disabled people carry the connotations of the postmodern condition. I do not propose a similarity or coincidence between these two *fin-de-siècle* moments. Rather, I attempt to make sense of some current images through recourse to the ways that people at the end of the last century engaged with personae who contained 'elements of grace, wisdom, wit, reserve, nervousness, masochism and perversion mixed in strange but attractive proportions', as Fletcher remarked on the dandy, Ronald Firbank, in Horder (1977: 23).

I employ the mechanism of 'constellation' which does not seek correspondences and mirroring, but instead searches for illuminating differences, connotations and generative echoes. I am embracing a methodology that understands the creation of meaning in a field of movement: meaning is created in acts, and is neither fixed nor stable or unitary, but part of the shifting, realigning field of simulacra. Attention to the playing field of meaning, the realms of the legible, can help to focus on the mechanisms that complicate attempts to categorize images into specific social and political agencies. In keeping with the politics of simulacra, I do not attempt to engage with the question of whether specific images of disabled people are 'positive' or 'negative'. I open up my enquiry to questions that need to be answered if we want to move on representational politics, and address the representational economics of our times. What makes images legible, what is the condition of beauty, power and strength in these images, how does the construction of categories such as disability and gender interact with the very construction of the concepts of 'beauty', 'truth' and 'agency'? What new maps emerge?

The images that are at the core of this investigation are fashion photographs created by fashion designer Alexander McQueen and photographer Nick Knight in 1998. The feature, which casts some disabled people as fashion models bedecked in expensive haute couture clothes, was the cover story 'Fashion-Able' of the September 1998 issue of the magazine *Dazed and Confused*. The shoot reverberated through the British and international press, and coverage of the images was given in the *Guardian*, *The Sunday Times* and other newspapers.

These images accompany a rising interest in disabled people – not as benefit recipients, not as politicians, not as social commentators, but as style icons. Certain phenomenological aspects of impairing conditions have previously interested performance artists and avant-garde film-makers (for instance, around the figure of Bob Flanagan; see Kauffman, 1998), but the mainstream reception of disability (real or not) as sexy, stylish, interesting is more recent. The database that allows me to make this claim is still relatively small. It includes films such as David Cronenberg's *Crash* (1996), where the sexual attractiveness of amputees and car crash victims is playfully or offensively invoked. Detective novels have discovered the disabled person as hero rather than victim. *The Coffin Dancer* (1998) and *The Bone Collector* (1997) by Jeffery Deaver feature Lincoln Rhyme, a paraplegic detective surrounded by expensive equipment and a sexy, also disabled, love interest. Rhyme's portrayal and narrative placing seem to exceed the various categories of 'crip' as narrative device. Another example of the glamorous disabled person can be found in Sally Potter's *The Tango Lesson* (1997). In this film, David Toole, a highly visible disabled dancer, well known in Britain, appears as a fashion photographer in a dream sequence, racing on his hands through a park, accompanied by lifeless high fashion beauties. TV productions, such as the dance film *Outside In* (1995) by the dance group CandoCo, also work with aesthetics that cite the history of the freak but query any one narrative of disability as well as conventional understandings of 'positive images' and 'normalization'. Whether legislation such as the US's ADA (Americans with Disabilities Act) or the DDA (Disability Discrimination Act) in the UK is cause or effect of the increasing visibility of disabled people is secondary to my argument – I am interested in the kinds of images that comprise 'Chic Disability'.

The image of the 'Fashion-Able' shoot that I discuss depicts Mat Fraser, a rock musician and actor who describes himself as a 'Thalidomide Warrior', and who has short upper arms and no forearms. Fraser is one of a group of

UNIVERSITY OF WINCHESTER
LIBRARY

disabled people who are relatively visible in the UK. He has been featured on the various disability magazine programmes on UK television, and he and his music have appeared in the short film *Freak Fucking Basics* (1995), which has been screened at venues such as the British Film Institute and the Norwich Film Festival as well as in disability specific contexts. In 2000, Fraser's moderation of a Channel 4 show *Freak Out* led to accusations within the disability scene of 'selling out', embracing a disempowering freak stereotype in order to make trash television. These accusations were answered by other viewers, who saw any mainstream visibility of disabled people as a powerful statement (National Disability Arts Forum, 2000). These discussions surrounding Fraser as 'commercial star' bring to the forefront the need to work on what contemporary image politics might be.

In the photograph (see Fig. 1), we see Fraser in a relatively close shot, lying on his side. His head, shaved apart from a strip of longer hair running over his scalp, takes up the most space in the image. Under his face, with his intensely blue eyes and a generous, red, wet mouth, are his two hands. He rests his chin on one of them, the other is lying by his side. We also see the upper part of his torso, clad in a golden-green waistcoat, which the accompanying text identifies as a 'hand-made plastic waistcoat

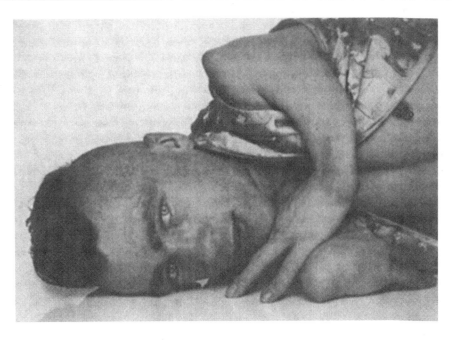

Figure 1 Mat Fraser. Photo: Nick Knight; art direction: Alexander McQueen for *Dazed and Confused* magazine.

by Catherine Blades'. The waistcoat reveals one of his nipples, which is pierced with a small silver ring. The image connotes intimacy: it is unconventionally close to the viewer. This makes it hard to take in the whole picture at once. My own gaze travelled from Fraser's face to the right of the photo, from the lustre of his hair, to the shine in his eyes to the shiny silver in his nipple.

In the *Guardian* issue in which this image appeared, a quotation by Fraser ran beneath the image: 'As disabled people, we are invisible, we're suffering from apartheid . . . You've got to declare yourself disabled and beautiful.' The image declares Fraser beautiful, indeed. But what are the conditions of that male beauty? Several categories mix and merge in Fraser's photo: he is depicted within the visual conventions and image repertory of femininity. He is passive, lying down, lit beautifully to emphasize the colouring of his eyes and mouth, and dressed in gold (the waistcoat) and silver (the ring). Wearing jewellery is another gender-bending attribute of the image. The 'punk' connotations of the nipple ring and the shaved hair and lock are usurped by the feminizing, soft aspects of the image. Although Fraser does not look androgynous himself (the *Guardian* describes him as 'six-foot tall, with an athletic physique and a startlingly handsome face'; Frankel, 1998: 16), the appeal of the photo is androgynous. Contemporary fashion photography delights in upsetting gender categories, and current advertisements ranging from Gap to the toiletries of Armani create a 'unisex' look underscored by the long hairdos of young male models and the thinness of the women. But the effect here is different. I would posit that the photo does not so much create a unisex appeal, but that it echoes a register of male fashion iconicity that goes back to the figure of the dandy.

Artificial delight

The dandy is a figure that excited French, and later English, commentators on society. A development of the Renaissance and Regency beau, the dandy became a focal point for the heated discussions about the relationship between society and art in the second half of the nineteenth century. At the core of dandyism is the delight in artifice, and the celebration and cult of self in careful presentation and self-stylization. The self became simulated – indistinguishable from the 'real' body, and more 'real' and present than weak copies of conventional masculinity. Dandyism is predominantly associated with modes of masculinity – the issues regarding control and the balance between the 'artificial' and the 'natural' are historically and discursively different for modes of femininity.

Richard Pine quotes Charles Baudelaire, whose work *The Painter of Modern Life* became a core text of a debate in which the relationship between aesthetics and ethics is traced, and which influenced dandy figures such as Oscar Wilde:

> 'Evil' says Baudelaire, equating 'evil' with 'crime', 'happens without effort, naturally, fatally', where 'Good' which he equates with 'beauty', 'is always the produce of some art'. Baudelaire can then announce: 'I am thus led to regard external finery as one of the signs of the primitive nobility of the human soul' – a brilliant extrapolation of the outward adornment of the dandy as the sign of an inner 'beauty' or 'goodness' which is a noble superiority of man to nature. (Pine, 1988: 20, quoting Baudelaire, 1964: 32)

The representation of Mat Fraser recalls some of these attributes: the body as a self-fashioned art object, the 'otherness' worn outwards on one's sleeve. Identity is fashion, but fashion is more than just outer style, it also reveals itself as inner attitude, as Jules Barbey d'Aureville writes of the dandy:

> Dandyism is social, human and intellectual. It is not a suit of clothes, walking about by itself! . . . It is the particular way of wearing these clothes which constitutes Dandyism. One may be a dandy in creased clothes . . . Dandyism is a complete theory of life. (1897: 20)

Disability, gender, clothes, jewellery, hairstyle, the body itself can become 'a complete theory of life', a foregrounding of the wearing, not the being. Dandyism refers to the artifice, not to the registers of 'the natural'. To make artificial the natural, to blur the boundaries, is the aim of the Wildean dandy. The cult of the self foregrounds the constructed nature of selfhood. Fraser's self-aware referencing and playful citing of the categories of female traditional beauty and male counter-culture beauty creates for me a sense of artifice, even if Fraser's photo reveals more flesh than it conceals in clothes. The connotations of the flesh and the clothes become one: style, surface through and through. Micheál mac Liammóir describes Oscar Wilde as 'dandy of dress, dandy of speech, dandy of manner, dandy of wit, dandy even of ideas and intellect' (1978: 22) – fashion embraces everything, flesh, thought *and* clothes.

The Fraser photo clearly creates an intensity of sensual encounter, a field of textures and colour, which destabilizes gender connotations without obvious recourse to the conventions of drag. This attention to detail and surface pleasure links to the dandyism of the senses, which delights in the hypersensitive openness to exquisite stimulation. Oscar Wilde gave the name 'Orchid' to his friend and the illustrator of his books, Charles Ricketts, who, together with his partner Charles Shannon, inhabited 'The Vale', a house in London famous for its collections, its catholic splendour, its visual sensuality. It was the details, sumptuousness, proliferation of objects, surfaces, textures and colours associated with 'the connoisseurs' or Aesthetes which were ridiculed by the 'tweedy, pipe-smoking "Hearties" such as W. E. Henley or Rudyard Kipling' (Calloway, 1997: 44). Even in contemporary fashion photography, the viewer is likely to encounter male models in black and white, in austere arrangements or surrounded by woods, jungles or women, who are the carriers of the textured, sensual audience address. The open sensuality of Fraser's photograph marks it as 'other' even before the disability is read as a sign of social otherness.

The 'dandy of thought' can also be found in the presentation of Fraser's image. In order to trace this tradition, I need to refer to the intertextual framework of the photo. In the quotation that frames the photo, 'beauty' and self-stylization are referenced: the dandy is in pursuit of beauty, effortlessly, arriving on a wave which defines 'beauty' according to his standard, setting the trend. Disability, culturally linked to invisibility and the 'ugly', needs reperforming, reclaiming, remapping if it is to appear in the registers of the beautiful. The narcissistic body, beautiful *against* 'nature', is created. As was seen in the Baudelaire quotation, for the dandy of the late nineteenth century, the need for self-emancipation from the natural was imperative.

Rocking nature

In Fraser's artistic persona, this destabilization of the natural has been a recurrent theme. Fraser became known in the disability arts circuit through his in-your-face rock performances, in which he attacked the 'body fascism' of non-disabled culture. His texts courted offence, and his delivery equally played on the stereotype of the 'disabled beast'. The lyrics of his song *Outsiders* include:

> So! Let's strip down to the freak-fuckin' basics
> And address the ones to whom this idea makes sick [*sic*]
> Yes I have a penis why should it seem incredible
> That I'd like to have access to someone who'd find it edible?
> Does my physical difference put up a barrier?
> Are you scared I'll fuck your sister or even worse marry her?
> That's right I said fuck – do you find that offensive?
> I just wanna shake you up and maybe you will then give
> Consideration to the concept, that disabled people have passion
> And personally I'd like to work towards it becoming high fashion
> Please don't label me a perverted vulture
> All I've done is reject your body fascist culture . . . (Fraser, personal
>   communication)

In the genre of rock, Fraser addresses very similar issues to the ones that are referenced in his work with Alexander McQueen and Nick Knight. The effects of being labelled 'disabled' are here coupled with the citation of the hypersexual figure of the rock star, out to corrupt young girls. The audience address of rock – shock tactics, references to sexuality, the (particularly) American hysteria surrounding naming of genitalia and 'offensive content' in hard rock and metal lyrics – is brought together with the vocabulary of the disability movement which maps out a new territory ('barrier', 'access', 'disabled people', 'label', 'body culture').

Masculinity and its construction and the convention of the body beautiful are both at stake in the representation of men in the rock and fashion industries. The two industries create potentially opposing images of men. Within the rock world exists the figure of the rock beast, so aptly caricatured in the Jim Henderson Muppet, and hysterically referenced in the spoof rock documentary *This Is Spinal Tap* (1983). The figure refers to a voraciousness which deals with music, drum sticks, young female groupies, cocaine and guitars in similar fashion: they are all consumed and destroyed by the wild hero, by the man out of control, a law unto himself.

In the fashion world, though, masculinity is often referenced through control. This control and reticence creates a deep structure within the male fashion apparatus:

> [T]he rhetoric of men's fashion takes the form of a set of denials that include the following propositions: that there is no men's fashion, that men dress for fit and comfort, rather than for style; that women dress men . . ., that men who dress up are peculiar (one way or another); that men do not notice clothes; and that most men have not been duped into the endless pursuit of seasonal fads. (Craik, 1994: 176)

As an effect of homophobic fears, anxiety about gender roles and the need to be aloof, male fashion, with noticeable deviations such as the dandy period, has often been characterized by 'an aggressive indifference to dress and a silent avoidance of bodily display' (Pumphrey, 1989: 96). Even where that control is relaxed, it is only relaxed on the condition that it is already vouchsafed by other references. Thus, Barbara Vinken analyses Armani clothing and its nostalgic, postmodern citing of Italian neo-realism and working-class culture as well as sensual textures – this relaxation of male, body-denying discipline is only possible because of the references to power and riches embedded in the label Armani. The brand evokes a feudal past, a moment before the bourgeois emphasis on the work ethic.

> Armani's fashions suggest that one can have both: the new power consists in the fact that one can perform relaxed sensuality. 'Masculinity' is

guaranteed through citation of a heroic, male history, the history of the industrial proletariat, on whose labour modernity is founded. (Vinken, 1993: 90, my translation)

In her study of fashion, Craik delineates how new images of masculinity, such as the gentle 'new man' and the hedonistic 'new lad', transgress the codes of masculine restraint and control, but acknowledges that, ultimately, male fashion remains embedded in the registers of discipline, not in the all-embracing display of the peacock.

But the fringe spaces of social self-representation have often provided the source for playfulness, and relatively safe exploration of 'dangerous' images. This is the other side of Stallybrass and White's argument that the 'Other' has such an important status for the centre, for

> the top *includes* that low symbolically, as a primary eroticized constituent of its own fantasy life. The result is a mobile, conflictual fusion of power, fear and desire in the construction of subjectivity: a psychological dependence upon precisely those Others which are being rigorously opposed on the social level. It is for this reason that what is *socially* peripheral is so frequently *symbolically* central. (Stallybrass and White, 1986: 5)

Thus, the archetypal man-beast of rock (and, of course, the either disavowed or beastly sexuality of the construction of the disabled man) holds powerful connotations for a male identity which is held in place through careful control mechanisms. The collision of rock music and fashion has spawned surprises before – in 1991, *Vanity Fair* published a fashion shoot supplement on Calvin Klein jeans which depicted members of a rock band undressing themselves and a group of groupies in a wild orgy (Grant, 1992). In a similar fashion, Fraser's liminality as rock musician, actor and disabled man allows for a shoot which articulates sensitive areas of male self-representation.

What becomes symbolically central in this meeting of fashion, rock and disability with masculinity is the concept of the 'natural'. The natural becomes a pose, an artifice, a style; it becomes transposed into the world of the simulacra. Just as the 'rock beast' is a performance, not a 'natural' expression of overbearing masculinity, the 'natural' of the disabled body becomes problematic. Fraser adorns his body not only with silver rings and golden vests, but also with the conscious performance of his physicality. His physical difference, the short arms, is not naturalized, but is central to his presentation. The arms are central to the photo of his body – his hands frame his expressive mouth, the arm which reaches down from the top of the image to the floor dissects the image, providing a strong counterbalance to the eye that reads the image from left to right. In the song lyrics quoted above, when Fraser sings of his sexuality, it seems to be the sexuality of a 'disabled man', framed as a 'category', a social text, rather than of 'Mat Fraser' – his physicality is politicized, put into discourse, mapped and performed in his acts.

In the manner of camp performance, 'disability' and 'masculinity' are two categories that are cited in Fraser's performance. Framed within the discourse of fashion, both markers of identity become destabilized as 'natural' attributes – they enter the style of the dandy who plays on the limits. This foregrounding of the performative over the natural does not point to the absence of the performed (gender and disability) but to the heightening of the identity signs, those markers of social meaning, into style and fashion. Fraser's beauty is based on a complex negotiation of categories, and the emergent style owns more to the tactics of the play between categories than to the content of any of them.

Image nostalgia

At this point of my discussion, I have crossed from the nineteenth-century moment of the dandy into the late-twentieth-century/early-twenty-first century moment of the performative: this master sign of contemporary identity theory given contemporary currency in critical theory by Judith Butler. But my constellation of the two *fin de siècles* doesn't aim to conflate these two moments, but instead endeavours to bring out aspects of each that might illuminate the other. To see performativity within the horizon of a *fin-de-siècle* moment imbues it with the sadness of 'endings'. Like the dandy, the play with Fraser's image is bound by melancholia. For Baudelaire,

> Dandyism, an institution beyond the law, itself has rigorous laws which all its subjects must strictly obey . . . What then is this passion, which, becoming doctrine, has produced such a school of tyrants? (Baudelaire, 1964: 27)

The creativity of the dandy is always circumscribed. Activity and passivity are implicated in each other. Fraser can state that he wants to choose his 'constructed' image, perform his disability, not become normalized or invisible, but, at the same time, the choice is not fully his, and as one image complex, of disability, is undermined, another potentially equally repressive one, of masculinity and commodity, is cited. For the man of fashion, the dandy, holds the same problem that plagues contemporary identity politics. Fashion works within the realm of the legible, and therefore draws its material from the structures and meaningful signs of culture. In the age of the simulacra, this legible realm is the legend of the maps. Judith Butler is aware of the limits of the performative as a source of innovation:

The power of discourse to materialize its effects is thus consonant with the power of discourse to circumscribe the domain of intelligibility. Hence, the reading of 'performativity' as willful and arbitrary choice misses the point that the historicity of discourse and, in particular, the historicity of norms (the 'chains' of iteration invoked and dissimulated in the imperative utterance) constitute the power of discourse to enact what it names. (Butler, 1993: 187)

The playfulness of fashion, intent on realigning cultural signs into pleasurable new ensembles, has curious effects on people who embrace its methods. When the dandy mobilizes his whole being into style, into parade, into artifice, he is the powerful herald who proclaims that there is no 'innocence', no origin, no nature, no core truth. Aesthetics become ethics: the moral imperative is to embrace the artifice as the only possible human act. Executing a simulated hold-up, showing the construction of all images, is the political act of Baudrillard's order of simulacra.

Dandyfying disability does not mean to move away from the embodied experience of disability, but to place one's body fully within the stream of discourse. Contemporary theorists such as Baudrillard and Virilio have used the disabled body as metaphor for the postmodern condition – a move critiqued by disability scholars. But our bodies and our difference enter the market place of meaning, and it is more interesting to see how disabled people themselves (or manipulated by others interested in yet new forms of otherness) can explore the mechanisms of metaphor. In these pages, I have read one particular example of contemporary disability images as an attempt not to 'narrativize' disability, make it stand for something else, but as a potentially radical gesture of displaying the discursive character of bodies and identities by embracing the 'natural' as 'artifice'. The dandy stands on the limits of the individual and the norm. In the same way, the Fraser image is not merely a statement about either disability or masculinity, nor an individual image about one person's difference, but is instead an oscillating, complex play which potentially shows up either identity category as discursive and simulated. Framed by the institution of fashion photography, it is not easily readable – its politics are shrouded and, like the dandies of the 1890s, it is easy to dismiss the disabled fashion models as freaks and poseurs. Baudelaire's manifesto for the high dandies, such as Wilde and his friends, captures the curious mixture of agency and victimization, of ability and inability, which characterizes the passionate yet careless play of the dandy: 'Dandyism is the last glimmer of heroism and decadence; like the sunset of a dying star, it is glorious, without heat and full of melancholy' (Baudelaire, 1964: 29).

At the dawn and sunset of a millennium, many identity performances are equally characterized by glorious self-display while dimly aware of the spectre of powerlessness. After having shown the complexities and problems in reading an oppositional stance in a film which showcases black dandies and queer voguing, *Paris is Burning* (1991), Judith Butler writes:

> Performativity describes this relation of being implicated in that which one opposes, this turning of power against itself to produce alternative modalities of power, to establish a kind of political contestation that is not a 'pure' opposition, a 'transcendence' of contemporary relations of power, but a difficult labor of forging a future from resources inevitably impure. (Butler, 1993: 241)

An historic perspective on a particular phenomenon of self-stylization, and of the will to art, shows how the historic practice of performativity can be traced in lived negotiations between identity markers and social actors. This historic understanding of contemporary images and their problematic status within identity politics can help us as disabled scholars and artists to place ourselves within commodity culture, and within the postmodern order of the simulacrum. 'Purity' or, to refer to Baudelaire, 'innocence' needs to be given up as an aim, and instead the interventionist, situated and specific mobilization of categories can be embraced as the political aims of self-representation. As disabled people become stylish in the market place of global culture, even if on compromised terms, it is up to disabled artists to enter shifting territories.

A different version of this chapter was published in *Disability Studies Quarterly*, Summer 1999, 19(3): 196–202.

References

Barbey d'Aureville, J. A. (1897) *Of Dandyism and of George Brummell*, trans. Douglas Ainslie. London: J. M. Dent.

Baudelaire, C. (1964) *The Painter of Modern Life and Other Essays*, trans. Jonathan Mayne. New York: Da Capo Press.

Baudrillard, J. (1983) *Simulations*. New York: Semiotext(e).

Baudrillard, J. (1988) *Selected Writings*, ed. Mark Poser. Cambridge: Polity Press.

Butler, J. (1993) *Bodies That Matter: On the Discursive Limits of Sex*. New York: Routledge.

Calloway, S. (1997) 'Wilde and the dandyism of the senses', in P. Raby (ed.), *The Cambridge Companion to Oscar Wilde*. Cambridge: Cambridge University Press, pp. 34–54.

Craik, J. (1994) *The Face of Fashion: Cultural Studies in Fashion*. London: Routledge.

Frankel, S. (1998) 'Body beautiful', *Guardian*, 29 August: 14–19.

Grant, L. (1992) 'Can Calvin Klein escape?', *Los Angeles Times Magazine*, 23 February: 16–22.

Hevey, D. (1992) *The Creatures That Time Forgot: Photography and Disability Imagery.* London: Routledge.

Horder, M. (ed.) (1977) *Ronald Firbank: Memoirs and Critiques.* London: Duckworth.

Kauffman, L. (1998*) Bad Girls and Sick Boys: Fantasies in Contemporary Art and Culture.* Berkeley: University of California Press.

Liammóir, Micheál mac (1978) *The Importance of Being Oscar.* Dublin: Dolmen Press.

Mitchell, D. T. and Snyder, S. L. (1997) *The Body and Physical Difference. Discourses of Disability.* Ann Arbor: University of Michigan Press.

National Disability Arts Forum (2000) *EtCetera,* Issues 69–70, August–September, e-mail list.

Pine, R. (1988) *The Dandy and the Herald: Manners, Mind and Morals from Brummell to Durrell.* Houndsmill: Macmillan.

Pumphrey, M. (1989) 'Why do cowboys wear hats in the bath? Style politics for the older man', *Critical Quarterly,* 31(3): 78–100.

Stallybrass, P. and White, A. (1986) *The Politics and Poetics of Transgression.* London: Methuen.

Thomson, R. G. (1996) *Freakery: Cultural Spectacle and the Extraordinary Body.* New York: New York University Press.

Vinken, B. (1993) *Mode nach der Mode. Kleid und Geist am Ende des 20. Jahrhunderts.* Frankfurt am Main: Fischer.

15

De-gene-erates, Replicants and Other Aliens: (Re)defining Disability in Futuristic Film

Johnson Cheu

Introduction

Popular media is already pushing society toward a Utopian model of bodily perfection and cure. One need look no further than such movements as *Cure Autism Now*, the telethons to find a cure for various birth defects, impairments and illnesses, or the 'I'll-Walk-Again-Anything-Is-Possible' rhetoric of Christopher Reeve, to 'see' this medical 'truth'. With the recent cracking of genetic coding, opening up the possibility of genetic manipulation, a future where medical technology and genetic engineering will have advanced to the point where bodies can be genetically manipulated before birth, or treated and cured so as to make 'disability' obsolete, is not beyond the realm of possibility. In this 'medical model', disability becomes non-existent.

The eradication of disability is not a new theme in media. In early twentieth-century film, eugenics, in its various forms, was a recurring theme. Among the most famous of these films is a 1916 film, re-released in 1927, entitled *The Black Stork*. In the wake of the death of baby Bollinger, a 'defective' baby who was permitted to die at the urging of doctors, *The Black Stork* reaffirmed the public fear of 'defectives', thus spurring the idea that death is better than disability, if medical cure is not possible. Medical treatment was, in fact, available to baby Bollinger, but the 'gross physical and mental abnormalities would remain', and thus death was better (Pernick, 1996: 3–4). *Stork* traces the lives of two couples. One couple, despite doctors' orders that they should not marry because of the man's 'hereditary' disease, go ahead with marriage and give birth to a 'defective' baby with multiple deformities. His disabilities supposedly make his life miserable, so he eventually shoots the doctor who saved his life. The woman of the other couple, Miriam, believes her mother to have hereditary epilepsy, and refuses to marry. Later, she discovers her stepmother has epilepsy. A healthy Miriam marries, and she has a 'very fat and happy' baby.[1] The message is a clear one: death is preferable to disability, unless cure is possible.

I begin my discussion of film with *Stork*, not as an indictment of eugenics in American history. Rather, films like *Stork* clearly place a value on the possibility of medical cure over a disabled life. The theme of medical cure permeates many films to this day, particularly science fiction.

Much of the scholarship on disability and film has centred on analysis of disabling stereotypes, such as the 'evil cripple' or 'saintly sage' (Norden, 1994). Some work – for example, Paul Longmore's 'Screening stereotypes: images of the disabled in television and motion pictures' (1987) and Paul Darke's 'Understanding cinematic representations of disability' (1998) – has attempted to show how these stereotypes pervade the way in which disability is perceived in society at large, and thus universalize how disabled people should feel about being disabled. Longmore uses a 'realigment/readjustment' narrative in which the character must either accept or reject his disability, whereas Darke employs what he calls the 'normality drama'. This, Darke states, 'specifically uses abnormal – impaired – characters to deal with a perceived threat to the dominant social hegemony of normality. The normality drama follows its own genre conventions: a physically or mentally impaired character is represented to reinforce the illusions of normality: a normality exhibited either in a film's non-impaired characters, or by the impaired character's rejection of their impaired self.' If impairment is an undesirable state of being, and being disabled an undesirable life, we can begin to understand – to see – the premium placed on medical cure, and the weight of the medical model in the eradication of disability in science fiction films.

Recent disability studies scholarship, however, has looked beyond the medical model to a broader and more culturally based understanding of disability. As Rosemarie Garland Thomson and other scholars have noted, from a culturally based paradigm, disability becomes a 'representational system rather than a personal misfortune or bodily flaw' (Thomson, 2000: 181). In other words, disability signifies more than a bodily impairment, a curable or treatable medical condition; it is a socially created and culturally perpetuated phenomenon. For instance, the acts of teasing or staring that are part of many disabled people's experience are based on what society has defined as an 'abnormal' body. The stigma of that 'abnormal' body that makes it the object of staring and teasing is socially constructed. Some scholars have referred to this as the *social constructionist model* of disability.[2]

If one employs a social constructionist model of disability, then disability would still exist even in 'medically advanced', futuristic societies. In other words, if we think of disability as not just a medical condition or bodily affliction which can be medically cured or genetically manipulated, but as an identity which is largely defined by society at large, then disability, in cultural terms, should be present in societies of the future.

The premiss that cure is constructed and disability, in the metaphorical sense if not literal/physical sense, is still present in the future is the greater part of the argument of this chapter which looks at science fiction films such as *Blade Runner, The Matrix* and *Gattaca*. Using a postmodern framework, I explore how cure is constructed, and how disability is redefined, and thus still present in these visions of the future.

In science fiction films, such as *Blade Runner, The Matrix* and *Gattaca*, we are presented with glimpses of our future, of a perfect Moore-like Utopia (Moore, 1992: 60). At first glance, in these postmodern worlds, populated largely by what Donna Haraway has termed 'cyborgs', or genetically engineered bodies, disability appears to be eradicated.

However, a closer examination of these films shows that disability as a societal, if not medical, construction, continues to dominate. Theories of postmodernism, particularly Fredric Jameson's analysis of the construct of Utopia, and those of Haraway, will ground my analysis. Through articulating the presence of disability as a societal construction in these films, I hope to show how we might rethink not only constructions of disability, but also medical 'cure' as a socially and culturally constructed concept.

Postmodern concepts: reading the future

Much controversy has surrounded the origins of postmodernism and its various characteristics.[3] Aesthetically, these films are generally considered postmodern, both in locale and theme. The mixing of architectural styles, such as the gritty, Gothic-like buildings existing in close proximity to the Techno-lit bar in *Blade Runner*, for instance, creates a very postmodern city-scape. Similarly, the unilaterally bland cubicle offices in *The Matrix*, and the antiseptic offices of *Gattaca*, while recalling visions of Fritz Lang's 1927 film *Metropolis*, symbolically denote a postmodern society – what Irving Howe has called a 'mass society . . . [in which] passivity becomes a widespread social attitude: the feeling that life is a drift over which one has little control . . . [where] reflections upon the nature of society are replaced by observations of its mechanics' (Howe, 1992: 25). The films also employ postmodern narrative plot structures, such as the blending of history and memory, and non-linear shifts in time and place.[4] While these elements help to place the films within a postmodern framework artistically, it is theories of postmodernism, as they apply to the films' respective themes and characters, which will frame my analysis and will, ultimately, help us to discern the presence of disability in the future.

While many theories of postmodernism exist, and it is somewhat differently defined in relation to art and literature, in particular two tenets of postmodernism will serve as the primary way of interpreting these films. First is what is commonly referred to in art history circles as the 'Andy Warhol effect', or Warhol's use of the 'multiple', meaning his silk-screens of movie stars and cultural artefacts that have become icons of popular culture. In some of Warhol's famous silk-screens of Marilyn Monroe, the image of her face is continuously repeated so that, instead of having one image of her for the viewer to focus on, there are multiple copies of the same image recurring on a single canvas.[5] The effect of these repetitions, or what Fredric Jameson calls 'the disappearance of the individual subject', is a questioning of what is real and what is imagined (Jameson, 2000c: 201). In an era of mass reproduction, the *original*, the *real*, becomes a much more valuable commodity. The emphasis on the 'real' versus the imagined, coupled with technological innovations and mass production, in a postmodern 'mass society' leads to a questioning of *knowledge* – of who we are, and what we know.[6]

Secondly, I want to consider the presence of a 'Utopia', in Fredric Jameson's terms, as it relates to visions of our postmodern future. While his primary concern was an examination of the concept of a Utopia in economic (Marxist) terms, his articulation of the failings of Utopian society will further my own argument of the presence of disability in the Utopian societies presented in futuristic film. Jameson argues that a 'false consciousness' exists in Utopia because of the 'bulk of production of a mass or media culture'. He says the purpose of material products is 'to distract readers and viewers from the nature of their own lives and the relationship of the latter to the socio-economic system in which they live' (Jameson, 2000a: 365–6).[7] Utopia, though, ultimately fails because 'commodities' are still valued differently. A 'class' system, a system of privilege, still exists. Relationships, too, instead of being free from political and individual will-power, are still driven by emotions and values such as 'violence, hate, love, sex, or whatever' (Jameson, 2000b: 376).

It is important to understand the relationship between Jameson's assertion of a 'class/value' system in Utopia and disability. If disability is a socially constructed phenomenon, the existence of a class system would demand a system of 'have and have-nots'. As theorists such as Erving Goffman, Lennard Davis and Harlan Lane have noted, the 'have-nots' occupy a stigmatized place in society.[8] Although there may be a physical difference upon which stigma is based, the stigma is socially created. It is assigned by one group to another based upon a specific valued body structure in much the same way other 'commodities' are valued or devalued within society. Further, as Haraway suggests, the production of cyborgs – 'a cybernetic organism, a hybrid of machine and organism, a creature of social reality, [lived social relations] as well as a creature of fiction' (Haraway, 1991: 149) – relates directly to Jameson's notion of a class hierarchy, where technological knowledge and genetic manipulation, resulting in a hybrid between human and machine, become the very foundation upon which a class structure and societal stigma is based. Haraway writes:

Another critical aspect of the social relations of new technologies is the reformulation of expectations, culture, work, and reproduction for the large scientific and technological work-force. A major social and political danger is the formation of a strongly bi-modal social structure, with the masses of women and men of all ethnic groups, but especially people of color, confined to a homework economy, illiteracy of several varieties, and general redundancy and impotence, controlled by high-tech repressive apparatuses, ranging from entertainment to surveillance and disappearance. (Haraway, 1991: 169)

For Haraway, the reconstruction of humans as cyborgs – products of and bound to technologies in ways previously unimaginable – leaves women and ethnic minorities especially occupying particular places in the socio-economic strata of a new genetically and technologically driven world. If we venture to include people with disabilities – the very population for whom wheelchairs, ventilators, pacemakers and the like are vital for literal survival and forged identity – into Haraway's configuration, her use of the 'cyborg' as a central figure around which class and stigma are based has implications for people with disabilities, as we will see shortly in explorations of the films.

If disability, as a social construction, exists on more than a theoretical plane, disability should be present as a social stigma in the future. This is not to suggest that bodies are immaterial in Utopian societies. Quite the contrary, bodies exist in Utopia which occupy a societal stigma of being unfit, sub-human, inferior, that shows the very existence of disability as a social construction.

To reiterate briefly: a rethinking of disability in social terms, either through a redefinition of 'reality' and knowledge of identity, or an examination of bodies in terms of societal stigma in futuristic 'Utopias', will allow us to understand how disability, far from being medically cured or eradicated, will still be present in the future.

My analysis of these films is chronological. I begin with *Blade Runner*, in part because our ideas of science and disability have changed with the times. In the Regan-era Star Wars-driven 1980s, and the aftermath of the Cold War, America was much more concerned with the idea of an 'Other' (Soviets) and the ability of technology to destroy humankind. We see these ideas featuring prominently in *Blade Runner*, where cyborgian technology and scientific progression are portrayed as a threat to humankind. In the 1990s, with the advances in technologies such as cloning and genetic manipulation, the central concern is not how technology will destroy humankind, but how it will alter our identities as human beings. We see this latest concern reflected in *The Matrix* and *Gattaca*. In her book, *Imagenation: Popular Images of Genetics*, José Van Dijck traces the evolution of genetics as cultural image, and society's responses to the changing image of genetics (Van Dijck, 1998).

In the 1950s, she contends, the discovery of DNA configured genetics as a structured 'code' based in biology, while in the 1980s and beyond, the image of the gene became one of a 'potentially dangerous micro-organism – a string of manipulated DNA escaping from a lab, unleashing its evolutionary powers onto the environment. The gene, in the environmentalist definition of engineered bug, became the designated enemy of nature, thus amplifying the punitive opposition between "nature" and "science"' (Van Dijck, 1998: 179–80). Later, with the rise of genetic manipulation by industry, genes could be viewed as 'potential lucrative resources, goldmines for capital investment and profit' (Van Dijck, 1998: 180). The concept of gene as commodity – as part and parcel of a Jamesonian class system – can be seen most clearly in the film *Gattaca*. But it should be pointed out that there are also 'real world' implications with this idea, as current debates surrounding such issues as the possibility of the 'gay gene' and finding the 'defective' gene for Down's syndrome suggest. In these debates, sexuality and disability respectively are, again, reduced simply to medical 'defect' or impairment, curable by gene therapy and manipulation. The concept of either sexuality or disability as social/political identity, or as 'social construction', is ignored in favour of a more pervasive scientific representation. The changing image of the gene and science, and humankind's responses to those changing images and, in turn, the changing response to genetics and its relationship to disability and medical cure are clearly evident in the three films under examination in this chapter. To see the relationship of science and genetics to the construction of disability and of medical cure more fully, let us turn now to a closer inspection of the films, and their visions of the future.[9]

The problem of replicants: 'belonging' in the world of *Blade Runner*

The quintessential postmodern science fiction film, and one that has received much analysis, is *Blade Runner*. While much critical attention has centred on issues of the film's production, marketing and the various versions, including the controversial *Director's Cut*, little attention has been paid to reading it in terms of disability.[10] Haraway's blurring of the human and machine in the form of a cyborg is clearly evident in the films *Blade Runner* and *The Matrix* explored in this chapter, but her ideas surrounding cyborgs certainly factor in to 'real world' configurations of disabled persons – and mainstream society's response to them as well. In this vein, the notion of 'replicants' as cyborgs has been the focus of analysis in such critical collections as *Retrofitting Blade Runner: Issues in Ridley Scott's 'Blade Runner'*.[11] If we figure replicants – literal cyborgs – as disabled, as minority, in a technologically advanced society, we can see the reformulation of disability as a social and class stigma centred on the cyborgian replicants.

Blade Runner has a comparatively simple premiss. In the future, the Tyrell Corporation has created a race of androids, called 'replicants'. These are technological, man-made organic doubles of humans. They are superior to humans 'in body strength and agility, and equal in intelligence'. They resemble humans in nearly every way, except they are created with a four-year lifespan. The main motive for their short lifespan is that, if made to last longer, it is feared that they would become emotionally too much like humans and would have human desires, such as love. As it is, they are enslaved by humans, and used to help colonize other worlds. There is an eventual mutiny. They are declared to be 'illegal' on Earth, and a special band of police known as 'Blade Runners' is created to execute any 'trespassing replicants'. These executions are known as 'retirements'. As the movie opens in 2019 in Los Angeles, former Blade Runner Deckerard (Harrison Ford) is drafted to retire some suspected trespassing replicants.

The replicants can be considered 'disabled' from several standpoints. At its base, such a storyline reaffirms some common stereotypes of disability. First, disabled people are overcompensated in one sense when another is deficient – one hears better if one is blind. The replicants make up in superior strength and agility what they lack in emotional depth and lifespan. Second, disabled people are bitter about being disabled, causing them to be either depressed or angry, and are consumed with the desire to be 'normal'. After all, what threat do the replicants pose? The replicants are only a problem when they desire to escape the boundaries of their fate, their enslavement, their bodies and be more human, more 'normal'. As replicant Roy tells his creator – a human he calls 'Father' – 'I want more time.' In addition to all the scientific reasons 'Father' gives for this impossibility – why, in other words, replicants cannot be 'cured' – hinting at overcompensation, he offers this as a balm: 'A light that burns twice as bright burns half as long. And you have burned so very brightly, Roy.' Third, if one cannot be 'cured', it would be better to die. Death is preferable to being disabled. It is not that the replicants want to die, rather that this idea is imposed by humans whose response to the replicants' desire to be more human is to use Blade Runners to kill them.[12] When Roy cannot become 'human', he murders 'Father', but not before he gouges his eyes out, blinding him. Deckerard eventually kills Roy. Similarly, the replicant, Priss, is designed as a 'pleasure unit' for humans. When she desires to escape that function, she is killed. In this Utopia, replicants are considered second-class citizenry and stigmatized as such.

Down the rabbit hole and beyond: disability in *The Matrix*

The Matrix is probably best known for its special effects. But there is much more to the story. It is a story about the subjugation of humankind to technology, a futuristic Christ fable, and about finding out who we are.[13] It is also a film in which we can see the postmodern principles of the real versus the imagined, and the construction of a 'false consciousness' at work.

In *The Matrix*, the future of our world is a dream world. That is, Artificial Intelligence has created a computer construct (called the Matrix) of our human world. Artificial Intelligence has hard-wired this reality into the minds of humans, and this is the 'consciousness', the 'reality', that most humans 'live in' and 'believe'. The truth is that humans are kept in incubators and used as power sources for the Artificial Intelligence. In other words, machines dominate humans, and our 'experiences' exist only in our minds. Of course, there is a small band of 'freed' humans, the Resistance, led by Morpheus (Laurence Fishburne) and Trinity (Carrie-Ann Moss) who want to destroy the Matrix, and end the machines' domination. As Morpheus explains, 'The Matrix is a world that has been pulled over your eyes to blind you from the truth . . . the truth that you are a slave, that you were born into bondage . . . a prison for your mind.' This shows traces of a social/class hierarchy at work.

The Resistance seeks a saviour, known mythically as the Chosen One. Enter Neo (Keanu Reeves) who will lead them. Morpheus gives Neo a choice: 'Take the blue pill, and you'll wake up in your bed, and believe what you want to believe. Or take the red pill, stay in Wonderland, and I'll show you just how deep the rabbit hole goes.' (There are many references to *Alice in Wonderland* throughout the film.) Neo, of course, chooses the red pill. A great 'rebirth' or cure scene follows, with Neo sliding down tubes, landing awash into a sea of red, where his body is unhooked from machines which have been using him as an energy source. The Resistance trains Neo, feeding programmes into his brain that allow him to learn such skills as kung fu at a rapid rate. Ultimately, however, the fate of the Resistance and all 'humankind' rests in Neo's ability to believe that he is the Chosen One, something he, at first, resists.

There is then a scene that conveys a powerful metaphor for how to foster one's belief. Morpheus takes Neo to see the Oracle, a clairvoyant omnipotent being (think God to Reeves's Christ), and, while he waits for her, he walks into a room with the other 'potentials'. One of these 'potentials' has a row of spoons laid out in front of her, and she bends one. Neo is impressed, but she tells him:

POTENTIAL: Do not try to bend the spoon. That is impossible. Instead, only try to realize the truth.
NEO: The truth?
POTENTIAL: There is no spoon.
NEO: There is no spoon? [holding the spoon]

> POTENTIAL: Then you will see it is not the spoon that must bend. It is only yourself. [Neo begins to bend the spoon]

Here is the principle of the 'real' versus the 'imagined' at work. In other words, what controls 'reality' is what you 'believe', not necessarily what you 'know' is physically in front of you. If Neo believes it is the spoon that must bend, the spoon will not bend because the laws of physics, as Neo knows them, have not changed. However, if he recognizes that he, not the spoon, needs to change – in this case, what he believes is physically possible within the Matrix – the spoon can and will bend.

In the end, Neo *is* the Chosen One. In the Matrix, his 'body' becomes impervious to the bullets that the Artificial Intelligence is shooting at him, because he believes, in essence, there are no bullets. He ends the film saying, 'I will show you [meaning humans] the truth . . . a world with no borders and boundaries. A world where anything is possible. Where we go from there is up to you.' There is an ending shot of 'unfreed' humans walking around in the Matrix. Neo, it is presumed, will show them their 'false consciousness', to question *knowledge* of who they are and what they know, what is real.

Disability, then, works on two levels in this film. On the one level, it can be argued that 'unfreed' humans are disabled due to their subjugation. Human beings are, after all, hard-wired to a massive computer that acts as a huge incubator. Their sole ability, by virtue of their subjugation, is to act as a power source for the dominant normative group (Artificial Intelligence). From the point of view of the Artificial Intelligence – the dominant unmarked group – 'humans are a virus, and we [machines] are the cure'. Human beings have a stigmatized status. In terms of the body, to become 'freed' is to become not only self-aware, but to be 'cured' of one's automaton status and bodily subjugation.

On another level, we can see the principle of social construction in terms of identity politics. Indeed, there are 'disabled' persons in the Matrix. However, if we understand that within the Matrix reality is a 'constructed', computer-generated reality, and bodies look, move and respond the way the individual *believes* his/her body looks, moves and responds, then disability, if it is merely a physical or mental impairment, should cease to exist. But disability continues to exist within the Matrix. As Morpheus explains to Neo, within the Matrix, 'your appearance now is what we call residual self-image. It is the mental projection of your digital self.' The blind man, for example, is blind because this is how he identifies, sees himself, and this belief may or may not have anything to do with his actual body.

What I feel *The Matrix* shows us is that what we believe about what bodies can or should be able to do – as in Neo's belief that he can stop bullets – is as much about how society has defined what a body can do, as it is about what the body can, in actuality, do. In this way, 'disability' has not disappeared. Its socially constructed status has, instead, become more clear.

Questions of genetics and ability: disabling possibilities in *Gattaca*

Perhaps the most troubling and complex of the science fiction films is *Gattaca*. The film tells us much, for example, about genetic technology, eugenics, 'passing' and identity, the representation of physically disabled characters, a 'classed' society. While there is more to the film than I will be able to examine, the central issue I will look at is the creation of a 'class' system within Utopia, and the idea of disability as a social stigma in this version of Utopia.

Unlike *Blade Runner*, in the world of *Gattaca*, it is the genetically manipulated beings who are considered 'normal'. The naturally conceived humans are stigmatized and belong to a socio-economic underclass. This is a world of 'Valids' (genetically manipulated) and 'In-valids' or 'De-gene-erates' (naturally conceived), as the movie calls them. The protagonist of the film is an 'In-valid' called Vincent, played by Ethan Hawke, who dreams of working for the elite corporation known as Gattaca, and of being chosen for one of its space exploration missions.[14] Of course, given the stigma of his natural conception, visibly noted by his need for glasses and his non-visible heart problems, this is an impossibility. In Gattaca, the closest that the 'In-valids' will get to a mission is working as janitors. 'Don't clean the glass too well,' warns Vincent's custodial boss, 'you might get ideas.'

Vincent does 'get an idea', however. In the world of *Gattaca*, Valids who 'fall on hard times' participate in a black-market system where they can sell their identity – DNA, blood, urine, hair – to In-valids who wish to assume their identity. Here, the fallen Valid is Jerome Morrow, played by Jude Law. Morrow is a first-rate athlete who, because of a broken back, now uses a wheelchair. The general populace is unaware of the accident 'because it happened out of the country'. Vincent's dream of space leads him to broker a deal with Morrow, and after some leg lengthening and blue contact lenses, Vincent assumes Morrow's identity. As the black-market broker says, it does not matter that Vincent does not look like Jerome: 'When was the last time anyone looked at a photograph? . . . It doesn't matter where you were born, just *how*.' In 'Jerome's' interview for admission to Gattaca, the interview consists of screening a drop of 'his' urine (which Vincent now carries in hidden packets), resulting in the computer identifying Jerome Morrow as 'Valid'.[15] Thus begins the deception and the passing of Vincent as Jerome.

Reviews of the film focus largely on the ethical questions of technology. If disability is mentioned, it is either in relation to 'flawed' Vincent or 'crippled', wheelchair-using Jerome, as the characters who are defined as 'disabled'. In the film, however, there are other notable 'disabled' characters. For example, Irene (Uma Thurman), Jerome's love interest and colleague at Gat-taca, is a woman with an imperfection – 'an unacceptable likelihood of heart failure'. And the bald, fedora-wearing detective, who, although he discovers 'Jerome's' true identity before anyone else, and solves the murder of Gattaca's director, is not promoted, but is still accountable to his superior, Vincent's genetically enhanced brother, Anton.[16] But I now want to examine the twelve-fingered man, and Jerome Morrow's interaction in the real world 'as a cripple', and his eventual death, in order to highlight the manifestations of disability as societal stigma.

The twelve-fingered man is an interesting example of disability in *Gattaca*. His disability, unlike either the real or passing 'Jerome', is not only known, but also displayed in society. In contrast, viewers are never altogether clear who knows or how much is known about Irene or the detective. Unlike these characters, the twelve-fingered man's disability (though it is never clear whether it is the result of a natural or technological aberration) is precisely what permits him to exist in mainstream society. He is a pianist whose sole purpose, it seems, is to perform pieces that 'can only be played with twelve [fingers]'. In the single scene he appears in, he performs that piece under spotlights with an adoring crowd of Valids looking on. Afterwards, he tosses one of his white gloves into the crowd, a glove which Irene then puts on her own hand, the extra digit flopping awkwardly. Also, to focus further on his difference, viewers see a shot of the posters advertising his performance. In these, his face is completely covered by his hands, so that what is visible is little more than his twelve fingers. He *is* his disability, and the sole attraction in this glimpse of a futuristic freak show. Like Priss in *Blade Runner*, his only function is to entertain the Valids. Like his predecessors, his difference becomes performance art. He is not considered 'human' in any real sense by the Valids. While it could be argued that disability is portrayed in a positive light, from an economic standpoint, his worth is still based on his ability to perform for Valids, to entertain what Rosemarie Garland Thomson has called 'the normate', and on their willingness to allow him to entertain.[17] He, literally, embodies not only his stigma, but also he reminds us of a class system, a system of differently valued commodities.

Jerome, Vincent and Irene remind viewers of the negative effects of stigma. For example, while Jerome and Vincent do go out to a local bar together, no one knows the wheelchair-using Jerome as 'Jerome Morrow'. Everyone believes Vincent is 'Jerome', a Valid, a 'made-man' and not disabled. The real Jerome, when he is spoken to, is only called 'sir' (not Eugene, as he is called by Vincent in public). This suggests that, even in a bar they both frequent, Jerome is not worth knowing, not quite human. This less-than-human status in society is also shown in Vincent's inability to attain a position above janitor without Jerome's helix 'tucked under his arm', and in comments made to Irene that her 'place is assured'. Jerome, Vincent and Irene's places in this society are assured as a result of what society perceives and not as a result of any particular ability. Although all are stigmatized by society, because Vincent and Irene's disabilities are not physically apparent, they are not as stigmatized as Jerome. In the end, Vincent and Irene are allowed to live. However, Jerome, according to film etiquette, must die – supposedly because he cannot be 'cured'. Although Jerome is suicidal prior to becoming a paraplegic, he tells Vincent upon returning from the bar that '[he] wasn't drunk when [he] stepped in front of that car'. The film, though, does not examine his depression and self-hate, attributing it solely to his accident, the moment of impairment; thus implying that his incineration, his suicide, at the film's end, is linked to his disability. Clearly, being a cripple, unless one becomes a freak show attraction, is unacceptable in *Gattaca*'s Utopia.

Conclusion

The idea that, because of medical technology and genetic manipulation, the future will be 'free' of disability and disease is not new, nor, given current strides in medical technology, as far-fetched as it might seem. The punchline to many jokes about cryogenic technology, for instance, is 'Freeze me till they find a cure.' This line of thought presumes that disability is nothing more than impairment. If, however, we shift our definition of disability to a social construction, through the presence of second-class citizenry, as in *Blade Runner* or *Gattaca*, to a more inclusive definition of identity as in *The Matrix*, we might begin to rethink how we understand the representation of disability.

This shift necessitates not only a rethinking of how we understand 'disability', but also how we conceptualize 'cure'. In the films, the concept of 'cure' is seen from a medical perspective, as something that can be garnered through the use of technology. However, if we begin to understand that disability is largely socially constructed, then cure, and the values it embodies, must be understood as likewise constructed. Like the metaphor of the spoon in *Matrix*, if you believe there is no spoon, if you do not believe there is anything that *needs* to be bent, then you are 'free'. If you do not believe there is a disability, if you do not believe there is anything that needs to be 'cured' or genetically prevented – that disability is indeed little more than a social construction – then you will likewise be freed from the need for cure. Science is making great strides in genetics and other technologies. In the race for bodily perfection through technology, the question is not what science can 'do' for us. The questions underlying these science fiction films, and other films where cure is or is not a realistic option, are these. In the face of such technologies, who will we become? Is medical cure, indeed, worth waiting for?

Notes

1. Pernick (1996: 144). There is only one known surviving copy of the film, housed at the University of Michigan. My comments are based on Pernick's account.
2. For a general introduction to social constructionism, see Vivien Burr (1995), *An Introduction to Social Constructionism* (New York: Routledge). For further explanation of the impairment/disability distinction and the theory of social constructionism, see texts such as Mairian Corker and Sally French (1999), 'Reclaiming discourse in disability studies', in *Disability Discourse* (Buckingham: Open UP); Simi Linton (1998), *Claiming Disability: Knowledge and Identity* (New York: NYU Press); Michael Oliver (1990), *The Politics of Disablement: A Sociological Approach* (New York: St Martin's Press); and Tom Shakespeare *et al.* (1996), 'Introduction', in *The Sexual Politics of Disability: Untold Desires* (London: Cassell). For my purposes here, my use of the term disability encompasses a cultural understanding.
3. For further reading, Perry Anderson (1998), *The Origins of Postmodernity* (London: Verso), has been a helpful text.
4. See the introduction in Cristina Degli-Espositi (1998), *Postmodernism in the Cinema* (New York: Berghahn), for further explanation. See also Judith B. Kerman (1997), 'Technology and politics in the *Blade Runner* dystopia', in Kerman, *Retrofitting Blade Runner* (Bowling Green, OH: Bowling Green University Popular Press), p. 16.
5. The term 'the Andy Warhol effect', referring to his repetitive technique, has become common parlance in art history circles. For further discussion of Warhol, see Anne Friedberg (1993), *Window Shopping: Cinema and the Postmodern* (Berkeley: University of California Press), pp. 170–4.
6. I forego a more detailed discussion of the past, the present and history as it relates to postmodernism here. See the writings of Jean-François Lyotard, Jürgen Habermas and Fredric Jameson for reference.
7. See the 'Utopia' section of *The Jameson Reader* for further reading about Utopia.
8. See Erving Goffman's (1963) seminal work, *Stigma: Notes on the Management of a Spoiled Identity* (New York: Simon and Schuster), and later thinking on the concept of stigma as it applies to disability in such works as Lennard J. Davis (1995), *Enforcing Normalcy: Disability, Deafness, and the Body* (New York: Verso), and Harlan Lane (1993), *The Mask of Benevolence: Disabling the Deaf Community* (New York: Vintage).
9. My analysis of the films is based on the DVD-released versions which, at times, contain deleted scenes and supplemental materials like interviews, etc. In particular, I am working from the 1992-released version of *Blade Runner: The Director's Cut*.
10. See Paul M. Sammon (1996), *Future Noir: The Making of Blade Runner* (New York: HarperCollins).
11. Judith Kerman (ed.) (1997), *Retrofitting Blade Runner: Issues in Ridley Scott's 'Blade Runner' and Philip K. Dick's 'Do Androids Dream of Electric Sheep?'* (Bowling Green, OH: Bowling Green University Popular Press).

12. For more on cinematic stereotypes of disability, see the introduction to Martin F. Norden (1994), *The Cinema of Isolation: A History of Physical Disability in the Movies* (New Brunswick: Rutgers University Press).
13. For more on religious interpretations of *The Matrix*, see Paul Fontana's 'Generation exile and neo restoration', as well as on-line articles located at: <*http://awesomehouse.com/Matrix/parallels.htm*>.
14. When referring to the film, I use italics. When referring to the corporation within the film, Gattica is in regular typeface.
15. Henceforth, when I refer to Vincent passing as Jerome Morrow, I will denote 'Jerome' in quotation marks. When referring to the 'real Jerome Morrow' (Jude Law), I will refrain from using quotation marks.
16. My thanks to Carolyn Tyjewski, whose discussions helped clarify my own thinking.
17. See Rosemarie Garland Thomson (1997), *Extraordinary Bodies: Figuring Physical Disability in American Literature and Culture* (New York: Columbia University Press).

References

Blade Runner: The Director's Cut (DVD, 1999) Dir. Ridley Scott. Perf. Harrison Ford, Rutger Hauer. Warner Bros.
Darke, P. A. (1998) 'Understanding cinematic representations of disability', in T. Shakespeare (ed.), *The Disability Reader: Social Science Perspectives*. London: Cassell, pp. 181–97.
Gattaca (DVD, 1997) Dir. Andrew Niccol. Perf. Ethan Hawke, Uma Thurman, Jude Law. Columbia.
Haraway, D. (1991) *Simians, Cyborgs, and Women: The Reinvention of Nature*. New York: Routledge.
Hardt, M. and Weeks, K. (eds) (2000) *The Jameson Reader*. Boston: Blackwell.
Howe, I. (1992) 'Mass society and postmodern fiction', in P. Waugh (ed.), *Postmodernism: A Reader*. New York: Routledge, pp. 24–30.
Jameson, F. (2000a) 'To reconsider the relationship of Marxism to Utopian thought', in M. Hardt and K. Weeks (eds), *The Jameson Reader*. Boston: Blackwell, pp. 362–7.
Jameson, F. (2000b) 'World-reduction in Le Guin: the emergence of Utopian narrative', in M. Hardt and K. Weeks (eds), *The Jameson Reader*. Boston: Blackwell, pp. 368–81.
Jameson, F. (2000c) 'Postmodernism, or the cultural logic of late capitalism', in M. Hardt and K. Weeks (eds), *The Jameson Reader*. Boston: Blackwell, pp. 188–232.
Longmore, P. (1987) 'Screening stereotypes: images of the disabled in television and motion pictures', in A. Gardner and T. Joe (eds), *Images of the Disabled, Disabling Images*. New York: Prager, pp. 65–78.
The Matrix (DVD, 1999) Dir. the Wachowski Brothers. Perf. Keanu Reeves, Laurence Fishburne, Carrie-Ann Moss. Warner Bros.

Moore, Sir T. (1992) *Utopia*, trans. Robert M. Adams, rev. 2nd edn. New York: Norton.

Norden, M. (1994) *The Cinema of Isolation: A History of Physical Disability in the Movies.* New Brunswick, NJ: Rutgers University Press.

Pernick, M. (1996) *The Black Stork: Eugenics and the Death of 'Defective' Babies in American Medicine and Motion Pictures since 1915.* New York: Oxford.

Thomson, R. G. (2000) 'The beauty and the freak', in S. Crutchfield and M. Epstein (eds), *Points of Contact: Disability, Art, and Culture.* Ann Arbor: University of Michigan Press, pp. 181–96.

Van Dijck, J. (1998) *Imagenation: Popular Images of Genetics.* New York: New York University Press.

Waugh, P. (ed.) (1992) *Postmodernism: A Reader.* New York: Routledge.

16

Naming and Narrating Disability in Japan

James Valentine

Naming and narrating postmodern identities

Names and narratives are central to the project of postmodernism to distance itself from modernity, that is characterized in universalistic terms and is crucially challenged by human and societal types at variance with predominant classifications. Disability is at the forefront of this challenge. This chapter explores names and narratives of disability in a society that falls outside the Western discourse of modernity. Japanese society, commonly represented as uniquely different, provides the focus for an examination of postmodern identities. Within this context, the discussion proceeds with an analysis of disability in terms of disorderly bodies that defy modernist classification and supposedly partake in a celebration of difference.

In subsequent sections, disabled naming is explored – initially by contrasting fluidity of identity with modernist impositions of essential identity: viewing Japanese classificatory practices in a comparative context undermines claims for cultural uniqueness here. The Japanese cultural principle of wrapping (Hendry, 1993: 172) has encouraged the development of euphemistic expressions for disability, yet these too can be compared with equivalents elsewhere. A genuine distinctiveness, however, is shown in the complexity of a written system that promotes multiple transformations of name. Nevertheless, the narratives implicit in naming, and expounded through media representations, continue to trace a line of moral progress through special disabled characteristics that imply identity fundamentalism rather than a celebration of multiple identities.

Differences in a different society

Difference is at the core of characterizations of postmodern identity. Identity is seen as multiple and fluid, defined through difference, without differences becoming essentialized. Characterization is through diverse names and particularistic narratives. The same is claimed of postmodernity itself, which is presented as a new and different time, after modernity, breaking with the grand narratives of modernism. Nevertheless, as with other eras, postmodernity is defined through difference that identifies fundamental change and locates this in a sequential narrative: 'modernity remains on the polluted side, representing "the other" in postmodernism's narrative tales' (Alexander, 1994: 180). Our advance is contrasted with other times and other places, in narratives that are both historical and geographical. Constructing the category of postmodernity gathers together all those societies that have surpassed modernity, or that are dissolved in globalization, in contrast to those who remain outside, in the past.

In this classification, some societies remain marginal, ambiguously defined either as stragglers or harbingers – as needing to catch up or as at the forefront. Japanese society is represented in this dualistic manner: as still facing the challenge of an internationalization and globalization that have ironically reinforced assertions of Japan's uniqueness (Befu, 1983: 261; McCormack, 1996: 283), and as already 'a most exemplary instance of the postmodern' (Wolfe, 1989: 224). Commonly contested accounts of Japanese society are in accord on one matter: Japan's difference. Japan is seen as different from the rest, which tends to mean 'the West'. This lumps together those seen as Japan's other, and thus fails to recognize differentiation amongst the contrasting viewpoints from which the 'othernesses of Japan' are set up (Befu, 1992: 17). At the same time, Japan's celebrated difference, according to its internal and external commentators, is based on a claimed homogeneity that fails to recognize internal differentiation, including disability.

The acknowledgement of difference within Japan is held back by circumspection in naming the other within: direct designation is frequently shunned. Names and their avoidance must be acknowledged as a crucial aspect of identification of self and other in every society: whether, how and what we call others says much about our selves. In this, it is vital to avoid considering Japan in isolation, as an exceptional case, uniquely different, as promoted by special 'theories of the Japanese people' (*Nihonjinron*). At the same time, the study of Japanese society, in its cultural contingency that survives or even thrives through globalization, can help to cast doubt upon universalistic accounts in social science. The apparent contradiction between universalism and relativism here is brilliantly resolved by Lebra (1992: 105): the ubiquitous social construction of self entails differential formation in particular contexts. In a similar way, disability is characterized as different, and as challenging universalistic discourses in a celebration of difference. With reference to disability in Japan, this chapter reflects on supposed postmodern bodies in a purported postmodern society.

Classification, control and cure

Disability challenges modernist pretensions to universalism, standardization and regulation, yet at the same time becomes subject to attempts to classify, control and 'cure'. Naming is a crucial part of this classification process. 'Who has the right to decide how a person shall be called decides how that person shall be classified and defined' (Romaine, 1999: 298). Definitional power – the power to name and classify – reveals the mutual construction of knowledge and power: 'language is critically linked to issues of knowledge, and ultimately power, because particular forms of knowledge are privileged' (Corker, 1999: 193). The modernist emphasis on classification of types of people has been explored by Foucault, who notes the way in which this kind of knowledge specifies who we are by what we do or 'fail' to do. On the basis of acts we become cases of species that are given 'strange baptismal names . . . fine names for heresies' (1981: 43), that assign an essential identity: doing becomes being.

The proliferation of types of being is associated with the growth of expertise in the modernist sciences that are engaged in classification of variant types: criminal types (for criminology), psychiatric types (for psychiatry) and sexual types (again for psychiatry or medicine or, more specifically, sexology). The archetypal modernist science is medicine, which attempts to classify, control and cure. Durkheim exemplifies this approach, where he adopts the medical model of science in sorting out sickness and structural defects in the body social (1984: lv): the use of the metaphor of bodily 'defects' is noteworthy here. Sorting out is suggestive of the rationale of modernist science: sorting into types, producing order and control and treating the wayward by ensuring they are cured and restored or else eradicated. Those who do not fit in must be ruled out.

Rooting out the wayward suggests a gardening metaphor. Gardening creates the very weeds which trouble it so greatly: the concept of weeds makes no sense outside the bounds of the garden. Weeds are the enemy within, strangers, those on the margins who do not belong properly and must be transformed or excluded – those we have to classify, control and cure. The modernist project of taming the wild, creating order out of wasteland, designing and rationalizing, reaches its pinnacle in the 'gardening state' (Bauman, 1991: 26). In its most monstrous form, as in Nazi Germany, it plots a final solution to the weeds, marking out Jews, Gypsies, homosexuals and disabled people for radical eradication.

If disabled people represent the disorderly bodies that challenge modernist classificatory schemes, then the postmodern rejection of absolute standards and universal applicability, in the context of the growing recognition of the social construction of the body, promises to place disability at the forefront of the celebration of difference. There is a fine line here between the optimism that affords the hope that struggle requires, and a Utopianism that persuades us that we have arrived in the best of all possible worlds and that no further action need be taken. Despite the acclamation of postmodernity, there is still power in modernist pretensions to classify, control and cure. Those who argue that power has been dispersed – that there is no longer a centre and hence no longer marginalization and social exclusion, no mainstream or systematic domination, no overriding classifications or narratives – are indeed living in a different world. Could this be Japan? Notwithstanding its mythical status as far out and 'faraway' (Barthes, 1982: 3), Japanese society does not presently constitute such a different world. In Japan, as elsewhere, disability is still subject to the controlling designs of naming and narrating.

Disabled naming

Naming is a vital part of the identification process. Names imply not only qualities of the person but also patterns of relationship, indicating an identification with and against others. This is especially significant for groups defined by dominant systems of classification as other, and thus employed to draw the boundaries of mainstream selves. Identification by type of person – typification – groups together a variety of individuals under a common name or label: they are classed with others regarded as sharing the same characteristics. Even with individual identification, some notion of sameness over time is assumed. To have an identity is not to differ too much from a former self: continuity is presupposed, so that, as Strauss suggests, transformations have to be announced and accounted for, or, indeed, discounted (1997: 148). Diversity is reconciled with identity through narrative, that constitutes constancy of character through emplotment (Ricoeur, 1992: 143). Through names and narratives identity is 'fixed' – plotted, repaired and secured.

Fixity of identity is belied by its alteration in time and scope: it is not just that things (and people) change, but categories may be more or less inclusive, from the modernist dream of watertight Western individuality to the broad bands of inclusion (and exclusion) such as ethnicity, sexuality and disability. These encompassing identities, that include one as belonging to a larger grouping, are situationally relevant, evoking and evoked by contrasts with 'others' with whom in different contexts one may be seen as sharing the same identity. Identification, by virtue of establishing sameness, establishes difference. Homogeneity and heterogeneity already imply each other: sameness and difference are different sides of the same. If identification draws at least temporarily the boundaries of sameness and difference, this means that identification *of* and *as* already implies identification *with*, as well as identification *against*, and that *ego* can become one with *alter* through alteration of compass.

This fluidity, already implied by interactionist and postmodernist recognition of multiple identities, is not yet impervious to modernist impositions of essential identity. Even in an era where difference is supposed to be celebrated, there is a fine line between celebrating difference and essentializing it, as Shakespeare observes in disability politics (1996: 106), and a pivotal identity is still imposed on those who are seen as different in a fundamental way. The selection of terms for those conceived as other has implications for the definition of mainstream selves: discussion of disability (*shōgai* in Japanese) induces the concept of able-bodied (*kenjō*). Able-bodied, however, is able to elude the frame of a fundamental identity through which all aspects of the person are defined.

The definitional power of dominant classifications means that names may not only be applied, but be made to stick, summing you up and implying a whole discourse. A good example of this is the way in which Deaf people are named disabled, and thus become subject to the predominant discourse of disability (Lane, 1995: 177). Disability is a contested domain, yet the presence of struggle should not delude us into assuming equality of the discordant parties. The refrains of the mainstream are difficult to block out, especially when orchestrated by experts. Overarching diagnoses can identify and exclude (Bartlett, 2000: 34). Disabled people, subject to social barriers as recognized in the social model of disability – a model for which the battle remains to be won (Shakespeare and Watson, 1997: 293) – are further disabled in the naming process.

This disabled naming occurs at its crudest in mainstream terms of abuse. Mainstream selves, and their boundaries of identification, are defined in opposition to negatively constructed others. While differences are central to disabled identities, the negative meanings attached to difference constitute prejudice (Morris, 1993: 101). Naming the other promotes 'normal' self-image and status through implied contrast of 'us' with a discriminatory name given to those on the margins (Valentine, 1998). A common form of insult is to administer the short, sharp shock of an abbreviation. Negative Japanese abbreviations include *gai* instead of *shōgaisha* (disabled person), *rezu* instead of *rezubian* (lesbian) and *Senjin* instead of *Chōsenjin* (Korean person). Similar derogatory abbreviations can be found in English: Jap, Paki, Abo, Yid, spas/spazzie, les/lezzie and homo. Terse or truncated terms of abuse may, however, be appropriated by marginalized groups themselves: 'queers' and 'crips' deflect definitional power and bounce back blatant names with added force, demonstrating not only pride but an explicit and unresigned recognition of dominant discriminations.

Abusive name-calling may bolster mainstream identities, but it is crude and may not be the most effective means of marginalization. In Japan the process of naming is carried out with considerable subtlety, especially in official discourse. Whereas insult may be characterized by abbreviation, formal bureaucratic terminology encourages the proliferation of lengthy euphemisms.

Disabled euphemisms

Marginal people who challenge modernist classificatory schemes may be ter-minologically ignored, abused or refined. In Japan, while lesbians and gay men may be ignored or plainly abused, and reluctance to acknowledge minority ethnic groups leads to clumsy circumlocutions or silence, disabled people are less readily ignored, and especially at times of official concern (such as *shōgaisha no hi*, Disabled People's Day, 9 December) there is an obligation to show consideration. This requires recognition and designation of disability in a way that demonstrates care.

Careful use of terms, so as not to cause offence when referring to those who, in terms of the dominant categorial system, are deemed offensive and embarrassing, may take the form of euphemistic expressions. Those who upset the system, and have the power to show up the polite progressive façade, are wrapped in delicate designations that are frequently the province and progeny of experts, whose euphemisms may be as disabling as more blatantly discriminatory terms. The disabling effects of language are not eliminated by the mere removal of offensive words (Oliver, 1996a: 43). Lan-guage may indeed be more liable to confirm discriminatory practice than to effect change: while paternalistic language enhances discriminatory practices, the rhetoric of integration may not of itself change practice but rather mystify or obscure the unaltered reality (Oliver, 1996b: 76, 85).

Through use, euphemistic labels may lose some of their linguistic coating, and thus periodically need upgrading as they take on derogatory connota-tions that reveal discriminatory attitudes towards those they latently degrade. Bureaucratic demand for ever more guarded designations, distending in length and indirectness, results in an inflation of euphemisms (Valentine, 1998). Without suggesting that every new name for marginalized groups be regarded as a euphemism, it is possible to trace a familiar process, that begins in the avoidance of a popular discriminatory term by substituting an expert label that appears neutral. This in turn through popular usage begins to assume common derogatory undertones, and calls for the elaboration of a euphemism. For example, *katawa* (whose closest English equivalent would be 'cripple', and which implies oddness) can be written with the *kanji* (Chinese-derived characters used in writing Japanese) for *kata* (one/side) and *wa* (wheel), conveying the image of a (vehicle with a) single wheel, hence not operating 'properly'. The use of *katawa* has declined in favour of *shōgaisha* (handicapped person/people – written with three *kanji*), or, in an elaborated euphemism, *karada no fujiyū na kata* (person with a physical disability).

In British English a similar movement can be traced from the use of cripple and spastic to (physically) handicapped, and then disabled people, or people with a disability. The rationale behind this last form (unavailable in Japanese grammar, where the predicate precedes the person) stems from regarding 'the phrases "a disabled person", "disabled people" and "visually impaired people" as discriminatory on the ground that they still attract too much attention to the disability or impairment by mentioning it first' (Pauwels, 1991: 60). To draw too much attention is precisely what euphemizing attempts to avoid. In the same way, it is contended that to drop 'people' from such expressions dehumanizes, as in 'the disabled', 'the blind', 'the elderly' or 'the poor'. Significantly, there is no impetus to replace 'the rich' with 'rich people': their elevated position does not require condescending concern.

In Japanese reference to blind people, the former Japanese term *mekura* is now recognized as discriminatory and has given way to *mōjin*. *Mōjin* is now regarded by many sighted Japanese as too direct and is coming to be replaced by the more lengthy euphemism *mōmoku no hito* (blind person), or by expressions that refer, as in similar English terms, to 'people with a visual handicap/disability': *me na fujiyū na kata; shikaku ni shōgai no aru kata*. These latter terms are also supposed to provide a more 'accurate' reference to degrees of visual impairment, but in practice are often used as lengthy euphemisms for blind.

While a change of names may be legitimated in terms of 'accuracy', more recent labels are not necessarily more accurately descriptive or less stigmatizing (Jenkins, 1998: 8). Accuracy depends upon social context. Notions of what is accurate change over time, and may be compounded with euphemizing, so that, for example, it is considered more accurate to use a nicer term, or a more accurate term may be more indirect or couched in technical language that makes meaning less directly apparent for lay users. Accuracy may thus be an expert rationalization for the inflation of euphemisms. Accuracy is indeed used as a legitimation on both sides of the political correctness debate: by those who want to defend the latest euphemistic inflation, and by those who wish to use direct terms of abuse: the charge of political correctness is commonly made by those who want to retain the right to be freely abusive.

Contending with 'common-sense' abuse is not the only challenge that experts face. Contention between sets of expert classifiers may ensue where their legitimacy derives from different sources of 'knowledge', as in the dispute between medical experts and educational and psychological experts over 'mental handicap' versus 'special needs' and 'learning difficulties'. The mode of classification became contested by two kinds of authority: medical specialists, who claimed the problems they diagnosed were medical in origin and solution; and educationalists and educational psychologists, who argued that the way to tackle difficulties (which, whatever the source, could not be treated medically) had to be educational, involving the provision of special educational support. As an example of a shift in categorial legitimacy, in Britain the various Education Acts reveal the domination of medical conceptions of special education, until the 1981 attempt to break away from medical classifications (Oliver, 1988: 19–20).

Terminological transformations reflect not only paradigm shifts but also the urge to develop more indirect and delicate designations to veil the derogatory connotations that begin to show through a succession of euphemisms. In Japan, *seishin hakujakusha* ('feeble-minded people', a dated bureaucratic term still in use in Japanese government regulations) was replaced by *seishin shōgaisha* (mentally handicapped people), and more recently by *chiteki shōgaisha* (intellectually handicapped people), an official term that avoids the suggestion of illness. In Britain, from the late nineteenth century, people with more than mild 'feeble-mindedness' were categorized, by decreasing degrees of severity, as 'idiots' and 'imbeciles', with 'morons' as the least severe level in early twentieth-century American usage. Such categories are now understood as common terms of abuse. Notions of 'mental deficiency' and 'defectiveness' predominated in England and Wales up to 1945, when the administrative category of 'educational subnormality' (ESN) was created (Tomlinson, 1981: 194) as one of eleven categories of handicap. The reference to handicap (as in Japan with *shōgai*) was found in Scotland too, where 'mental handicap' replaced educational subnormality as one of the categories of handicap (Williams, 1988: 130). Legislation in 1981 supposedly abolished such categorization, along with degrees of subnormality, substituting notions of 'special needs' and 'learning difficulty', which, however, were subdivided into mild, moderate and severe. As Oliver notes, 'it could be argued that only the labels have changed' (1988: 20). Marková and Jahoda suggest:

> such changes in terminology would be fruitless if they were not accompanied by implicit and explicit changes in societal values and representations of mental handicap. The changes in labels and names would only be temporary because the new terms would quickly acquire the meaning of the discarded terms and the renaming could start all over again. (1992: 13)

The aim to abolish labelling merely developed longer labels – 'people with learning difficulties' or 'people with special needs'. Moreover, the expression 'special needs' puts together two of the terms most commonly used in patronizing euphemisms. Corbett notes that 'needs' implies 'dependency, inadequacy and unworthiness' (1996: 3), while 'special' renders 'powerless but nice' (1996: 49). The euphemistic use of 'special', also found in the Japanese discriminatory concept of 'people of special communities' (*tokushu burakumin*), carries apparently positive connotations of being singled out for especially elevating treatment; yet this in itself indicates the need for elevation, and hence the actual subordination. 'Special' segregates.

More recently, learning difficulties have been incorporated within the discourse of disability as 'learning disabilities', though in American use this is generally defined as excluding 'mental retardation', which is increasingly subsumed in ‘developmental disabilities’ – a broader term whose incorporation of less disparaged disabilities encourages its use as an indirect reference. Disability currently encompasses 'intellectual disability', as in references to 'intellectually impaired people' (Lonsdale, 1990: 36), 'people with intellectual impairments' (Baird, 1992: 23) and 'people with intellectual disabilities' (Pauwels, 1991: 60; Baird, 1992: 7). The earlier shift from handicap (which could refer to physical or mental handicap) to disability removed any association between physical and intellectual impairment. The notion of learning or intellectual disabilities reintroduces the ambiguity into the term disability, while applying the discourse of disability to people who may reject disabled labels. Self-advocacy groups such People First demonstrate awareness of the labelling process by describing themselves as 'people who are labelled as having a learning difficulty' (Carlisle People First) or 'people labelled with learning disabilities' (People First Birmingham). It will be interesting to see if those who wish to refer to physical disability will attempt to distance the expression from association with learning disabilities. Names are used to differentiate discriminated people from each other, as well as from the presumed norm, especially if there are fears of contamination through association. Experts in modernity foster multiple distinctions that cannot pass as a postmodern celebration of difference.

Naming multiplicity

Multiple transformations of name are encouraged by multiplicity of linguistic sources. Languages that can draw upon two or more major linguistic sources may be able to develop euphemisms more readily, using a source that is less everyday and more erudite. Both English and Japanese are languages with multiple sources, where formal identification uses names derived from a more prestigious foreign source. Thus in English, euphemisms, especially where medicalized, tend to employ words taken or derived from Greek and Latin, as in paraplegic, invert, dementia, retardation and non compos mentis. In contrast, indecent and abusive terms commonly comprise shorter Anglo-Saxon words and 'monosyllables denoting familiar animals' like cock and ass: 'The use of phonetically complex terms for "close" animals seems always to be the result of a euphemistic replacement of a tabooed word' (Leach, 1972: 56).

In Japan, a complex written system further encourages the growth of fresh euphemisms. With the multiple readings of its Chinese-derived characters (*kanji*), Japanese tends to articulate euphemisms with the *on* reading – the

Japanese borrowing and adaptation of the Han dynasty Chinese reading. The *kanji* for deaf can be read as *rō* or *tsunbo*, and the *kanji* for blind can be read as *mō* or *mekura*; but it is the *on* reading (*rō*; *mō*) that is used in euphemistic expressions for deaf or blind people (*rōsha*; *mōjin*). The *on* reading is more formal, intellectualized and distanced, and hence is suited for euphemizing. New *kanji* combinations are also easy to construct, thus allowing the generation of fresh euphemisms, such as *mōmoku* (blind) and *shōgaisha* (disabled person). New ways of writing old terms are also possible: a *kanji* with derogatory connotations may be replaced by a different *kanji* with the same reading, or abandoned for *hiragana*, a syllabary that avoids ideographic representation. *Mekura* (now considered a discriminatory term for blind) might be slightly less offensive when written in *hiragana*, rendering the sounds for 'eye' and 'dark', rather than in the *kanji*, that places 'dead' over 'eye'.

Alternative ways of reading and writing facilitate not only the amendment of old and the construction of new Japanese expressions, but also the easy importation of foreign words that can be used as euphemisms. Words borrowed from foreign languages (except Chinese, for which *kanji* are used) are written in a special syllabary, *katakana*. Unlike in China, where the global discourse of disability is incorporated into Chinese characters (Stone, 1999: 145), *katakana* keeps loanwords visibly different. For a while this difference can impart the distance required for euphemizing. *Handikyappu* (from 'handicapped') and *hāfu* (from 'half', referring to the offspring of Japanese and non-Japanese parents) have been used in this way, not only euphemizing but segregating from native terms – and perhaps implicitly from mainstream Japanese people. The Roman alphabet (*rōmaji*) can also be used, especially in initials of terms, as in LD (learning difficulties). Such initials provide a triple distance from common Japanese terms: a foreign designation, written in foreign script, with initials for those in the know.

Capitalizing initial letters can, however, be used as an affirmation of distinct community. In English this is apparent in writing Deaf, that connects with identities capitalized through nationality, ethnicity, culture or language, such as French, German or Spanish – languages that do not themselves capitalize such identifications. In American English there is a tendency to capitalize on the ability within disAbility. Japanese, while lacking its own capital letters, possesses a wealth of resources for rewriting: the multiplicity of homophones, especially where derived from Chinese, along with different meanings specified in writing by selected *kanji*, facilitates the redefinition of some marginalized groups in favourable terms. For example, disabled people and those working with them have recently come to use a different *kanji* in writing *shōgaisha* (disabled person). The *gai* here has usually been written with a *kanji* that implies harm, injury or damage, and thus carries negative overtones, that become even more apparent where *gai* is used on its own as a derogatory abbreviation. The recent substitute *kanji* for *gai* in *shōgaisha* signifies obstacle, thus suggesting social obstacles rather than individual injury or damage: in accordance with the social model of disability, the responsibility for disability is located in inadequate social provision. Thus a popular uncomplicated term is retained, while its reference is redirected through appropriate selection of written symbols. In names and accounts of disability, disabled people are clearly not passive. Indeed, postmodernism encourages new knowledge of disability from disabled people themselves, who may turn the linguistic tables and assertively name the Others as 'temporarily able bodied' (Peters, 1996: 219), while mainstream power and expertise continues to frame disability within dominant definitions and established narratives.

Narrating disability

Names do not just indicate qualities of the present person, but suggest narratives of becoming. For example, the obstacles literally written into *shōgaisha*, and flagged up by the social model of disability, suggest a number of possible lines of development, both collective and individual. Despite the social model's implication that collective socio-political action is needed, narratives of disability commonly suggest individual action to overcome barriers. This type of narrative is implied by the name 'challenge': disability (even if the social context is recognized) is represented as a challenge for the disabled person, upon whom is placed the burden of solitary struggle.

'Physically challenged' is a much parodied American euphemism. Challenge suggests a struggle, sport or game in which disabled people can heroically persevere to success, thereby acting as paragons of unprotesting individuality with the independence that suits official disengagement and government cuts in societies West and East. Imported designations may indeed be employed to endorse local narratives. Challenge (*charenji*) has become a common imported term in the discourse of disability in Japan, and is aligned with a dominant narrative of perseverance, sustained through Japanese mass media representations, in which disabled people act as role models for a non-disabled audience (Valentine, 1997: 8).

Narratives of perseverance are also applied to deafness: popular Japanese representations incorporate deafness into mainstream accounts of disabled qualities and personal history, that involve heroic perseverance through tragedy, armed solely with the hallmarks of inner purity and special talents. Compensatory artistic skills and the virtue of endurance, observed in Chinese impairment-related characters and proverbs (Stone, 1999: 141–2), are evident in traditional Japanese views of disability. Narratives of deafness are constructed within this conventional discourse of disability, that is endorsed through naming and renaming. Popular television dramas and documentaries in Japan are careful to use lengthy expressions such as *mimi no fujiyū na kata* (person whose ears are disabled) or *chōkaku ni shōgai no aru kata* (person who has a disability in the sense of hearing) that accord with the pattern of disabled euphemisms. In contrast, programmes by Deaf people for Deaf people are more likely to use *rōsha* (Deaf person), or even the imported word *defu* (Deaf). Such programmes may share a general cultural value of perseverance, but are able to eschew the stereotyped virtues that pervade non-disabled narratives of disability, which persist in telling moral tales of individual fortitude and progress.

Narratives that trace a line of moral development, a staged advance over obstacles, still pervade popular culture, and academia is not immune. Despite the claim of an end to grand narratives, sequential stories (of which post-modernism is ironically an example) continue to thrive and preside, as witnessed by the current taste for describing our era as late or post. Obituaries of the age provide concluding narratives (McColgan *et al.*, 2000). Commentators on the times like to be good conventional storytellers, telling us what happened next and whether they ended up living happily ever after.

After words

After modernity's claimed demise, we have not moved beyond the reach of the framing power of words, as witnessed by names and narratives of disability. Although postmodernism can appear 'viciously Utopian' (Harding, 1992: 347), this does not mean that its contribution is without value. The portrayal of a different society, in terms that envisage the celebration of difference, a collapse of boundaries and an end to exclusion by centralized power, can be held up as a critical model to the prevailing social order. This is the manner in which the view of emancipated and participatory communication in a fully egalitarian and democratic society is used as a transcendental ideal by critical theory (Frisby and Sayer, 1986: 83–8). Such an ideal has clear implications for a critique of disabling social situations.

Beyond its value as critique, postmodernism reaffirms the significance of narratives in the construction of the multiple identities of self and others. Nevertheless, we are not unbound in the authorship of ourselves. Despite the challenge that disability presents to modernist pretensions, this chapter has argued that there is still a strong impetus to classify, control and cure, and that names and narratives are fashioned through definitional power. Dominant designations of disability suggest a pivotal identity through terms of abuse or a progression of expert euphemisms that draw upon multiple linguistic sources. Characteristic names invoke narratives of disability in terms of heroic challenge, yet are themselves challenged by disabled people in developing identities through naming and narrating themselves.

Disabled people are neither passive in naming and narrating, nor naïve enough to assume that redefinition is a magical solution to an ongoing legacy of discrimination in a world where, despite the claimed postmodernity of Japanese or Western societies, some differences are a cause for identity fundamentalism rather than the celebration of fluid multiplicity. The power of words and tales should be neither neglected nor overestimated. As Marx contended, there are many problems that defy solution in terms of merely interpreting the world; yet if the point is to change it, we must not underestimate the continuing significance of names and narratives in framing the lives of disabled selves and others.

References

Alexander, J. C. (1994) 'Modern, anti, post, and neo: how social theories have tried to understand the "new world" of "our time"', *Zeitschrift für Soziologie*, 20(3): 165–97.

Baird, V. (1992) 'Disabled lives: difference and defiance', *New Internationalist*, 233: 4–28.

Barthes, R. (1982) *Empire of Signs*. London: Cape.

Bartlett, R. (2000) 'Dementia as a disability: can we learn from disability studies and theory?', *Journal of Dementia Care*, 8(5): 33–6.

Bauman, Z. (1991) *Modernity and Ambivalence*. Cambridge: Polity Press.

Befu, H. (1983) 'Internationalization of Japan and *Nihon bunkaron*', in H. Mannari and H. Befu (eds), *The Challenge of Japan's Internationalization: Organization and Culture*. Tokyo: Kodansha International, pp. 232–66.

Befu, H. (1992) 'Introduction: framework of analysis', in H. Befu and J. Kreiner (eds), *Othernesses of Japan*. Munich: Iudicium Verlag, pp. 15–35.

Corbett, J. (1996) *Bad-Mouthing: The Language of Special Needs*. London: Falmer Press.

Corker, M. (1999) 'New disability discourse, the principle of optimization and social change', in M. Corker and S. French (eds), *Disability Discourse*. Buckingham: Open University Press, pp. 192–209.

Durkheim, E. (1984) *The Division of Labour in Society*. Basingstoke: Macmillan.

Foucault, M. (1981) *The History of Sexuality, Vol. 1*. Harmondsworth: Penguin.

Frisby, D. and Sayer, D. (1986) *Society*. London: Tavistock.

Harding, S. (1992) 'The instability of the analytical categories of feminist theory', in H. Crowley and S. Himmelweit (eds), *Knowing Women: Feminism and Knowledge*. Cambridge: Polity Press, pp. 338–54.

Hendry, J. (1993) *Wrapping Culture: Politeness, Presentation, and Power in Japan and Other Societies*. Oxford: Clarendon.

Jenkins, R. (1998) 'Culture, classification and (in)competence', in R. Jenkins (ed.), *Questions of Competence: Culture, Classification and Intellectual Disability*. Cambridge: Cambridge University Press, pp. 1–24.

Lane, H. (1995) 'Constructions of deafness', *Disability and Society*, 10(2): 171–89.

UNIVERSITY OF WINCHESTER
LIBRARY

Leach, E. (1972) 'Anthropological aspects of language: animal categories and verbal abuse', in P. Maranda (ed.), *Mythology*. Harmondsworth: Penguin, pp. 39–67.

Lebra, T. S. (1992) 'Self in Japanese culture', in N. R. Rosenberger (ed.), *Japanese Sense of Self*. Cambridge: Cambridge University Press, pp. 105–20.

Lonsdale, S. (1990) *Women and Disability: The Experience of Physical Disability among Women*. Basingstoke: Macmillan.

McColgan, G., Valentine, J. and Downs, M. (2000) 'Concluding narratives of a career with dementia: accounts of Iris Murdoch at her death', *Ageing and Society*, 20(1): 97–109.

McCormack, G. (1996) '*Kokusaika*: impediments in Japan's deep structure', in D. Denoon, M. Hudson, G. McCormack and T. Morris-Suzuki (eds), *Multicultural Japan: Palaeolithic to Postmodern*. Cambridge: Cambridge University Press, pp. 265–86.

Marková, I. and Jahoda, A. (1992) 'The language of special needs', in S. J. Baron and J. D. Haldane (eds), *Community, Normality and Difference: Meeting Special Needs*. Aberdeen: Aberdeen University Press, pp. 12–24.

Morris, J. (1993) 'Prejudice', in J. Swain, V. Finkelstein, S. French and M. Oliver (eds), *Disabling Barriers – Enabling Environments*. London: Sage, pp. 101–6.

Oliver, M. (1988) 'The social and political context of educational policy: the case of special needs', in L. Barton (ed.), *The Politics of Special Educational Needs*. Lewes: Falmer Press, pp. 13–31.

Oliver, M. (1996a) 'Defining impairment and disability: issues at stake', in C. Barnes and G. Mercer (eds), *Exploring the Divide: Illness and Disability*. Leeds: Disability Press, pp. 39–54.

Oliver, M. (1996b) *Understanding Disability: From Theory to Practice*. Basingstoke: Macmillan.

Pauwels, A. (1991) *Non Discriminatory Language*. Canberra: Australian Government Publishing Service.

Peters, S. (1996) 'The politics of disability identity', in L. Barton (ed.), *Disability and Society: Emerging Issues and Insights*. London: Longman, pp. 215–34.

Ricoeur, P. (1992) *Oneself as Another*. Chicago: University of Chicago Press.

Romaine, S. (1999) *Communicating Gender*. Mahwah, NJ: Lawrence Erlbaum Associates.

Shakespeare, T. (1996) 'Disability, identity and difference', in C. Barnes and G. Mercer (eds), *Exploring the Divide: Illness and Disability*. Leeds: Disability Press, pp. 94–113.

Shakespeare, T. and Watson, N. (1997) 'Defending the social model', *Disability and Society*, 12(2): 293–300.

Stone, E. (1999) 'Modern slogan, ancient script: impairment and disability in the Chinese language', in M. Corker and S. French (eds), *Disability Discourse*. Buckingham: Open University Press, pp. 136–47.

Strauss, A. (1997) *Mirrors and Masks: The Search for Identity*. New Brunswick: Transaction.

Tomlinson, S. (1981) 'The social construction of the ESN(M) child', in L. Barton and S. Tomlinson (eds), *Special Education: Policy, Practices and Social Issues*. London: Harper & Row, pp. 194–211.

Valentine, J. (1997) 'The framing of marginality through Japanese media representations of marginality', *Japan Foundation Newsletter*, 25(1): 7–10.

Valentine, J. (1998) 'Naming the other: power, politeness and the inflation of euphemisms', *Sociological Research Online*, 3(4). <*http://www.socresonline.org.uk/socresonline/3/4/7.html*>.

Williams, P. (1988) *A Glossary of Special Education*. Milton Keynes: Open University Press.

Wolfe, A. (1989) 'Suicide and the Japanese postmodern: a postnarrative paradigm?', in M. Miyoshi and H. D. Harootunian (eds), *Postmodernism and Japan*. Durham, NC: Duke University Press, pp. 215–33.

17

The Crooked Timber of Humanity: Disability, Ideology and the Aesthetic

Anita Silvers

From the crooked timber of humanity, no straight thing can ever be made.
(Immanuel Kant)

Postmodernism, aesthetics and disability studies of the arts

The postmodern indictment of beauty

Ask not what postmodernism means, but what it does, postmodernists advise. What postmodernism does is to take all subjects of study to be continuously contestable and inescapably debatable. Some postmodernists urge us to convolute our considerations of the world in recognition of the disassociated, dispersed character of our experiences of it. However, other postmodernists go further and propose to abandon all attempts to comprehend the world in standard terms. They think that even the most convoluted interpretations misleadingly fix what is fluid and reduce what is multidimensional to a few impoverished aspects.

Jean-François Lyotard's *The Postmodern Condition: A Report on Knowledge* (1984) was the first influential rendition of postmodern theory. Lyotard identifies several theses with the postmodern perspective on life (Herwitz, 1998: 61):

- Postmodernists recognize the personal and political harms that totalizing ideas have visited on people who do not fit into or comply with them and therefore are suspicious of meta-narratives that dictate the terms in which we acknowledge each other.
- Postmodernists see their task as being to reveal what has been ignored, veiled or undervalued by being labelled 'different' or 'deviant'. To foreground what commonplace ideas obscure or conceal, they invent modes of observing, expressing and connecting that aim at shattering the bonds imposed by the rules of routine discourse.
- Postmodernists portray the world as shifting and our forms of knowledge as consequently lacking stability. As the practices that shape ideas realign themselves, renovations and revitalizations of our modes and standards of knowing become possible.

Postmodernism thus rejects the grand narratives of legitimation that were used to justify the old repertoire of restrictive social standards. Liberalism and Marxism fare no better than facism in postmodern critiques. All totalizing ideas are under suspicion because all construct discourses which, as Corker (1998: 41) points out, impose a few familiar patterns of social relations at the expense of many other ways in which humans could productively interact. So postmodernists seek discourses that are not dominated by static and categorical metadiscursive commitments.

One discursive domain within which humans engage with physical objects, as well as with each other, is the aesthetic. From Plato on, the delight humans take in sensuous and formal beauty has been considered an important human capacity. However, postmodernists, especially those influenced by Foucault, think that aesthetic discourse has been dominated by males, capitalists, nationalists and imperialists (Herwitz, 1998: 62). Their political power has imposed aesthetic criteria that sustain dominant group interests. Thus, standards of beauty are typically criticized by postmodernists for fortifying patterns of existing power. As a result, aesthetic discourse is condemned for being deeply implicated in the exercise of power. If this is right, we can expect that individuals who deviate from the types embraced by politically dominant groups will be disadvantaged whenever the value of beauty is invoked. In this vein, the cultural historian Sander Gilman asserts that 'much evil has been caused in the name of beauty' (quoted in Rothstein, 2000). Gilman identifies beauty with politically constructed ideals that are meant to be exclusionary. Other critics of beauty believe that judgements of beauty inevitably commodify the things that are judged (Herwitz, 1998: 62). A corollary of this last indictment is the assumption that aesthetic discourse is inescapably oppressive because it is designed to treat already marginalized humans, such as women (Rothstein, 2000) and people with disabilities, as objects.

The paradoxical aesthetics of disability
In promoting these criticisms, however, postmodernism produces a paradox. No underlying reality legitimates any representations as veridical or good. So nothing beyond the power-infested aesthetic of appearance seems available to prompt our selection of the objects we contemplate aesthetically.

Given postmodernism's assumption that beauty is an instrument of the interests of power, we would expect artists seeking to satisfy aesthetic standards to shun the subject of disability. For no group of people is less powerful, and has been more marginalized, than the disabled. In social situations, people with disabilities typically are rendered invisible. When they are present, other people often look away or refrain from interacting with them. Yet paradoxically for postmodernism, the history of art shows again and again that aesthetic representations of people with disabilities make for beautiful art.

An imitated object shares its properties, except those that make it real, with any completely accurate imitation of itself, the excepted properties being what differentiates the original from the imitation. So we would expect imitations of people we usually avoid looking at to be similarly ignored. Yet imitations of disabled people are prominent in works of visual, literary and dramatic art that command and gratify our attention. What accounts for the eagerness and enjoyment elicited by aesthetic imitations of people whose actual appearance is commonly impugned?

Some postmodern artists foreground such figures in their efforts to celebrate difference and exalt deviance. In other words, postmodernists rely on the aesthetic force of representations of disability to undermine precisely those power relationships from which they think the aesthetic draws its force. How can aesthetic imitations of people who are powerless be so powerful? Further, why do artists with disabilities enjoy such prominence in the history of the arts when stories of similarly disabled people who are not artists are otherwise absent from history? Feminists famously complain about the omission of works by women from the canons of the arts, but disability theorists have no ground for a similar complaint. Indeed, appreciation for artists from Homer to Van Gogh seems to be elevated in virtue of their having disabilities. What is it about disability that makes their aesthetic products seem more meaningful?

Resolving the paradox of postmodern disability aesthetics

Postmodernist disability studies of the arts must grapple with these paradoxes. Their usual response has been to deconstruct representations of disability in the visual, literary and dramatic arts. This scholarship has attempted to escape the paradoxes by claiming that aesthetic representations of disability 'signify' something other than disability's real self. In other words, the aesthetic is imagined to conceal disability by miring it in discourses of attractiveness. Images of disabled people are exploited to bolster dominant people's confidence in their own perfection. Postmodernist disability studies of the arts thus interprets all aesthetic representations of disability as fortifying the exclusionary applications of political power to which real disabled people are subjected. Art thereby becomes simply another kind of instrument for obscuring the experiences of people with disabilities.

I will argue, to the contrary, that such attempts to disempower the aesthetic rest on flawed interpretations of aesthetic portrayals of disability. For the idea of the normal holds so much less sway in art than in ordinary life. While everyday practical discourse is disturbed by anomaly, aesthetic discourse revels in the shock of the new. Understanding this capacity of aesthetic discourse can lead us to an aesthetic that makes disability powerful.

Subtracting reality from disability

Why do depictions of disabled people attract delighted attention when real disabled people encounter dismayed, pitying or averted gazes? This question relates to a more general puzzle that has perplexed thinkers who have theor-ized about art, namely the allure of perceiving imitations of objects that in themselves repel perception. Plato and Aristotle both struggle to explain this phenomenon, and Kant (1914: 195) comments: 'Beautiful art . . . describes as beautiful things which may be in nature ugly or displeasing.'

Two general kinds of answers have been proposed. The first, offered by theorists from antiquity to the modernist era, is that representations gain attractiveness by omitting displeasing features of the originals they replicate. For instance, a common explanation of aversive behaviour toward the dis-abled is that real disabled people, but not pictures or textual descriptions of them, seem disturbingly portentous to the non-disabled of their own impending physical and social decline. But in refraining from contemplating another person's impairment(s), our experience lacks that feeling of reprise characteristic of being haunted by threatening reveries or fears. Further, accurate representations can be even more portentous than the real thing.

The answer that art abstracts from the threatening particularities of reality founders once we notice that, as Aristotle (1989: 4, 1448b) first observed, detailed accuracy in imitations increases our delight in them. If the reality of one's potential for becoming disabled becomes tangible in the fleshly pres-ence of someone else who already is so, and one protects one's self from this reality by occluding that presence, it is hard to see why a picture or other depiction of that presence would elicit the opposite response. That is, it is hard to see why viewing imitations of anomalous bodies should be so much less portentous than viewing real anomalous bodies as to be so much more enjoyable. Similar arguments can be made for other disagreeable correlates of disability, for instance its associations with incompetence, moral depravity or burdensomeness. All equally easily attach to portrayals of disabled people, yet such portrayals are by no means disagreeable.

Disabled people sometimes protest that art rarely reflects the lumpy, bumpy, dumpy realities of their lives. But relatively few artistic works about any subject are so very realistic. Versions of the thesis that artistic representa-tions of disability lack the disagreeable aspects of real life with a disability all fail because it is hard to see what kind of disagreeableness can inhere in real disabled people but cannot do so in artistic imitations of them. Moreover, from a postmodern perspective, fidelity to the real is no criterion by which to judge art. For postmodernism, the reality of disability is no more natural, and no less a social product, than is the depiction of disability in literary, dramatic and visual art.

Adding signifying to disability

The second answer, which can be traced to the eighteenth century but has become virtually scriptural for postmodernists, holds the advantage of artistic imitations to lie in what has been added to, rather than subtracted from, them. Art is said to be transformational of its subject matter. Art then is accused of being manipulative in so doing by enhancing imitations to distract us from or camouflage distasteful aspects of their originals.

Disability studies scholars have applied this assumption when deconstructing the portrayal of disability in visual, dramatic and literary works. They characteristically analyse artistic depictions of disabled people as invoking signifiers that transcend disability. Such beautiful dissimulations of disability are supposed to soothe the same non-disabled people who are repelled by real disability. A signature thesis of disability studies thus is that art inherently appropriates and exploits the figure of disability. Visual, literary and dramatic art that portrays disabled people is charged by disability studies scholars with using disability symbolically to signify something other than itself, and thus with diverting attention from disability in order to hide it.

This conspiratorial interpretation of how disability is treated in art assumes that society's disregard of disabled people cannot help but pervade our art. To illustrate, literature scholars Mitchell and Snyder (1997) launch a volume on the cultural study of disability – the keystone volume of a series on disability published by a major US university press – by characterizing the record of representing disability in the arts as a history of 'metaphorical opportunism' (p. 17). They claim there is a 'pervasive cultural and artistic dependency on disability' (*ibid.*). They indict society for colonizing people with various kinds of impairment and exploiting their images in order to nourish non-disabled people's fictions about their own perfections (p. 12).

Artistic marginalizing by association

Disability studies indicts art
The indictment they tender is repeated throughout their edited volume. Several key thoughts are echoed by many of the contributors. First, it is contended that disability cannot be other than disruptive or transgressive of the social order. The argument for this claim is that, because current social organization is structured so as to marginalize people in virtue of their corporeal or cognitive anomalies, the prospect of their full social inclusion or participation cannot be other than threatening to the non-disabled audience. Based on this assumption, the artistic effectiveness of representations that portray disabled people as frail and vulnerable is imagined to reduce the threat supposedly posed by the disabled by making them out to be too weak

to thrust themselves into ordinary civil and commercial life. This artistic device exacerbates stereotyping and thereby entrenches the real-life conditions that curtail disabled people's access to social opportunity.

Second, Mitchell and Snyder believe visual art, drama and literature veils the realities of disability to make its thought or image palatable. They say that impairment is veiled by being treated as broadly symbolic of disempowerment. In literature, drama and visual art, disability is manipulated to serve as the stereotypical signifier of the disempowerment of all those, whether or not impaired, whom the dominant society excludes and oppresses:

> the disabled body also serves as the raw material out of which other socially disempowered communities make themselves visible. [But] once the [deformed] bodily surface is exposed as the . . . facade that disguises the workings of [dominant] class norms, the monstrous body itself is quickly forgotten . . . [which] further entrenches the disabled as the 'real' abnormality from which all other nonnormative groups must be distanced. (p. 6)

Signifying defeats aversion, it thus is thought, by disconnecting representations of impairment from disabled people and assigning them more widely appealing meanings. For, of course, people are not repulsed by disagreeable seeming things when it is evident that they are not what they seem. Signifying not only diminishes people with disabilities but also privileges people who are not disabled by serving a therapeutic purpose for them.

In its usual assignment as a signifier, Mitchell and Snyder insist, disability is embellished until it is a generalized symbol for undeserved misfortune. This usage creates what they call the 'representational double bind of disability' (p. 6). That is, the limitations of people with impairments are put on display to be manipulated by others in order to assuage societal guilt and to permit non-disabled people to congratulate themselves on their own superior assets. Because of their role in inducing such therapeutic experience for the non-disabled, artistic representations of impairment acquire an appeal absent in their originals.

Another version of this signifying strategy is to use images of disability to call attention to the general repressiveness society visits on people who are different from those of the dominant group (Mitchell and Snyder, 1997: 6). Disability thus becomes a place-holder or marker for the political mistreatment of other groups which are of greater concern to the audience. Representations that are vehicles for larger meanings of this sort are understandably intriguing. But such signifying reprises the averted glance that disregards the particular experiences of disability. For, if this is really the prevailing way in which disability functions in art and literature, its uses are thoroughly figurative and, consequently, fail to illuminate the actual experience of disability and to enhance appreciation of real disabled people. For instance, in the 1951 film *Bright Victory* (Norden, 1994: 180), a racist soldier is blinded and, when he is rejected the way he himself has rebuffed black people, decides he has more in common with blind black veterans than with the non-disabled whites in his home town. Such signifying is exploitative according to Mitchell and Snyder's thesis because 'disability seldom has been explored as a condition or experience in its own right; instead, disability's psychological and bodily variations have been used to metaphorize nearly every social conflict outside its own ignoble predicament in culture' (1997: 12).

Countering the indictment

Literary, dramatic and visual art undoubtedly present many stereotypical figures of disability. But enumerating egregious examples, as is characteristic of disability studies analyses, is far from demonstrating that the arts make disability presentable only by diverting attention to more palatable meanings. Not all manifestations of disability in the cinema and other arts achieve their meaningfulness in the same way. Indeed, there are cases where an actor's actual impairment becomes, of necessity, his character's impairment without signifying or representing anything beyond itself. The severe arthritis which impaired Lionel Barrymore's mobility means nothing more than it is. At a time when no one in a wheelchair could be admitted to medical school, Barrymore the wheelchair-user was the wheelchair-using Dr Gillespie in fifteen Dr Kildaire films that show his condition but neither emphasize nor metaphorize it.

Furthermore, although characters with disabilities are often assigned stereotypical roles such as the Sweet Innocent, the Tragic Victim, the Noble Warrior (or Noble Wounded Veteran) and Abased Avenger, these familiar filmic figures are not usually people with disabilities. It seems odd to hold that, for instance, the Sweet Innocent with a disability Mary Pickford plays in *Stella Maris* is a more concealing and therefore exploitative signifier than the Sweet Innocent without a disability she plays in so many other films. So a more plausible analysis of the artistic representation of disability than that art illegitimately capitalizes on disability is that audiences are partial to suffering heroines, and illness and death are among the many kinds of events which can be used plausibly as plot devices to occasion the characters' suffering (Gates, 1998).

The many mechanisms of (counter)-hegemony

Diverting attention beyond the particularities of a depiction need not be malignant. Doing so may function as an antidote to exploitative scrutiny. As bell hooks (1995) reminds us, 'few American artists have worked with the black female body in ways that are counter-hegemonic . . . within sexist racist iconography, black females are most often represented as . . . caretakers whose bodies and beings are empty vessels to be filled with the needs of others.' For hooks, hegemonic depiction is fully frontal so as to induce a colonizing gaze, whereas counter-hegemonic depiction shrouds the body and turns it away (pp. 95–7). Thus, for hooks, exposure rather than concealment is the pre-eminent instrument of cultural tyranny. Veiling the black female body by representing it as indifferent or resistant to others' scrutiny is emancipatory. hooks praises the work of the photographer Lorna Simpson 'because so many of them are not frontal images. Backs are turned, the bodies are sideways, specific body parts are highlighted – repositioned from the start in a manner that disrupts conventional ways of seeing and understanding black womanhood' (p. 98).

Black women typically have had access to sexual, procreative and nurturing roles but the social construction of their race has devalued their participation in them. hooks tells us: '(I)n this culture, black women are seen and depicted as down to earth, practical, creatures of the mundane' (*ibid.*). In contrast, the social construction of disability commonly prevents women with disabilities from assuming sexual and maternal roles, even in the belittling assignments reserved for black women (Shakespeare *et al.*, 1996; Barron, 1997; Silvers, 1998a, 1998b, 1998c, 1999). Therefore, portraying black women in these roles reprises the social practice that oppresses them, but failing to portray women with disabilities in these roles is equally dismissive.

This observation suggests one of the complications of categorically assuming that depictions of disability in art and literature do not signify disability but instead have other meanings. Representational conventions that are supposed to disempower the disabled are often the inverse of those thought to disempower other oppressed groups such as black women. Why would a culture oppressive to those individuals whose bodies do not fit the standard – whether because they are female, black, eyeless or legless – marginalize some such people by spotlighting and others by beclouding their representations?

Together with the counter-examples and objections made earlier, this point casts grave doubt on the contention that artistic renditions of impairment are attractive because they categorically direct our attention away from disability, and thus shadow rather than illuminate it. The counter-examples offered here are just a few, drawn from a very replete catalogue of representations of disability in literature and the arts. The number and variety of artistic representations of disability demonstrate that it is hyperbolic to characterize the history of representing disability in art as one of 'metaphorical opportunism' (Mitchell and Snyder, 1997: 17). Systematically (mis)-interpreting artistic representations of disability this way emanates from reading deterministically from the society, which incontrovertibly disregards individuals on account of their disabilities, to art, which does not necessarily do so. Politicizing the aesthetic this way clearly does not explain why painted corporeal anomalies can be beautiful when similarly configured real bodies are not so.

Granted that, both in life and in art, disability is associated with negatively valued states like suffering. But no one supposes that similarly connected conditions like slavery and poverty are categorically concealed and meta-phorized, rather than revealed and interrogated, in the various artistic media. For were this the case, art would be so much less able to elucidate the human condition, and therefore so much less valuable, than it clearly is. Granted also that art sometimes invokes disability as a signifier. But disability is often shown simply for what it is by the artistic media. Contrary to the disability studies account on which representing disability inescapably involves manipulative signifying, artistic representations which show disability as it is effectively elicit delight. This is so despite the reluctance of non-disabled people to engage in similar appreciation of their originals. How this is so is our yet unanswered question.

Artistic marginalizing by definition

Another version of the indictment

We have found no basis for holding that riveting (or, for that matter, pedes-trian) artistic representations of disabled people are signifiers that divert audi-ences' regard away from disability to more agreeable meanings. But there is another marginalizing role disability is reputed to play in art, namely, as 'one of the instrumental devices of . . . [artistic] production' (Mitchell and Snyder, 1997: 17). In regard to this role, disability studies scholars of literature and the arts continue to be guided by their signature thesis, namely that art must be oppressive when it references disability, for otherwise it could not be valued by a society that discriminates against disabled people. Here disability is prominent rather than occluded, but once again its portrayal is said to further the interests of non-disabled people against those of disabled people.

As opposed to the previously discussed role, in which art manipulates disability's circumstantial associations, in this role art exploits disability in virtue of its definitive conceptualization. Davis (1997) says, 'Disability is more than a background . . . it is . . . the basis on which the "normal" body is constructed . . . disability defines the negative space the body must not occupy' (p. 68). Thomson (1997a) explains that the 'subject position of cul-tural self [is] the figure outlined by the array of deviant others whose marked bodies shore up the normate's boundaries. The term normate usefully desig-nates the special figure through which people can represent themselves as definitive human beings' (p. 7). Notice that on these accounts the meaning of representing disability in art is the product of an inescapable conceptual struggle that places normalcy and disability in irresistible conflict.

Artistic representations of the body are said to rely on a syntactical process whereby 'the "normal" body always is in a dialectical play with the disabled body. . . . our representations of the body are really investigations of and defenses against the notion that the body is anything but a seamless, whole, complete, unfragmented entity' (Davis, 1997: 68). Thus, what is normal is thought to have no identity apart from its relationship to its own absence. That is, its identity depends on its contrast with impairment: 'the disabled figure operates as a code for insufficiency, contingency, and abjection – for deviant particularity – thus establishing the contours of a canonical body that garners the prerogatives and privileges of a supposedly stable, universalized normalcy' (Thomson, 1997a: 136).

Casting disability as a component of a binary definition construes it as a discrete concept but one that nevertheless is dependent on the concept of normalcy. Normalcy operates as the superior term on this construal, while disability is the inferior and consequently the repressed one. On this reading, representations of disability necessarily invoke what they are not and so always signify being in deficit. This is thought to be so because normal bodies are conceived as being unified, consolidated, whole. Their wholeness is foregrounded by their oppositional relation to the shattered and limited anomalous bodies of definitively non-normal disabled people (Davis, 1997: *passim*).

Although unimpaired bodies are privileged by being valued over impaired ones, neither can be discerned without reference to the other. So although the standard of normalcy is imposed on discourses of disability, not the least through non-disabled people's presumption that normalcy is a state disabled people covet, discourses of normalcy themselves are vitalized by the energy with which both non-impaired and (unenlightened) impaired people disclaim disability. Normalcy in bodies thus is embraced by means of the very same process through which disability is denied or distanced. For to define disability in terms of lack, and impairment in terms of incompleteness, implicitly makes normalcy regulative. So represented disability becomes one of the elements of a binary dynamic occurring within the artwork.

Proposing that representations of disability stimulate a dynamic explains the power of this category of appearances to engage our attention. The representations emit this energy by showing disability to be itself and not another thing; on this analysis, they can do so regardless of the details of the likeness because there can be no simulation of disability that fails to fall away from normalcy. This account situates the disruptiveness occasioned by disability within the work of art rather than in the world. For instance, Harold Russell's upper torso, with the harness that affixes his metal hooks, is explicitly oppositional to the physiques of heroes previously pictured on the screen. The image of Russell's composite body signals that the normalcy represented in *The Best Years of Our Lives* will be a post-war or newly challenging normalcy, not the complacency of the pre-Hitler era. Art shapes, and therefore can reshape, which appearances seem familiar and commonplace, as well as which strike us as strange and disturbing.

More drawbacks to the indictment

There are, nevertheless, several drawbacks to viewing normalcy and disability as definitively locked in struggle. The most obvious is that conceptualizing their relation this way constructs a dualism that tends to force all cases into one or the other camp. Representations must show their originals as normal or else as deviant; they must present either normalcy or its transgressive, defective opposite. However, to bind the significance of disability to such a structure impoverishes it by reducing it to a confrontation between privilege and inferiority. Furthermore, this analysis is intolerant of borderline cases because their undecidability defeats the binary dynamic.

On this account, disability inescapably is in disadvantageous contention with normalcy. Conceptualizing disability this way forestalls, by definition, the possibility of its transcending limitation and necessarily mires it in deficit. However, normalcy and disability need not be antithetical. The privilege of being normal is that one has a claim on having one's commonness respected. The equivalent, and compatible, privilege of being disabled is acknowledgement of a claim to having one's difference respected. Thought about this way, normalcy and disability not only are concordant (rather than oppositional) but are vitally so.

Artistic centring by means of aestheticizing

The deficiencies of normalcy

The previous discussion suggests the virtue of seeking another analysis of the meaningfulness of the dynamic between normalcy and disability. The analysis we need should explain why normalcy appears to be a regulative ideal affecting our social responses to other people's corporeal configurations, but not of aesthetic reactions to representations of those same bodies. Mitchell and Snyder approach an important thought regarding this, but almost immediately back away. Their volume, they say, 'seeks to demonstrate that disabled bodies and lives have historically served as the crutch upon which artistic discourses and cultural narratives have leaned to ensure the novelty of their subject matter' (1997: 13). Subsequently, however, they avoid grappling with the notion of novelty by eliding it with deformation and distortion. In doing so, they revert to worrying about literature's 'often hazardous complicity in the "ideology of the physical"' (*ibid.*).

Of course, if one assumes that advantage always lies in being normal, the slope from novelty to blemish is lubricious. But unlike in life, in art normalcy is seldom prized. Novelty rather than normalcy, and uniqueness rather than typicality, are artistic desiderata. That singularity emancipates imagination and frees the exceptional individual from the expectations to which the group is held is an artistic commonplace. To illustrate, this understanding was expressed in nineteenth-century literature by the figure of the invalid. From Harriet Martineau's *Life in the Sickroom: Essays by an Invalid* (1844) to Charlotte Yonge's *The Clever Woman of the Family* (1865), confinement to the couch empowered women thus limited by freeing them from reproductive roles and thereby redefining their productivity as intellectual.

Promoting novelty over normalcy

Why does the normal hold so much less sway in art than in life? We see a painted face in cubist style as beautiful, but see a similarly configured fleshly face as deviant (Silvers, 2000). Carroll tells us that 'the anomalous nature of [objects of art-horror] is what makes them disturbing, distressing, and disgusting. However . . . the very fact that they are anomalies fascinates us' (1990: 188).

Even in art, however, anomaly is not necessarily received favourably. It is not unusual for the initial reception of anomalous art to duplicate the aversion with which anomalous real objects are received. For instance, when Caravaggio started painting from dead bodies, art viewers were shocked at his depictions being too real or natural. The famous painting by Thomas Eakins, *The Gross Clinic* (1875), was rejected by jurors from an exhibit in the art section and hung in the medical section (Silvers, 2000).

What eventually altered apprehending works like these (and so many other initially shocking but currently canonical art works) so that they attract rather than repel attention? Kimmelman (1998: 35) advances a strategy for accommodating to, and enjoying, the shock of the new in art. He recollects a remark by the pianist and essayist Charles Rosen, who 'demonstrates how we may actually be sickened when something is truly unfamiliar to us, when it thwarts our expectations'. The initial shock evoked by novel art, Kimmelman observes, 'isn't specifically about grotesque or horrible . . . effects. It's about incomprehension' (*ibid.*).

What then permits configurational anomaly to transcend incomprehension and become attractively lucid when it pertains to the artistic representation of people? And is the strategy appropriate for confronting the shock we experience in perceiving configurational anomalies in real people? Thomson gestures in the direction of a response. She remarks that, in art, anomaly can 'neutralize alienation and repugnance (in order) to highlight the potential for an iconoclastic liminality that can accommodate new forms of identity' (Thomson, 1997b: 247). Innovative art calls into question the prescriptive authority of the historical contingencies that shape our expectations and thereby broadens what we previously have imagined to be normal, even – indeed, especially – what we consider normal in regard to art itself. Thus, what is agreeable about the artistically engendered shock of the new is not its disruptiveness but instead that sensation's aftermath.

Non-normal art is transfigured into something that appears beautiful through an aestheticized discourse that discloses its relational properties and foregrounds it. An important step or element in appreciating anomalous art is the insight that it is indeed art. This is a kind of experience that supersedes our initial perplexity and perturbation. We are gratified that what is unexpected is yet orderly, provided we are able to construct an order into which the unexpected fits.

Making anomaly powerful

We experience neither anomalous artistic representations of people, nor anomalous real people, with an innocent eye. Each individual viewed – whether artwork or human being – is limned by its lineage and kin; these outline what is expected of it and what it is expected to be, that is to say, what is normal for it. That anomaly presents as originality rather than deviance depends on the way we conceptualize the connectedness of successors with their heritage and, specifically, on the prescriptiveness with which individuals are obliged to conform to their predecessors.

As Danto (1964) points out, the state of art's history at the time a novel object is introduced determines whether it is accepted as art. We can see Picasso the Cubist as the artistic successor of Cézanne, pressing beyond his predecessor's exploration of the shapes of volumes. But if Picasso had lived immediately after Caravaggio, it is unlikely that his seventeenth-century contemporaries would have affirmed that his cubist works were art, for, unlike Picasso's twentieth-century contemporaries, their eyes would not have been acclimatized by their previous familiarity with Cézanne's and Matisse's paintings.

Novel art remains connected to its predecessors despite differing disruptively from them. To embrace art, yet be respectful of its history, is to comprehend how historical precedent can be of consequence for future art without commanding conformity. Art's history has been theorized in various ways that facilitate the firm but free connecting of novel objects with their aesthetic predecessors. Art's history thus receives rather than repudiates new forms of identity, for art's history is interpretive, not coercive. Is it possible for human history to do so as well?

We can now begin to understand how aesthetic responses to representations of human anomaly differ from the usual social responses to real anomalous people. Aesthetic responses to anomaly do not occlude it. As novel works are tied to other works of art, so novel figures within works are tied to the work's other figures. For example, in Velasquez's *Las Meninas* the small stiff figure of the Infanta initially centres the viewer's eye, but almost immediately the far-right figures of the dwarfs Maribarbola and Nicolasito become dominant in the scene. The latter figures have been variously described by art historians as disturbing, energetic and in the first plane of reality. Almost all art historians speak of the dwarfs in terms of their links to the other figures, of Nicolasito's suppleness counterpointing the rigidity of the Infanta, of the independent Maribarbola as more substantial than the ephemerally reflected queen and king. While in everyday life people typically either look away from figures like Maribarbola and Nicolasito or fasten them with an isolating stare, the aesthetic response to such anomalous human figures is to create a more inclusive perceptual order that embraces them.

Making impairment powerful

What theorizing of human beauty would facilitate our perceiving disabled people as enlivening, rather than depreciating, the human collective in a manner similar to that which permits us to see novel configurations as invigorating art? Understanding how art empowers its own unexpected products suggests how impairment can also be powerful. The philosophy of art makes available a variety of applicable proposals for bringing novelty and precedent into contiguity for this purpose. Applying any of these requires recognizing that (some) novel people advance how we understand humanity as (some) novel objects expand how we understand art.

Such an idea occasionally surfaces in disability studies, but it is treated as an exceptional and unreliable manifestation rather than as a familiar achievement of art. For instance, Thomson (1997b) observes that a few African-American writers create characters for whom 'disability neither diminishes nor corrupts . . . [but instead] affirms the self in context [and] augments power and dignity . . . [thereby] inspiring awe, and becoming a mark of superiority' (p. 250). For these writers, 'difference, not sameness, is [the] principle of identity. Being outside the ordinary is both essential and emancipatory in . . . self-definition' (p. 241). The upshot is that 'disabilities, then, are not metaphors for lives twisted by oppression, but the identifying, affirming, and valued manifestations of bodily uniqueness and personal history' (Thomson, 1997a: 125). Yet Thomson is reluctant to follow through this thought. Not the imaginative aesthetic understanding of beauty for which I have been arguing, but, instead, the impoverished politicized one that currently prevails in disability studies prompts her to pull back from giving priority to an expanded idea of beauty. Instead, she cautions that 'aestheticizing disability . . . precludes analysis of how these representations support or challenge the sociopolitical relations that make disability a form of cultural otherness' (1997a: 112; 1997b: 247).

My analysis should put this kind of worry to rest. Understanding how beauty really matters should quiet concerns about the aestheticizing of inter-personal conduct by showing that aestheticizing disability elevates otherness to originality. Such a conception is a powerful antidote to the hegemony imposed by 'normal' socio-political relations. In contrast to the prevailing methodology of the postmodernist disability studies scholars referenced here, the approach I am recommending neither assumes nor requires disability to be confined to 'cultural otherness'. To view anomalously configured people as we do novel art, we must appreciate them both as originals and as heirs of human biological history. As we master human genetics and learn more about the variables involved in the inheritance of various human traits, we will need to emphasize the diversity of effective human functioning. Doing so requires that we avoid the errors of simple-minded Darwinian functionalism in formulating both our biological and our social history.

Further, molecular biology offers techniques to intervene at the genetic level to make attributes such as having blue or brown eyes, being hairy or bald, or possessing the Picasso-like triangular-shaped face associated with osteogenesis imperfecta rather than the Raphaelite oval-shaped face a matter of human artifice rather than natural selection. As molecular biological engineering is perfected, being like a Picasso rather than a Raphael, or having a Rubenesque rather than a Modiglianish body, has the potential to become as much an expression of personal taste as choosing to shave one's head or wear one's locks long. To be appreciated, human diversity must be seen as the product of creative human choice, not merely as the outcome of uninspired intention. Thus, to be fully appreciated, the human variations we call disabilities must be interpreted as being meaningful.

At this time, the beguilement of normalcy continues to be influential. Yet even now the propriety of drugging a Van Gogh to subdue the extraordinariness of his manner is by no means obvious. We apprehend Van Gogh as an original, an amplifier of culture, rather than as a cultural other (Silvers, 1994). So, although disturbing, the extraordinariness of Van Gogh's manner is seen as being meaningful.

Unlike feminist and ethnic studies of literature and the arts, disability studies is deplorably in deficit in respect to formulating histories that show how the diversity occasioned by disability is meaningful in furthering enduring human purposes. As I have argued here and elsewhere (Silvers, 2000), postmodernist disability studies is too much obsessed with existing socio-political relations and too little inspired by the potential of aestheticizing. No doubt postmodern students of disability are rightly suspicious of the discursive terms that influence how we currently acknowledge each other. But showing that disability is often obscured and undervalued does not suffice to shatter the bonds imposed by routine discourse. To do so we need to develop a new stage of disability studies. We need to shift from repudiating socio-political relations to realigning them by reshaping beauty into a more expansive idea that revitalizes the meaning of disability (Silvers, 2000).

References

Aristotle (1989) *The Poetics*, trans. S. Butcher. New York: Hill and Wang.

Barron, K. (1997) 'The bumpy road to womanhood', *Disability and Society*, 12(12): 223–4.

Carroll, N. (1990) *The Philosophy of Horror or Paradoxes of the Heart.* New York: Routledge.

Corker, M. (1998) *Deaf and Disabled, or Deafness Disabled?* Buckingham: Open University Press.

Danto, A. (1964) 'The artworld', *Journal of Philosophy*, 15 October: 571–84.

Davis, L. (1997) 'Nude venuses, medusa's body, and phantom limbs: disability and visuality', in D. Mitchell and S. Snyder (eds), *The Body and Physical Difference: Discourses of Disability.* Ann Arbor: University of Michigan Press, pp. 51–70.

Gates, A. (1998) 'Ready for my fade-out, Mr. De Mille', *New York Times*, 21 June, pp. 15, 29.

Herwitz, D. (1998) 'Postmodernism', in M. Kelly (ed.), *The Encyclopedia of Aesthetics.* Oxford: Oxford University Press, pp. 57–63.

hooks, b. (1995) *Art on My Mind: Visual Politics.* New York: The New Press.

Kant, I. (1914) *The Critique of Judgement*, trans. Bernard. London: Macmillan.

Kimmelman, M. (1998) 'How the tame can suddenly seem wild', *New York Times*, 2 August, Arts p. 35.

Lyotard, J.-F. (1984) *The Postmodern Condition: A Report on Knowledge*, trans. Geoff Bennington and Brian Massumi. Manchester: Manchester University Press.

Martineau, H. (1844) *Life in the Sickroom: Essays by an Invalid.* Boston: Leonard Bowles and William Crosby.

Mitchell, D. and Snyder, S. (eds) (1997) *The Body and Physical Difference: Discourses of Disability.* Ann Arbor: University of Michigan Press.

Norden, M. (1994) *The Cinema of Isolation: A History of Physical Disability in the Movies.* New Brunswick, NJ: Rutgers University Press.

Rosen, C. (1994) *The Frontiers of Meaning.* New York: Hill and Wang.

Rothstein, E. (2000) 'Two faces of beauty: timeless and timely', *New York Times*, 6 May, A15–16.

Shakespeare, T., Davis, D. and Gillespie-Sells, K. (1996) *The Sexual Politics of Disability.* London: Cassell.

Silvers, A. (1994) 'Vincent's story: the importance of contextualism in art education', *Journal of Aesthetic Education*, 28(3): 47–62.

Silvers, A. (1998a) 'Disability', in A. Jaggar and I. M. Young (eds), *Blackwell's Companion to Feminist Philosophy.* Oxford: Blackwell, pp. 330–40.

Silvers, A. (1998b) 'Reprising women's disability: feminist strategy and disability rights', *Berkeley Women's Law Journal*, 13: 81–116.

Silvers, A. (1998c) 'On not iterating women's disabilities: a crossover perspective on genetic dilemmas', in A. Donchin and L. Purdy (eds), *Embodying Bioethics: Feminist Advances.* Lanham, MD: Rowman & Littlefield, pp. 177–202.

Silvers, A. (1999) 'Ageing fairly, feminist and disability perspectives on intergenerational justice', in M. Walker (ed.), *Mother Time: Women, Ageing, and Ethics.* Lanham, MD: Rowman & Littlefield, pp. 203–26.

Silvers, A. (2000) 'From the crooked timber of humanity, beautiful things can be made', in P. Brand (ed.), *Beauty Matters: New Theories of Beauty*. Bloomington: Indiana University Press.

Silvers, A., Wasserman, D. and Mahowald, M. (1998) *Disability, Difference, Discrimination: Perspectives on Justice in Bioethics and Public Policy*. Lanham, MD: Rowman & Littlefield.

Thomson, R. G. (1997a) *Extraordinary Bodies: Figuring Physical Disability in American Culture and Literature*. New York: Columbia University Press.

Thomson, R. G. (1997b) 'Disabled women as powerful women in Petry, Morrison, and Lorde: revising black female subjectivity', in D. Mitchell and S. Snyder (eds), *The Body and Physical Difference: Discourses of Disability*. Ann Arbor: University of Michigan Press, pp. 240–66.

Yonge, C. (1865, 1985) *The Clever Woman of the Family*. Reprinted in New York: Virago.

Index

UNIVERSITY OF ...STER
LIBRARY

Printed in the United Kingdom
by Lightning Source UK Ltd.
133110UK00001B/10-33/P